EMILY A. HOLMES is Associate Professor, Department of Religion and Philosophy at Christian Brothers University and co-author of *Women, Writing, Theology: Transforming a Tradition of Exclusion* (Baylor University Press, 2011). She lives in Memphis, Tennessee.

FLESH MADE WORD

FLESH MADE WORD
Medieval Women Mystics, Writing, and the Incarnation

Emily A. Holmes

BAYLOR UNIVERSITY PRESS

Cover Design by Steve Kress
Cover Art: Detail from Weyden, Rogier (Roger) van der (c.1399–1464), The
Magdalen Reading, before 1438. Oil on mahogany, transferred from another
panel, 62.2 x 54.4 cm. Bought, 1860 (NG654). National Gallery, London,
Great Britain. © National Gallery, London / Art Resource, NY

Library of Congress Cataloging-in-Publication Data

Holmes, Emily A., 1974–
  Flesh made word : medieval women mystics, writing, and the incarnation
/ Emily A. Holmes.
  246 pages cm
  Includes bibliographical references and index.
  ISBN 978-1-60258-753-3 (alk. paper)
  1. Incarnation—History of doctrines—Middle Ages, 600–1500. 2.
Mysticism—History—Middle Ages, 600-1500. 3. Hadewijch, active 13th
century—Authorship. 4. Angela, of Foligno, 1248?–1309—Authorship.
5. Porete, Marguerite, approximately 1250–1310—Authorship. I. Title.
  BT220.H59 2013
  282'.40820902—dc23
                                            2013007939

Printed in the United States of America on acid-free paper with a minimum
of 30% post-consumer waste recycled content.

To Paul

"To write as if your life depended on it:
to write across the chalkboard, putting up there in public words
you have dredged,
sieved up from dreams, from behind screen memories, out of silence—
words you have dreaded and needed in order to know you exist."

—Adrienne Rich, "As if Your Life Depended on It"

"And we must constantly encourage ourselves and each other to attempt
the heretical actions that our dreams imply, and so many of our old ideas
disparage. In the forefront of our move toward change, there is only poetry
to hint at possibility made real."

—Audre Lorde, "Poetry Is Not a Luxury"

CONTENTS

PREFACE

In the 1987 film *Le Moine et la Sorcière*,[1] the Dominican friar Étienne de Bourbon enters a village in southern France in search of heretics. There he meets a woman who attracts his attention. A midwife, herbalist, and healer, she cares for the bodies of the villagers. Intrigued, and not a little suspicious, he seeks her out for conversation. Their talk turns to the many books he has read. She would like to know how to read but doubts she ever will. Perhaps the curé could teach her to read prayers? But to write. Could he teach her to write? Well . . . what would she write about, anyway? "Plants and rocks . . . I'd tell how the flowers turn toward the sun which they love." "One writes about God's truths, not about plants." For the herbalist and midwife, those subjects are not opposed. Will he teach her? Teach her to write, at least to write the letters of God's name, here, with a stick in the earth that sustains her. "We don't write God's name in the dirt." Instead, he writes her name, Elda, short for Eldamere. "Do you write about God's truths?" Elda asks. Someday, after hard study and reading many, many books, he will write, perhaps even about a village like this one, there where she learns new things every day.

What are the conditions of medieval women's writing? Of a woman writing botany, or theology, or fiction? How many women, like Eldamere or, as Virginia Woolf imagines, Shakespeare's sister, perished as a result of their hidden genius, their lack, as Woolf put it, of money and freedom, a room

---

[1] *Le Moine et la Sorcière*, directed by Suzanne Schiffman (Cambridge, Mass.: Lara Classics, 1987), DVD. Screenplay by Pamela Berger and Suzanne Schiffman, based in part on a passage in Étienne de Bourbon (d. 1262), *De Supersticione*.

of one's own?[2] We might follow Woolf's thought experiment in imagining a sister of Thomas Aquinas, a woman who also had an aptitude for theology, a brilliant and orderly mind. Would her parents have offered her to a monastery where she might have received an education? Or would she have languished in an unhappy arranged marriage? Even had she learned how to read and write, what forms of theological support would be required for Thomas' sister to think she had something worth saying, something to teach? In a deeply misogynistic culture, in which the question of whether women were created in the image of God was a serious topic of debate, what would she have had to believe about God and herself in order to consider herself worthy of writing?[3]

Writing demands certain material conditions: financial support, a place in which to write, raw materials—parchment, pen, ink. Less tangible, but no less important, are the necessity of time, education, literacy—whether the medieval gold standard of Latin or the local tongue. The luxury of books: scripture, Augustine, Bernard of Clairvaux, tales of romance and poems heard and sung, memorized, read. The elusive writings of other women, perhaps shared and distributed along informal reading and writing communities and networks in the growing towns and cities of the thirteenth century. More subtle still but most crucial of all—belief in the value of what one writes, in one's right to write. That she—that anonymous if not fictional woman—has something worth saying. The authority to speak, an eager audience to hear. That she is not the devil's gateway, but the image of God. If she were to escape the fate of Shakespeare's sister, who "killed herself one winter's night and lies buried at some cross-roads where the omnibuses now stop outside the Elephant and Castle"[4]—then she must believe that her existence is not a mistake, her talent is not wasted, but beloved by God. That her very flesh is embraced by the God who loved flesh so much that he became flesh, taking it on for his own. Contrary to all expectations, there, the images and words that mirror her body—broken, bleeding, birthing, feeding—there on the cross, the one who whispers my beloved, you are beautiful, you are sweet to me. You are loved. And in response—her words pour out.

———

[2] Virginia Woolf, *A Room of One's Own* (New York: Harcourt Brace Jovanovich, 1929).
[3] This question is no less pressing today. See Sarah Sentilles, "The Pen Is Mightier: Sexist Responses to Women Writing about Religion," *Harvard Divinity Bulletin* 40, nos. 3–4 (2012): 42–51.
[4] Woolf, *Room of One's Own*, 48.

Central to Christian theology, history, and practice is what French feminist philosopher Luce Irigaray calls "an incarnational relationship between the body and the word."[5] For Christians, this relationship is named in the prologue to the gospel of John as Christ the "word" who "became flesh and lived among us." The doctrine of the incarnation has traditionally focused on the salvific significance of Jesus Christ as the uniquely incarnate Word, one person in two natures, divine and human. This book wants to expand Christian understanding of the incarnation beyond the particular male body of Jesus—through the writings of medieval women. In the writings of medieval women mystics and, sometimes, in those of contemporary feminist theorists, concepts of "word" and "flesh" strain beyond their classical christological boundaries. Rather than examining the metaphysics of the Word that became flesh, we find in writing incarnations of female flesh becoming word. Some medieval women learned how to write the body of Christ with their bodies and with their words, and they invite other Christians to follow.

Women's Theological Writing

One question this volume addresses is of the ideological conditions of medieval women's theological writing: what enabled women to write and interpret Christian doctrine? Considering the place of women's writing in the history of literature, Hélène Cixous speaks to the fears of many women writers when she asks, "Wouldn't you first have needed the 'right reasons' to write? The reasons, mysterious to me, that give you the 'right' to write?"[6] Similar questions can be asked of women who began to write theology: excluded from ordination to the priesthood and from the universities that granted authority, lacking formal education in Latin (outside monasteries) and therefore technically illiterate, living in a patriarchal and misogynistic Christendom that blamed women for the downfall of man—what gave women the right to write theology?

To address this question it is worth briefly considering the conditions of medieval women's writing more broadly. Since the emergence of women's studies as an interdisciplinary field of scholarship, a great deal of attention has been paid to women's writing and, increasingly, to women's writing prior

---

[5] Luce Irigaray, "The Redemption of Women," in *Key Writings* (London: Continuum, 2004), 150.

[6] Hélène Cixous, "Coming to Writing," in *"Coming to Writing" and Other Essays*, ed. Deborah Jenson, trans. Sarah Cornell et al. (Cambridge, Mass.: Harvard University Press, 1991), 9.

to the fourteenth century.[7] Whereas Peter Dronke's *Women Writers of the Middle Ages* (1984) identified women's motivation for writing as an "urgently serious . . . response springing from inner needs, more than from an artistic, or didactic, inclination,"[8] more recent accounts see less "immediacy" and more craft, collaboration, and didactic and artistic influence in the production of medieval texts.[9] It is true that the medieval conception of "*auctor*" as "a marker of doctrinal authority, signifying an ancient theologian or approved classical writer who commanded deference and obedience" excluded women (and most men) from the chain of signification linking "*auctoritas*, authority, to tradition, defined as a stream of continuous influence by its root *tradere*, to pass on."[10] Women did, however, participate in a wide range of "authorial activities," including occupying the roles of visionaries who made use of scribes and secretaries; collaborators with confessors and spiritual directors who mediated their texts; patrons commissioning texts; the subjects of men's writing; compilers of the writings of others; and as readers who glossed and supplemented texts for new audiences.[11] These activities created a variety of entry points to the Christian tradition. When we loosen our definition of "author" (for the modern definition applies to medieval women no better than the medieval *auctor*), of literacy (to include not only Latin but also the vernacular), and of the value of the signature (to include pseudonymous and anonymous works), we gain a much clearer sense of the participation of women as writers in the Christian Middle Ages.

But this loosening also requires an expansion of our understanding of what counts as *writing*. Here the "French feminists," such as Cixous, Irigaray, and Julia Kristeva, are particularly helpful for theorizing the role of the body, of flesh, and of matter in the practice and effect of women's writing.

---

[7] Diane Watt, *Medieval Women's Writing: Works by and for Women in England, 1100–1500* (Cambridge, UK: Polity, 2007), 1.

[8] Peter Dronke, *Women Writers of the Middle Ages: A Critical Study of Texts from Perpetua († 203) to Marguerite Porete († 1310)* (Cambridge: Cambridge University Press, 1984), x.

[9] See Watt, *Medieval Women's Writing*, 11–18; see also Joan M. Ferrante, *To the Glory of Her Sex: Women's Roles in the Composition of Medieval Texts* (Bloomington: Indiana University Press, 1997); Jennifer Summit, *Lost Property: The Woman Writer and English Literary History, 1380–1589* (Chicago: University of Chicago Press, 2000); Carolyn Dinshaw and David Wallace, eds., *The Cambridge Companion to Medieval Women's Writings* (Cambridge: Cambridge University Press, 2003); and Carolyne Larrington, *Women and Writing in Medieval Europe: A Sourcebook* (New York: Routledge, 1995).

[10] Jennifer Summit, "Women and Authorship," in *The Cambridge Companion to Medieval Women's Writings*, 92.

[11] See Summit, "Women and Authorship," 93–105.

Influenced by Jacques Derrida's broad conception of writing (or "Writing") to include the speech and gestures of the body,[12] the French feminists, in different ways, consider how women's bodies influence, resist, and enter language and "write"—whether by putting words to paper or parchment, through gestures and symptoms, or through laughter, tears, and speech. Expanding our understanding of what counts as "writing" gives us a much better appreciation of women's contributions to Christian theology beyond traditional definitions of authorship.

It is with this broad sense of writing that I approach the medieval women theologians considered in this book. The case for including Hadewijch and Marguerite Porete is relatively clear-cut, although with both women we must recognize the role of the audience(s), both inscribed and real, to whom they wrote, and with Porete, we must take account of the history of her manuscript, which circulated for over six hundred years, in numerous translations and without her signature. Identifying Angela of Foligno as a writer is more difficult because of the high degree of influence of her confessor, Brother Arnaldo, who first recorded her words to assist his own memory and for other men to read. *The Book of Blessed Angela* that resulted from their collaboration, however, is as much hers as it is his, and, in the end, it is God who signs the book, just as God is the Author to whom both Hadewijch and Porete attribute their works. Instead of seeing self-effacement, humility, or the oppression of women in attributing authorship outside themselves, however, we instead see the complexity of the premodern conception of writing (and authorship), which includes active collaboration and positioning the human being not as an originator but as a recorder of "divinely inspired text that originates elsewhere."[13] For these medieval women, all (legitimate) authority stems from God; writing comes from the Other and merely passes through the human voice, whether she dictates words to her scribe or holds the pen herself. This broad and inclusive notion of writing resonates in many ways with postmodern literary theory, much more so, at least, than with modern forms of literary criticism that identified the author as the unique origin of his work.[14]

---

[12] See Jacques Derrida, *Of Grammatology*, trans. Gayatri Chakravorty Spivak (Baltimore: Johns Hopkins University Press, 1974); idem, *Writing and Difference*, trans. Alan Bass (Chicago: University of Chicago Press, 1978); Cixous, "Coming to Writing"; and idem, "Le rire de la Méduse," *L'Arc* 61 (1975): 39–54.

[13] See Summit, "Women and Authorship," 99.

[14] See Roland Barthes, "The Death of the Author," in *Image-Music-Text*, trans. Stephen Heath (New York: Hill & Wang, 1977), 142–48; and Michel Foucault, "What Is an

In choosing these sources, there is an implicit claim, as well, for a broad interpretation of what counts as theology.[15] When medieval women write theology, that term cannot be restricted to the recognized and authoritative theology of the monastery or the university. "Theology" refers to speech about God, and that "speech" can be stretched to include writings by women in the vernacular, using forms of secular literature (lyric and romance), as well as narratives about women's miraculous visions, bodies, and words, and (though more difficult to trace) the lived experience of women and men in the architectural space of cathedrals, in the ritual space of the liturgy, and on the literal and metaphorical journey of the pilgrimage. The interaction of bodies with Christian words, doctrines, symbols, and spaces, within a highly visual and oral culture, composed the lived theology of the Christian medieval period. Women contributed to this form of theology-making in multiple ways as full participants in their religion and should be viewed as agents in cocreating the popular piety of medieval Christianity.

But here I choose to focus on *writing* theology precisely because it is a category that, until recently, has excluded women officially, if not always, as we now know, in practice. To restate the question: What are the conditions that enabled women's theological writing? To anticipate the answer: writing emerges as a spiritual practice in response to the incarnation. Writing allows women's flesh to become word(s) in response to the Word made Flesh. It also grounds an inclusive and expansive interpretation of the incarnation that can be retrieved for diverse feminist theologies today. The transcendence of God is revealed in multiple forms and genres of speech and writing; likewise, the incarnation, the revelation of God in human flesh, requires multiple bodies in which to appear and delights in our human differences.

Method and the Path Ahead

In what follows, I begin with a discussion of the way the doctrine of the incarnation has been critiqued and interpreted in contemporary feminist theologies, offering my own constructive interpretation through writing as an inclusive way of practicing the encounter of word and flesh. In each chapter that follows, we meet two writers, one medieval, and one postmodern, whose writings support this interpretation. These writers are juxtaposed and

---

Author?" in *The Foucault Reader*, ed. Paul Rabinow (New York: Pantheon Books, 1984), 101–20.

[15] See Margaret Miles, *The Word Made Flesh: A History of Christian Thought* (Oxford: Blackwell, 2005).

read together for their particular resonance—and at times, dissonance—
on the particular theme of the incarnation of Christ and the more general
relation of bodies to language, of flesh to word. Chapter 2 pairs Hadewijch
with Kristeva to examine the maternal generativity that is the source of
both poetic language and (divine) love, incarnate through Mary in Christ.
In chapter 3, Angela and Cixous trace the transition from the symptomatic
and paramystical body of the holy woman to the teacher and writer who
embodies the Word with authority. Chapter 4 examines Porete's description
of the annihilated soul, who becomes the place of divine love, in conversation
with Irigaray's writings on women becoming divine. The principle of these
pairings is not forced likeness or comparison, but interesting exchange. In
each case, this deliberate set of juxtapositions stages a dialogue between the
writers, weaving my discussion of their texts together, so that they mutually
illuminate one another. The aim is to demonstrate the fruitfulness of both
medieval women's writings and French feminist theories for contemporary
feminist theology, and in particular, for a theology of the incarnation. While
the French feminists are immensely helpful in thinking about questions of
writing, gender, and the body, and I wish to draw out the theological implications of their work, the mystics surpass them in many ways, not only in
their spiritual insights, but in their writings: beautiful and mysterious texts
that challenge and delight their readers. But including contemporary feminist theory leads us to reread the medieval texts more attentively; it broadens
the context in which we read, without reducing one set of writings to the
other. Both groups of texts provide support for an inclusive and expansive
view of incarnation.

This book has strong affinities with several recent books on religion that
address feminist concerns, particularly Grace Jantzen's *Becoming Divine:
Towards a Feminist Philosophy of Religion*[16] and Amy Hollywood's *Sensible
Ecstasy: Mysticism, Sexual Difference and the Demands of History.*[17] Although
my focus differs from theirs, it will be clear to the reader that this book is
indebted to both Jantzen and Hollywood in ways both implicit and explicit,
for we read similar sources (medieval women mystical writers, French

---

[16] Grace Jantzen, *Becoming Divine: Towards a Feminist Philosophy of Religion* (Bloomington: Indiana University Press, 1999) and *Power, Gender and Christian Mysticism* (Cambridge: Cambridge University Press, 1995).

[17] Amy Hollywood, *Sensible Ecstasy: Mysticism, Sexual Difference, and the Demands of
History* (Chicago: University of Chicago Press, 2002) and *The Soul as Virgin Wife: Mech-
thild of Magdeburg, Marguerite Porete, and Meister Eckhart* (Notre Dame, Ind.: University of
Notre Dame Press, 1995).

feminist theorists) and find them, if not uncritically, engaging for contemporary feminist concerns. What Jantzen has done with these sources for philosophy of religion, and what Hollywood (and, in different ways, Carolyn Walker Bynum and Margaret Miles) for the history and theory of religion, this book attempts in the field of constructive feminist theology. That is, I wish to draw out the implications of these particular medieval theologians (Hadewijch, Angela, and Porete), feminist theorists (Kristeva, Cixous, and Irigaray), and their interpreters (Jantzen, Hollywood, Bynum, and others), for contemporary theology. One way of reading this book, then, is as a translation of some of these recent insights into material that the church, in the broadest sense, might find useful for thinking about the implications of the incarnation for bodies today.

My guiding interest in the theology of the incarnation, with feminist commitments to the flourishing of all people, does not mean that those interests were necessarily shared by the medieval women here examined, or, for that matter, by my contemporary theoretical sources and conversation partners. Instead of reading those interests back into the primary texts, I see the medieval texts as supporting a range of interpretations, some of which I wish to draw out in light of contemporary concerns. Making my own commitments and interests explicit here will, I hope, allow the reader to distinguish my voice from my sources and to recognize the differences in perspective and historical context that shape what follows. Mine is but one voice among many, inevitably shaped by the particularity of my own experience and social location, and therefore eager to lift up and learn from the voices of other women through the medium of writing. The result is a dialogue of multiple voices, a type of heteroglossia: at times the voices of my medieval sources stand out, some over and against one another, and at other times they fade to the background as my own conclusions come to the fore.

One final note on method: To situate my interpretation of the incarnation in terms of mystical *writings* means that I am not asking about "mystical experience" itself. While I examine mystical theology and experience insofar as it informs the *content* of these texts, it is not the primary focus of the chapters that follow,[18] for what we have with the mystics is, in the first instance, a text that is the product of a discourse and not an account of raw experience.[19]

---

[18] For a feminist approach to mystical experience, see Beverly Lanzetta, *Radical Wisdom: A Feminist Mystical Theology* (Minneapolis: Fortress, 2005).

[19] Michel de Certeau, *The Mystic Fable* (Chicago: University of Chicago Press, 1992), and idem, *Heterologies: Discourse on the Other*, trans. Brian Massumi (Minneapolis: University of Minnesota Press, 1985).

This view of mysticism through its texts relies on Pseudo-Dionysius' description of "mystical theology" as a particular way of speaking and writing.[20] As discussed more fully in the final chapter, mystical writing functions as an interpretative and didactic discourse that attempts to speak what cannot be spoken, and then to "unsay" it in turn.[21] Insofar as the experience behind the text remains opaque to history, what is of primary interest is the letter of the text itself, its particular words, its images and ideas, its writing.[22] My theological interest in the mystics as guides to the incarnation thus gravitates to the question of their writing: what motivated women to write of their encounters with the embodied God? What makes that writing possible and what are its effects?

For women in particular, writing provides a path into the symbolic order of language, meaning, and tradition. Writing presents a direct challenge to the authority of the word when it is restricted to an elite. It creates the possibility of speaking to other women, of creating community, of teaching across temporal and geographic distances, and of telling a story.[23] And writing is a way for women to enter the Christian tradition without speaking from authority *ex officio*, just as it is a way to engage with the Christian tradition without being suffocated by it. When women discover their divine words, they find a way to live into the promise of the incarnation. And that, it seems to me, is what these particular medieval women achieve, remarkably, through their writings. Marguerite Porete would be known only as a woman executed for heresy had her book not survived the flames. Angela would be considered a minor holy woman inspiring a small circle of disciples had she not collaboratively written her book. Nothing at all would be known

[20] Pseudo-Dionysius, *The Complete Works*, trans. Colm Luibhéid and Paul Rorem (New York: Paulist Press, 1987).

[21] Michael Sells, *Mystical Languages of Unsaying* (Chicago: University of Chicago Press, 1994).

[22] Although Bernard McGinn uses the phrase "presence of God" to describe mysticism, his nuanced, multivolume study makes it clear that mystical theology was far from occasional or "extraordinary" for the life of those practicing contemplative prayer. He further notes that "experience" is a modern term and, at any rate, inaccessible to the historian. What we have are texts—that is, ways of speaking mysticism through language. Bernard McGinn, *The Foundations of Mysticism: Origins to the Fifth Century*, vol. 1 of *The Presence of God: A History of Western Christian Mysticism* (New York: Crossroad, 1991), xiv–xx.

[23] For instance, Harriet A. Jacobs, *Incidents in the Life of a Slave Girl* (1861; New York: Oxford University Press, 1988); Woolf, *Room of One's Own*; idem, *Three Guineas* (New York: Harcourt, Brace, 1938); and Dorothy Allison, *Two or Three Things I Know for Sure* (New York: Dutton, 1995) all describe the effects of writing for women in similar ways, despite the differences in their social locations.

xviii   PREFACE

of Hadewijch, apart from her writings. To encounter these women, we are indebted to generations of scribes, copyists, translators, and scholars transmitting the texts across temporal and linguistic borders.[24] For contemporary Christian theologians, writing emerges as a way to practice the incarnation. By transmitting flesh into word, following the medieval women here examined, we write the body of Christ.

---

[24] See Dinshaw and Wallace, introduction to *The Cambridge Companion to Medieval Women's Writing*, 5.

Acknowledgments

Writing about writing reveals the degree to which writing is not one's own, but utterly dependent on the inspiration, ideas, and labor of others. Nothing in this book would be possible without the multitude that has preceded me, surrounded me, and sustained me over this long and eventful journey.

Christian Brothers University has supported my research and writing beyond all expectations. Sean MacInnes assisted with a variety of tasks from proofreading to mailing to trips to the library; Melissa Verble obtained numerous books and articles through interlibrary loan; Marius Carriere secured funds for travel to conferences; Chris Peterson assisted research and read drafts; Daryl Stephens helped assemble the bibliography; Scott Geis and Frank Buscher approved the course reduction that allowed me to finish the final two chapters; and Leigh Pittenger agreed to teach additional classes. I am especially fortunate to be part of a supportive, collegial, and sociable department, and for that I am grateful to Scott Geis, Burt Fulmer, David Dault, James Wallace, and Max Maloney.

An earlier incarnation of this book developed through my dissertation work, and so I wish to thank my teachers and colleagues at Emory University, especially Dianne Stewart, Wendy Farley, and Mark D. Jordan, whose insight, advice, good humor, and support have extended far beyond my time as their student. I am grateful to Amy Hollywood for graciously reading and supporting my research, as well as to Luce Irigaray for her questions, her writing, and her wisdom. Emory's Graduate Division of Religion provided an ideal environment for theological formation. The camaraderie, conversations, and questions of my peers in theology have stimulated and sustained my thinking, and I am happy to see that community ever widening as the conversation continues through social media. Kent L. Brintnall, Michelle Voss Roberts, and Meghan Sweeney each deserve special mention for reading and commenting on chapters. I remain grateful for their encouragement, conversation, and friendship.

The Lindsay Young Visiting Fellowship from the Marco Institute for Medieval and Renaissance Studies at the University of Tennessee, Knoxville, supported the research for chapter 4. Portions of the book in progress were presented at meetings of the American Academy of Religion, the International Congress on Medieval Studies, the Southeastern Commission for the Study of Religion, the Luce Irigaray Circle, and the seminar of Luce Irigaray at the University of Nottingham; I am grateful to the audiences in these sessions for their keen questions and conversation. Funding from Emory University, the University of Nottingham, and Christian Brothers University made travel to those meetings possible.

I am grateful to Carey Newman, Jordan Rowan Fannin, and the entire Baylor University Press team for their hard work and professionalism. I owe a particular debt of gratitude to Nicole Smith Murphy, whose editorial wisdom, encouragement, and skill make her midwife to this book. Three anonymous readers provided invaluable suggestions; remaining errors and infelicitous expressions are all my own.

My friends and neighbors in Cooper-Young supported and sustained me with laughter, playdates, dinner, and wine, and I am especially grateful to Emily Fulmer, Laura Willemsen, Jenni Pappas, Laura de Velasco, and Penny Dodds. Cheryl Cornish and the community of First Congregational Church teach me weekly what an incarnational theology looks like in practice.

I am keenly aware that writing depends on a whole host of material conditions, and I am humbled by the work done by others that made my work possible—in particular Laura Holcomb, who empties the trash in my office and asks me about my boys every day; the teachers of Barbara K. Lipman School, First Baptist Day School, and Peabody Elementary, who care for and educate my children; my midwives, Amy and Andrea; Jenessa and Kyra, babysitters extraordinaire; and the Cooper-Young Community Farmers Market, and in particular Josephine and Randy from Tubby Creek Farm, who grow the food that feeds me.

This book was written in three cities and four academic institutions and frequently interrupted by teaching duties and family obligations. While I still wonder at the writing, I know that it never would have been possible without the constant support and love of my parents, JoAnne and Ron, my dear sister, Margaret, my late grandmother, Frances Schmand, and my parents-in-law,

Evelyn and Jack Haught—Jack who provides such an inspiring model of writing theology. As a working mother of two, I spent eight years in the making of this book, from initial proposal to complete manuscript. Perhaps there are better ways to balance academic work with family life, but I am acutely aware that this balance frequently eludes me. Time away from home has been a shared sacrifice, and one that my children did not choose, and so I am especially grateful to my family: to my children, Dominic and Jacob, who daily connect me to the joys and sorrows of growing up, who teach me presence, patience, humor, and perspective, and who give me reason to play, cuddle, and read children's books; to my parents, whose unfailing support made it possible for me to follow my vocation, who shower love on their grandchildren, and who regularly drive over from Little Rock to take care of us all; and finally to my partner, Paul, who kept the household humming along during intense periods of writing and who gave me the time and space that were needed to finish. To him, husband, father, friend, writer, and reader, I dedicate this book.

INTRODUCTION

The incarnation is the beating heart of the Christian message: God with us in a human body, Word made flesh in history, the good news proclaimed in Christ. As a theological doctrine, the incarnation has traditionally referred to Jesus Christ as the uniquely incarnate Word of God, one person in two natures, divine and human, the Logos who "took flesh" and became human for the sake of our salvation. But this classical formulation troubles many in the contemporary world. Naming the incarnation as the turning point of a world-historical narrative of fall and redemption contradicts our contemporary picture of the origins and evolution of the universe.[1] The affirmation of Jesus as the unique incarnation of God excludes the revelations of other religions, and Christology has been particularly problematic for its implicit, at times explicit, anti-Judaism.[2] Consequently, some theologians would prefer to interpret the incarnation as a myth, metaphor, or symbol for Christians rather than a historical event or ontological reality.[3] For many people, even many followers of Christ, the idea of an immaterial, preexistent divine being entering history in the very particular body of a first-century Palestinian Jew is simply unbelievable, if not downright offensive to reason.

---

[1] See Colleen Carpenter Cullinan, "In Pain and Sorrow: Childbirth, Incarnation, and the Suffering of Women," *Crosscurrents* 58, no. 1 (2008): 95–107; and John Haught, *God after Darwin: A Theology of Evolution* (Boulder, Colo.: Westview, 2000).

[2] Sallie McFague, *The Body of God: An Ecological Theology* (Minneapolis: Fortress, 1993), 159.

[3] See John Hick, *The Metaphor of God Incarnate: Christology in a Pluralistic Age*, 2nd ed. (Louisville, Ky.: Westminster John Knox, 2006).

Early in the history of feminist theology, the incarnation came under sharp critique. Along with doctrines such as the Fatherhood of God, sin, and atonement, the incarnation emerged as the site of struggle for many women with Christianity, a source of promise in its affirmation of the body as divine but also of peril in its restriction of the divine to one particular male body and exclusion of women from divinity.[4] For post-Christian feminists such as Daphne Hampson and Mary Daly, the incarnation is the decisive argument against the compatibility of Christianity with the full liberation of women. They reject the concept of a "single divine incarnation in a human being of the male sex"[5] because it "gives a male human being a status which is given to no woman."[6] This problem of how a unique divine incarnation can be salvific for all, including women, is classically described as the "scandal of particularity." The scandal involves both ontology and representation. How could Jesus' singular flesh incorporate all the human differences that mark our particularity, embodied differences of race, sex, ability, class, and sexuality? Womanists have pointed out how the traditional doctrine of the incarnation has not only upheld patriarchal views that subordinate women, but also supported white racism, particularly through images of Christ as a blond-haired, blue-eyed, northern European.[7] For many feminists and womanists, the incarnation begs the question of representation, of how our differences are represented by Christ, as well as who might, in turn, represent him. Rosemary Radford Ruether's classic expression of the theological problem asks whether a male savior can save women: if women cannot represent Christ, then does Christ represent women—or does he instead reinforce their oppression?[8] Many post-Christian women have rejected Christianity for precisely this reason, seeing the doctrine of the incarnation used as a

[4] Lisa Isherwood describes how the incarnation "declares the full flourishing/redemption of all, yet when viewed only as fully evident in Christ, laid such a reducing, restricting burden on the lives of women" in "The Embodiment of Feminist Liberation Theology: The Spiralling of Incarnation," *Feminist Theology* 12, no. 2 (2004): 140–56.

[5] Mary Daly, *Beyond God the Father: Toward a Philosophy of Women's Liberation* (Boston: Beacon, 1973), 71.

[6] Daphne Hampson, *Theology and Feminism* (Cambridge, Mass.: Blackwell, 1990), 76.

[7] See Jacquelyn Grant, *White Women's Christ and Black Women's Jesus: Feminist Christology and Womanist Response* (Atlanta: Scholars, 1989); and Kelly Brown Douglas, *The Black Christ* (Maryknoll, N.Y.: Orbis Books, 1993).

[8] Rosemary Radford Ruether, *Sexism and God-Talk: Toward a Feminist Theology* (Boston: Beacon, 1983), 81. See also Kelley A. Raab, *When Women Become Priests: The Catholic Women's Ordination Debate* (New York: Columbia University Press, 2000).

legitimation of male supremacy[9] and against the full humanity of women.[10] But problems with the traditional view of the incarnation exceed the scandal of particularity and the attendant question of representation.

The gospel of John draws on the Hellenistic Jewish philosophical tradition to describe the manifestation of God as the "Word" (*Logos*).[11] This Word, which became enfleshed in Jesus (John 1:14), signifies both the divine identity of Christ and the rational principle in the human soul that reflects its maker, theoretically making it inclusive of women. But this tradition, as Rosemary Radford Ruether notes, was shaped in a patriarchal and androcentric culture in which power, rationality, divinity, and normative humanity were all assumed to be male. These concepts interlocked with one another to define the Logos in masculine terms, cementing "the assumption that God is male and that the human Christ must be a male in order to reveal the male God."[12] Instead of opening up the doctrine of the incarnation to include women, logos-language was used to reinforce the identity of the maleness of Jesus with a patriarchal view of God.[13] The identification of the Logos with the maleness of Jesus took place in the context of an empire that, by the fourth century, made Christ the Logos, the master signifier of a hierarchical social-political order based on domination and subjugation. Christian understanding of the incarnation came to reflect the hierarchical order of imperial Roman society, with women representing the bodily realm that is ruled over by the masculine logos: power, rationality, and divinity.[14]

For the church fathers, the incarnation of Christ was theoretically inclusive of women, at least with respect to redemption. Jesus' humanity included femaleness—not because Jesus was androgynous or transgender but because an androcentric anthropology considered the male human being normative for both sexes.[15] When Gregory of Nazianzus wrote that "what is not assumed is not redeemed," he meant to emphasize the full and inclusive humanity of

---

[9] As Thomas Aquinas put it, "The male sex is more noble than the female, and for this reason he took human nature in the male sex." *Summa Theologica* 3.31.4 ad 1.

[10] See Mary Daly's famous sermon given in Harvard Memorial Church in 1971, "The Women's Movement: An Exodus Community," *Religious Education* 67 (1972): 327–33.

[11] Rosemary R. Ruether, *Introducing Redemption in Christian Feminism* (Sheffield, UK: Sheffield Academic Press, 1998), 82.

[12] Ruether, *Introducing Redemption*, 82.

[13] See Elizabeth A. Johnson, *She Who Is: The Mystery of God in Feminist Theological Discourse* (New York: Crossroad, 1997), 152–53; and Ruether, *Introducing Redemption*, 83.

[14] Ruether, *Introducing Redemption*, 90–91; cf. Ruether, *Sexism and God-Talk*, 125–26.

[15] See Thomas Laqueur, *Making Sex: Body and Gender from the Greeks to Freud* (Cambridge, Mass.: Harvard University Press, 1990).

Christ: redemption demands the ontological assumption of human nature in its entirety. The particular characteristics of the historical Jesus were unimportant in light of his full humanity, which, together with his full divinity, was essential for salvation. Some postcolonial theologians today take this approach in order to emphasize Jesus' generic and inclusive humanity.[16] But in the history of European theology, women are included in Christ's male body only because men are seen as both normative and representative of all humanity. Christ's humanity reflects and reinforces an androcentric anthropology that makes maleness both the human standard and superior to femaleness.[17] Today we have lost the philosophical framework (derived from both Aristotle and neo-Platonism) that makes this line of thinking comprehensible.[18] Our understanding of biology and anthropology recognizes a range of sexual differentiation and no longer takes the male human being as normative for humanity. The question of whether "what is not assumed is not redeemed" reemerges in this perspective and, for contemporary women, demands new interpretations of the incarnation.

The drama of redemption surrounding the traditional understanding of the incarnation additionally leaves highly problematic roles for women. In the form of Eve, woman is blamed for the fall and the subsequent necessity of the incarnation, and death, of Christ. Women are thereby placed within a theological framework of guilt as daughters of Eve.[19] But woman is just as problematically praised in the figure of Mary, whose virginity makes the incarnation possible in a traditional patrilineal genealogy of Father and Son. In this framework, Jesus' divinity is inherited from his father; paternity is guaranteed by the sexual purity of his mother.[20] All other female bodies appear as fallen, daughters of Eve, while Mary, alone of all her sex, makes possible the incarnation of the Son through her inimitable combination of virginity with

---

[16] E.g., see the postcolonial feminist theologian Monica Melanchton, who sees Jesus as the representative of new humanity, both women and men, through his incarnation; cited in Chung Hyun Kung, *Struggle to Be the Sun Again: Introducing Asian Women's Theology* (Maryknoll, N.Y.: Orbis Books, 1990), 60.

[17] Ruether, *Sexism and God-Talk*, 126.

[18] See Hampson, *Theology and Feminism*.

[19] See Isherwood, "Embodiment," 141; see also Cullinan, "In Pain and Sorrow," 95–101; and Tertullian (c.160–c.225), "On the Apparel of Women," trans. S. Thelwall, in *Ante-Nicene Fathers: Translations of the Writings of the Fathers down to A.D. 325*, Vol. 4, ed. Alexander Roberts and James Donaldson (Buffalo, N.Y.: Christian Literature Publishing, 1885), 1.1.

[20] Laurel Schneider, "Promiscuous Incarnation," in *The Embrace of Eros: Bodies, Desires, and Sexuality in Christianity*, ed. Margaret D. Kamitsuka (Minneapolis: Fortress, 2010), 238.

motherhood.[21] Women become, perhaps inevitably in this schema, the privileged representatives of sin, sex, and death—passively redeemed through their association with men, but reminders of the flesh God did *not* choose for his unique revelation.[22] The natural resemblance argument against women's ordination reinforces this view of women's bodies, which become "a prison that shuts them off from God, except as mediated through the christic male."[23] The incarnation appears to leave women's flesh bereft of sacramental significance, more sinful somehow than male flesh.[24]

These problems with the incarnation are real and pressing, and yet as feminists and womanists increasingly emphasize *embodiment* as a key value of their theology the powerful notion of incarnation beckons. Rather than rejecting the incarnation as a mere metaphor on the one hand, or becoming embroiled in arcane debates over the metaphysics of the hypostatic union on the other, many feminist theologians have been drawn to the liberatory potential in the words of the fourth gospel: "And the Word became flesh and lived among us." One of the most fascinating things about Jesus from a feminist perspective is the divinity of his body and the potential, indicated by the incarnation, for a divinization of flesh.[25] Because the historical Jesus was male, he is the manifestation of God made man. Flesh and blood, fully human and divine, his incarnation is richly suggestive of human potential, but it remains partial, limited to male flesh. The question is how we might extend our understanding of the incarnation to include women's flesh.

Inclusive Christologies

Feminists and womanists[26] have found a remarkable variety of ways to extend the incarnation from its traditional location in the historical body of Jesus

---

[21] See Marina Warner, *Alone of All Her Sex: The Myth and the Cult of the Virgin Mary* (New York: Knopf, 1976).

[22] See Ruether, *Sexism and God-Talk*, 134–35.

[23] Johnson, *She Who Is*, 153.

[24] See, for instance, the misogyny of Heinrich Kramer and James Sprenger's manual for witchcraft inquisitors, *The Malleus Maleficarum*, trans. Montague Summers (1484; New York: Dover, 1971), 47: "All witchcraft comes from carnal lust, which is in women insatiable."

[25] See Luce Irigaray, "Equal to Whom?" in *The Essential Difference*, ed. Naomi Schor and Elizabeth Weed, trans. Robert L. Mazzola (Bloomington: Indiana University Press, 1994), 72.

[26] In what follows, and for the sake of brevity, I use "womanists and feminists" as a shorthand for liberation theologies arising from the diverse experience of women, including Mujerista/feminista/Latina/Hispanic women's theologies, Asian and Asian-American women's theologies, African women's theologies, postcolonial and Third World (or Two/Thirds

of Nazareth to include other bodies, other flesh, as the bodies of Christ on earth. These inclusive Christologies have shown something of a revival of incarnation language in women's theological writings in recent years, perhaps against expectations.[27] With increasing focus on embodiment, womanist and feminist theologians have turned to the incarnation as the core message of the Christian gospel: the enfleshment of God in Jesus and his liberating and inclusive embodied practices. These practices show the way Christians might live as followers of Christ through sacrament and solidarity with others. Incarnation emerges as the interpretive heart of Christianity, the lens through which all other doctrines and practices appear, and, in Wendy Farley's metaphor, as a prism that "allows a world structured by love to be glimpsed" like the colors of invisible light.[28]

Womanists and feminists have held up this prism to reveal the myriad ways in which women's bodies can be included within the incarnation, from the figure of Wisdom to the experience of suffering, from the message and praxis of Jesus to our own practices of liberation. The following typology analyzes the rich variety of ways women theologians have discovered female flesh within the body of Christ. These are not mutually exclusive, and together they paint a rich and vivid picture of the incarnation. None, however, explores the central Johannine categories of Word and flesh and their potential significance for women's bodies and women's writing practices. Before considering writing the body along with other ways of participating

---

world) theologies, queer and lesbian theologies, and theologies of disability. In order to do justice to this remarkable theological, racial, ethnic, and sexual diversity, I refer to many specific theologians who identify with particular oppressed communities and also as feminists, with recognition that "feminist" is a contested term, not only but frequently associated with whiteness. My aim is not to assimilate difference among women to what Ellen Armour calls "whitefeminism," but to honor the diversity of women and their concern for the liberation of women as gender intersects with other forms of oppression. See Ellen T. Armour, *Deconstruction, Feminist Theology, and the Problem of Difference: Subverting the Race/Gender Divide* (Chicago: University of Chicago Press, 1999).

[27] For instance, two recent books in constructive theology take the incarnation as their primary locus: Wendy Farley's *Gathering Those Driven Away: A Theology of Incarnation* (Louisville, Ky.: Westminster John Knox, 2011), a systematic theology written from the underside and margins of Christianity, and M. Shawn Copeland's *Enfleshing Freedom: Body, Race, and Being* (Minneapolis: Fortress, 2010), a theological anthropology written with special attention to black bodies under slavery. While Farley's book can be seen as an extended meditation on Schleiermacher's *Christmas Eve Dialogue*, Copeland's is an extended meditation on Toni Morrison's *Beloved*.

[28] Farley, *Gathering*, 14.

in the incarnation, however, one must first grapple with the fact that Jesus' historical body was male.

The Maleness of Jesus

Most feminist and womanist Christologies begin with a frank acknowledgment of the maleness of Jesus. Beginning with that indisputable fact of the incarnation, it turns out, does not limit but opens up more inclusive interpretations.[29] Too much of Christian theology can be seen as "a long flight from the full consequences of its central profession" of the incarnation, a "vehement refusal to think Jesus' sex while insisting on his masculinity."[30] The problem with the incarnation is not the maleness of Jesus; it is the way Jesus' masculinity has been distorted and used to support male hegemony in both social structures and theology, including in the doctrine of God and theological anthropology.[31] When we turn our attention to the way Jesus himself performed his masculinity as portrayed in the Gospels, we see a radical subversion of patriarchy. Instead of reinforcing the Roman hierarchies of gender, class, and ethnicity, Jesus overturns them, associating with the poor and marginalized, with women and tax collectors. Mercy Amba Oduyoye writes that African women claim the "so-called feminine traits they find in Jesus—his care and compassion for the weak and excluded. The anti-hunger ministry, healing, and the place of children in his words and works—all go together to create a bonding around women's lives that African women feel with Jesus. He is one of us, knows our world, and can therefore accompany us in our daily joys and struggles."[32] Again and again, feminist biblical scholars and theologians have pointed out how Jesus' teaching and practices, his

---

[29] See, for instance, Shawn Copeland, who finds this blunt acknowledgment liberating for the full inclusion of lesbians and gay men in the Body of Christ. "Jesus of Nazareth had a human body," she writes, "his was a male body, he had the genitals of a male human being. To refuse to speak about his sex and gender far too often leaves us unable to speak well and compassionately about sex, about gender, about sexuality, and, especially, about homosexuality." Copeland, *Enfleshing*, 62.

[30] Mark D. Jordan, "God's Body," in *Queer Theology: Rethinking the Western Body*, ed. Gerard Loughlin (Oxford: Blackwell, 2007), 281–92, 283.

[31] See Elizabeth A. Johnson, "Redeeming the Name of Christ," in *Freeing Theology: The Essentials of Theology in Feminist Perspective*, ed. Catherine Mowry LaCugna (San Francisco: Harper, 1993), 134.

[32] Mercy Amba Oduyoye, "Jesus Christ," in *Hope Abundant: Third World and Indigenous Women's Theology*, ed. Kwok Pui-lan (Maryknoll, N.Y.: Orbis Books, 2010), 167–85, 181.

life and ministry, directly opposed and undercut expressions of patriarchal power, violence, exploitation, and exclusion.[33]

Rosemary Radford Ruether famously described Jesus' maleness as kenotic—that is, emptying—of patriarchy. While she argues that the maleness of Jesus has no ultimate theological significance, it does have social symbolic significance in a patriarchal social context. That is, Jesus dissociates maleness from patriarchal power in his life and ministry, which rejects hierarchical privilege and speaks for the lowly.[34] In this view, Jesus' maleness emerges as prophetic; his countercultural performance of masculinity challenges patriarchal forces of domination and empties them of their power. For other feminist theologians, Jesus' maleness was a downright advantage to his message. Surely if a woman had advocated love and service to others, the world would have yawned, while Jesus attracted attention with the same message because it emerged from a social position of male privilege.[35] Jesus teaches a new way of being human, by identifying with the poor and the despised, beginning with the subversive way in which he embodied masculinity. His incarnation was kenotic not only of patriarchy, but also of anything that would prevent full human liberation, and it is to this divine destiny, this new way of being human, that our flesh, too, is called.[36] In order to understand the full significance of the incarnation, we have to appreciate the maleness of Jesus' flesh.

But the maleness of the historical, earthly Jesus can be distinguished from other ways in which Christ is incarnate: the Wisdom that Christ embodies, the cosmic Christ, his embodied message and practice, the Christ who dwells in the church and in liberative community, the Christ met in the liturgy and sacraments, the Christ who suffers with the afflicted, and the incarnation of Christ through Mary, the Spirit, and the divinization of his followers. In these aspects, Christ is no longer restricted to the maleness of the historical, earthly body of Jesus. Instead, Christ's divinity can be encountered in gendered and nongendered ways, both embodied and transcendent.[37] An exploration of each of these various directions helps to expand our understanding of the incarnation.

[33] See, e.g., Copeland, *Enfleshing*, 63; and McFague, *Body of God*, 162-76.
[34] Ruether, *Sexism and God-Talk*, 137.
[35] See Johnson, *She Who Is*, 160.
[36] See Copeland, *Enfleshing*, 64–65.
[37] See Julius Gathogo, "Christology in African Women's Theology," *Africa Theological Journal* 31, no. 2 (2008): 75–92.

Wisdom/Sophia

One way of arguing for an inclusive incarnation is by reviving the biblical language of Wisdom or Sophia. The Wisdom literature of the Hebrew scriptures describes the immanence of God through the female metaphor of divine Wisdom or, in Greek, *Sophia*, which is theologically identical to the description of Jesus as the Logos or Son of God in the New Testament.[38] Wisdom is associated with creation, ordering the cosmos and offering life to all; she is in solidarity with human beings, and her paths are justice and peace. Early Christian writers such as Paul and the evangelists used this concept to explain the way in which God was present in Jesus. With a few notable exceptions (such as Hildegard of Bingen), however, most theologians in the history of Christianity have preferred the masculine symbols of Logos or Son to refer to the divine being that became incarnate in Jesus, cementing the erroneous idea that Jesus' historical maleness reflects an ontological connection with the maleness of the Son or Logos, which is itself seen as the necessary expression of a male (Father) God.[39] But there is no *theological* reason for this preference, and numerous feminist theologians have recovered this biblical language to describe Christ as the incarnation and prophet of Sophia/Wisdom.[40] Since the synoptic gospels and the writings of Paul identify Jesus' divinity as the Wisdom of God,[41] reclaiming this way of speaking about Jesus' incarnation allows feminist theologians to use flexible and inclusive language in their Christologies. It is a way of extending the incarnation—not through the particular flesh of Jesus, but through the divine figure incarnate in him.

Elizabeth Johnson developed this language most fully for systematic theology in her feminist classic, *She Who Is*.[42] Johnson retells the story of Jesus as the incarnation of Sophia, emphasizing Sophia's ordering of the cosmos, her offer of life abundant, and her solidarity with those who suffer. While the symbol of Sophia has both biblical foundation and orthodox provenance, she introduces gender fluidity into Christ, who even in his human maleness

---

[38] See Ruether, *Sexism and God-Talk*, 117.

[39] See Ruether, *Sexism and God-Talk*, 117.

[40] See in particular Elisabeth Schüssler Fiorenza, Elizabeth Johnson, and Rosemary Radford Ruether.

[41] E.g., in Luke 11:49, Mt 11:18–19, 1 Cor 1:24. See also Elisabeth Schüssler Fiorenza, *In Memory of Her: A Feminist Theological Reconstruction of Christian Origins* (New York: Crossroad, 1983).

[42] See Johnson, *She Who Is*, 86–100 and 124–87.

reveals God in female form.[43] Wisdom Christology also reverses the gendered categories of Greek metaphysics: in Wisdom, the feminine is associated with cosmic ordering and transcendence, while Jesus' maleness signifies the earthly and human. This gender fluidity dislodges any sense of a necessary ontological connection between the maleness of Jesus and a masculine God and thereby makes Christology more inclusive of women.[44] Reclaiming the biblical strands of Sophia Christology reinforces the ultimately inclusive intent, as some see it, of the doctrine of the incarnation as it developed through the councils of Nicaea and Chalcedon.[45] Although Johnson acknowledges the ways in which the doctrine has been used against women, Jesus as Sophia incarnate reveals the inclusive *intent* of orthodox Christology. Because divine Sophia incarnate in Jesus calls all people to be friends of God, she can be represented by anyone, women as well as men.[46]

The intent of the doctrine of the incarnation is indeed inclusive, nor is gender constitutive of its classical form: what is not assumed is not redeemed, and the assumption of humanity by Wisdom/Sophia signals redemption offered to all. But as particularity has received greater attention in recent years, feminists have wrestled with the problem of the universal—such as "humanity" or "woman"—and the dangers of obscuring differences through representation by one person. We now recognize that all of us are shaped and determined by the particularities of our social location: our sex, race, class, sexual orientation, ability, age, body size, religion, and so on. These details of our lives intersect and multiply;[47] they are ascribed social significance as we are positioned through these categories, frequently to our detriment.[48] We increasingly recognize the dangers of claiming to represent or speak for others, the assumed privileges of white racism, for instance, or of heteronormativity.[49] And yet, when it comes to the incarnation of Christ, historical

---

[43] See Johnson, *She Who Is*, 165.

[44] Johnson, *She Who Is*, 99; see also 165.

[45] See Johnson, *She Who Is*, 153.

[46] Johnson, *She Who Is*, 165.

[47] See Kimberlé Crenshaw, "Demarginalizing the Intersection of Race and Sex: A Black Feminist Critique of Antidiscrimination Doctrine, Feminist Theory, and Antiracist Politics," in *Feminist Legal Theory: Readings in Law and Gender*, ed. T. K. Bartlett and R. Kennedy (Boulder, Colo.: Westview, 1991), 57–80.

[48] See Nancy Hartsock, "The Feminist Standpoint: Developing the Ground for a Specifically Feminist Historical Materialism," in *Discovering Reality*, ed. Sandra Harding and Merrell Hintikka (Dortrecht, Holland: Reidel, 1983), 283–310; and Patricia Hill Collins, *Black Feminist Thought*, 2nd ed. (New York: Routledge, 2000).

[49] See Elizabeth V. Spelman, *Inessential Woman: Problems of Exclusion in Feminist*

particularities such as maleness, Jewish ethnicity, social class, native language, etc. do not have privileged significance. It is not somehow "more appropriate" for God to be incarnate in one particular social reality rather than another.[50] This is an important objection to those who would undercut the universal significance of the incarnation by claiming that men naturally resemble Christ better than women. And yet this approach, emphasizing the universality and inclusivity of the incarnation, risks evading the problem of particularity and representation. The figure of divine Wisdom or Sophia fruitfully expands our appreciation of the divinity incarnate in Jesus, but Jesus' historical body, his flesh, remains male. Although in this perspective women can represent Christ and share in his mission,[51] we still lack a representation of female flesh as divine. What should be the good news of the embodiment of the divine can be made still more inclusive.

The Cosmic and Ecological Christ

One distinct advantage, however, of the biblical Wisdom-language is the way in which Wisdom connects Christ to the natural world and indeed the entire cosmos.[52] Christ as Wisdom (and as Logos) is the principle through which the world was created as well as the power of new creation, renewing and reconciling the entire cosmos with God.[53] This view of the cosmogonic Logos, the creator, redeemer, and fulfillment of the world, is sometimes referred to as cosmological Christology or the cosmic Christ. In his battles with world-disparaging gnostic Christians, Irenaeus of Lyons, for instance, came to see creation itself as an incarnation of the Logos, reaffirmed and renewed through the incarnation in Jesus. In both creation and in Jesus the Christ, divine power makes a sacrament out of what is material and body.[54] Christ is incarnate in the world in both its origin and its telos; the particular incarnation of God

---

Thought (Boston: Beacon, 1988); and Adrienne Rich, "Compulsory Heterosexuality and Lesbian Existence," in *Blood, Bread, and Poetry: Selected Prose, 1979–1985* (New York: Norton, 1986), 23–75.

[50] Johnson, *She Who Is*, 166.

[51] Johnson, *She Who Is*, 167.

[52] See Johnson, *She Who Is*, 166.

[53] In this sacramental view of the cosmic Christ, salvation is not the least bit otherworldly. As Ruether notes, the "culmination of this process of . . . reconciliation of the cosmos with God, is, as Paul puts it in 1 Corinthians 12:25, 'So that God may be all in all.'" *Gaia and God: An Ecofeminist Theology of Earth Healing* (San Francisco: Harper Collins, 1992), 233.

[54] See Ruether, *Gaia and God*, 235.

in Jesus instantiates this more general incarnational relationship of the Logos to the world.[55]

The incarnation of Christ in both cosmos and in Jesus has tremendous potential for valuing the natural world and the bodies of plants, animals, and human beings. And yet, despite being so focused on embodiment, Christianity has, as Sallie McFague notes, "denied, subjugated, and at times despised the body, especially female human bodies and bodies in the natural world."[56] In response, McFague develops the implications of the cosmic Christ for a new model of the God-universe relationship in creation.[57] Rather than a king who is sovereign over his domain, God is immanent in the universe, making the natural world "the body of God." But this model must be specified through "the Christic paradigm"—that is, the particular incarnation in the historical body of Jesus. The Christic paradigm makes the story of Jesus exemplary for understanding God's relationship to creation.[58]

Both the particularity of the historical Jesus and the extension of the incarnation in the entire cosmos must be held together. Jesus' life and death are paradigmatic for a Christian understanding of how God is present in creation.[59] Just as Jesus practiced inclusive love for all, but in particular for the marginalized and oppressed, God's love for creation extends beyond humanity to nature in all its rich diversity, which McFague calls "the new

---

[55] This notion of the cosmic Christ is taken up by several more recent thinkers such as Teilhard de Chardin and Matthew Fox, although their writings are not without problems. Ruether, for example, critiques aspects of the theory of the cosmic Christ for its seeming denial of mortality, in its ancient form, and of materiality and equality, in its modern form. See *Gaia and God*, 234–37 and 242–45.

[56] McFague, *Body of God*, 163.

[57] McFague, *Body of God*, 160.

[58] McFague rejects the traditional narrative of the incarnation and proposes a constructive theological view that both "relativize[s] the incarnation in relation to Jesus . . . and maximize[s] it in relation to the cosmos." *Body of God*, 162.

[59] Although I do not have the space to discuss it here, an important aspect of McFague's discussion is the place of the cross and God's response to suffering—both human and within the natural world—in creation. Part of the Christic paradigm for the world as God's body involves the way of the cross—that is, suffering in solidarity with those who suffer, and advocating for their liberation, as signified by the resurrection. She writes, "In both forms of Christian solidarity with the oppressed, the active and the passive, liberation and suffering, the cross and resurrection of the Christic paradigm are central to an embodiment theology." *Body of God*, 173. In McFague's panentheistic model of the world as God's body, God feels the pain and suffering of all those who "live and move and have our being in God," including the suffering of the natural world, because "God, though assymetrically, lives in us as well." *Body of God*, 176.

poor" due to human exploitation, domination, and neglect.[60] Here feminist liberation theology can be logically extended in the direction of ecological concern. Brazilian ecofeminist theologian Ivone Gebara develops her incarnational theology in order to address both the poverty of the slums and environmental degradation, through a religion "rooted in human flesh and in the flesh of the earth."[61] It is through our bodies that we perceive God's presence in the bodies of others and in the body of the earth. The incarnation of particular bodies, bodies without access to running water or adequate sewage, concrete, suffering, and silenced bodies, therefore takes priority over metaphysical reflections on the mystery of the incarnation in Gebara's concern for the lives of the poor.

In an ecological perspective, the incarnation is not limited to the historical body of Jesus. The resurrected Christ is a manifestation of the cosmic Christ, through whom the world is created and redeemed. This power of God, the power of creation and redemption, is present in all bodies; it is incarnate in the world.[62] The image of the cosmic Christ means that salvation is not separated temporally or sequentially from creation as an otherworldly remedy for a fallen world; rather salvation takes place *in* creation, and creation always tends *toward* salvation. The incarnation was always the means of God's revelation of divine love, in the creation of the world and in the life and ministry of Jesus.[63]

Message and Praxis

In contrast to ontological extensions of the incarnation through the cosmos or the figure of Wisdom, many feminists and womanists have shifted focus away from Jesus' person entirely and to his message and praxis, which can be taken up and embodied by anyone. In this view, redemption and liberation come from Jesus' life and ministry rather than his incarnation or his crucifixion.[64] Critical of classical forms of Christology that emphasize Jesus' generic

---

[60] McFague, *Body of God*, 160–65.

[61] Ivone Gebara, *Longing for Running Water: Ecofeminism and Liberation* (Minneapolis: Fortress, 1999), 177.

[62] "The New Testament appearance stories attest to the continuing empowerment of the Christic paradigm in the world: the liberating, inclusive love of God for all is alive in and through the entire cosmos." McFague, *Body of God*, 179.

[63] McFague, *Body of God*, 180.

[64] Rosemary Radford Ruether is perhaps the most famous exponent of this perspective; see especially *Sexism and God-Talk*, 134–38. But see also the writings of Elisabeth Schüssler Fiorenza, such as *Jesus: Miriam's Child, Sophia's Prophet* (New York: Continuum, 1994); and

humanity and purported inclusion of women in his incarnation, many feminists have turned instead to the Jesus of the synoptic gospels and his prophetic message and ministry. Here one finds Jesus depicted as a prophet and iconoclast who overturns relationships based on domination.[65] What makes Jesus paradigmatic for Christians in this perspective is not his metaphysical incarnation or much less his maleness. Rather, it is the way he lives out and embodies his message of good news to the poor, of rejection of systems of oppression, and of love and liberation by God offered to the most despised.[66]

This "message" Christology is a powerful way of focusing on the ministry of Jesus, his reversal of social order, his practices of care, and his refusal of social division and relationships based on domination. It is also a way of avoiding the question of his sexed incarnation entirely. His male embodiment simply is not relevant for the view of Jesus as liberator; what matters instead is what he said and did. His body matters only insofar as it expresses the concrete embodiment of a set of liberative practices, replacing systems of domination with service, compassion, and empowerment of the least.[67]

Shifting attention to the message and praxis of the Jesus of the synoptic gospels makes the practices of the historical Jesus normative for the Christian understanding of Christ. "The Christ" is inclusive of women insofar as they too engage in prophetic critique and liberating practice. In this way, the notion of incarnation can be subtly reintroduced. That is, when Christians imitate Christ and share his message and practices, they participate in redemption and themselves incarnate Christ. Christ can then be seen in the face of every person and every group insofar as they struggle for liberation: as Black, as lesbian, as Latina, as disabled. The coming Christ is not a reiteration of the incarnation in Jesus of Nazareth, but rather "the fullness of human diversity gathered together in redemptive community."[68]

Redemptive Community

A common theme among both womanist and feminist theologians is finding the resurrected Christ incarnate in the community of all who share in

---

Carter Heyward, *The Redemption of God: A Theology of Mutual Relation* (Eugene, Ore.: Wipf & Stock, 2010).

[65] "His ability to speak as liberator does not reside in his maleness but in the fact that he has renounced this system of domination and seeks to embody in his person the new humanity of service and mutual empowerment." Ruether, *Sexism and God-Talk*, 137.

[66] See Ruether, *Introducing Redemption*, 93.

[67] Ruether, *Sexism and God-Talk*, 137.

[68] Ruether, *Introducing Redemption*, 94.

his compassionate love, participate in acts of justice and peace, and struggle for liberation in solidarity with those who suffer. This interpretation of the incarnation is a variation on the metaphors used by Paul in the first letter to the Corinthians—"now you are the body of Christ and individually members of it," (1 Cor 12:27)—and by John in his gospel: "I am the vine, you are the branches" (John 15:5). From the beginning, the community of disciples shares the confession that Jesus is the Christ and that the continuing Christian community participates in Christhood through baptism, taking on a christomorphic character as the body of Christ.[69] Jesus is the foundational representative of the way of love and liberation, but not its unique or exclusive manifestation. Each disciple must follow, and thereby become Christ to one another. As Ruether argues, "The church becomes redemptive community, not by passively receiving redemption 'won' by Christ alone, but rather by collectively embodying this path of liberation in a way that transforms people and social systems."[70]

While for most theologians Christ is preeminently the one who reveals, embodies, and teaches the way of redemption, his abiding incarnate connection to the community shows the power of his relationships with others. Divine incarnation and salvific power manifest in connectedness and relationality rather than individuals.[71] Finding salvation in the erotic power (as defined by Audre Lorde)[72] that emerges within community, Rita Nakashima Brock emphasizes the relational character of incarnation: the Christ continues through the community that embodies his love.[73] Shawn Copeland likewise deploys the language of eros in community to describe Jesus' incarnation, as he lived out of an embodied spirituality and gave his body out of love to and for others.[74] With particular reference to the bodies of those who have suffered in history, such as the enslaved, and the bodies of those who are excluded and marginalized today, such as lesbians and gay men, Copeland

---

[69] See Johnson, *She Who Is*, 161.

[70] Ruether, *Introducing Redemption*, 93.

[71] Rita Nakashima Brock, *Journeys by Heart: A Christology of Erotic Power* (New York: Crossroad, 1988), 52. Charlene P. E. Burns uses social-scientific research to argue for retaining the ontological definition of the incarnation through the concept of empathic relation in *Divine Becoming: Rethinking Jesus and the Incarnation* (Minneapolis: Fortress, 2002).

[72] See Audre Lorde, "Uses of the Erotic: The Erotic as Power," in *Sister Outsider: Essays and Speeches by Audre Lorde* (Trumansburg, N.Y.: Crossing, 1985), 53-59.

[73] Brock thereby ultimately (and unconvincingly) displaces Jesus as the locus and primary referent for the language of incarnation and salvation. See Brock, *Journeys By Heart*, 52–69.

[74] Copeland, *Enfleshing*, 65.

sees the power of the incarnation extended through all flesh.[75] Jesus calls Christians to break the bonds of oppression and to realize themselves as his own flesh, as the body of Christ on earth.[76]

But recognizing our own bodies as Jesus' own flesh, as the body of Christ, is hard for those who have been excluded, marginalized, and oppressed precisely because of their bodily differences. For that reason, the incarnation takes place only in the context of a hospitable, affirming, and radically inclusive community. "If my sister or brother is not at the table, we are not the flesh of Christ. If my sister's mark of sexuality must be obscured, if my brother's mark of race must be disguised, if my sister's mark of culture must be repressed, then we are not the flesh of Christ. . . . Unless our sisters and brothers are beside and with each of us, we are not the flesh of Christ."[77] The flesh of the marginalized is the prophetic witness of the body of Christ. Without them, the incarnation is incomplete.[78] Manifesting the flesh of Christ requires both radical inclusivity and imitation of Jesus' ministry through acts of justice, critique of domination, solidarity with the oppressed, and love of others.[79] These acts create redemptive community; even more, they incarnate Christ on earth. This form of incarnation is "promiscuous," mixing indiscriminately with the flesh of all those who suffer.[80] God is repeatedly incarnate wherever God's purpose of radical justice and promiscuous love for all suffering flesh is practiced and pursued.

---

[75] Unlike Brock, Copeland holds Jesus of Nazareth as the standard and measure for what the incarnation means in terms of concrete practices of justice. Jesus "is the clearest example of what it means to identify with children and women and men who are poor, excluded, and despised; to take their side in the struggle for life—no matter the cost. His incarnation witnesses to a divine destiny seeded in our very flesh . . . His incarnation . . . disrupts every pleasure of hierarchy, economy, cultural domination, racial violence, gender oppression, and abuse of sexual others." Copeland, *Enfleshing*, 65; see also 87.

[76] Copeland reads 1 Corinthians through the lens of Toni Morrison's *Beloved*, powerfully claiming that "We are the body raised up by Christ for himself within humanity; through us, the flesh of the crucified and resurrected Jesus is extended through time and space . . . We are all transformed in Christ: *we are his very own flesh.*" Copeland, *Enfleshing*, 82. Emphasis in original.

[77] Copeland, *Enfleshing*, 82.

[78] "The church requires the voices of those driven away because these are ones that Wisdom herself uses: lovers of Christ who were declared heretics or were burned or consigned to silence, those who are difficult to find in seminary curriculum, womanist, feminist, queer, activist. They may not make up the structure of the institutional church, but without them the body of Christ is hopelessly maimed and dismembered." Farley, *Gathering*, 5.

[79] Copeland, *Enfleshing*, 81.

[80] Schneider, "Promiscuous Incarnation," 245.

Extending the incarnation through redemptive community is a far cry from the patriarchal image of the church as the bride of Christ.[81] In contrast to that image, feminist and womanist thinkers extend the incarnation beyond the bounds of the Christian church to recognize liberating and revelatory events wherever they occur.[82] In Matthew 25, the Son of Man is incarnate, though unrecognized, in "the least of these," the hungry, the naked, the imprisoned. Christ is present in the bodies of the afflicted and in the gestures of those who come to their aid.[83] Wherever liberation is practiced, or justice is pursued, or love is shared, Christ is incarnate in the struggles of redemptive community.

Liturgy and Sacraments

Christ is incarnate in a distinctive way, however, in the liturgy of the church, which recognizes Christ's presence in word and sacrament. The risen Christ is encountered "through the Spirit wherever two or three gather, bread is broken, the hungry fed."[84] The Eucharist in particular makes Christ present in the elements of bread and wine and in the bodies of those who give thanks and eat. The Eucharist is a way of practicing the incarnation by making Christ present in the flesh of all who remember him in solidarity with the despised. It is also the reenactment of the dangerous memory of Jesus' torture, death, and resurrection in which the recipients incorporate his body into their own. Such practice is a form of solidarity with all who are tortured and put to death, an act of resistance to the forces of empire, a gesture of hope for new life as we "strive to become what we have received and to do what we are being made" through the sacrament.[85]

But Christ is present only when all are welcome to the table. While the Eucharist in theory recognizes the sacramentality of disabled bodies, celebrating the God whose body was broken for a broken people, in practice

[81] An image that Mary Daly rightly criticized as "another way of conveying that [the church] is 'the extension of the Incarnation,' since a bride or wife in patriarchy is merely an extension of her husband." Daly, *Beyond*, 139.

[82] For Daly, "The point is not to deny that a revelatory event took place in the encounter with the person Jesus. Rather, it is to affirm that the creative presence of the Verb can be revealed at every historical moment, in every person and culture." Daly, *Beyond*, 71.

[83] With reference to this passage, McFague includes "the least of these" in incarnation: "God is present when and where the oppressed are liberated, the sick are healed, the outcast are invited in . . . so also every creaturely body in need is Christ's body, if we can see it as such." McFague, *Body of God*, 195.

[84] Johnson, *She Who Is*, 163.

[85] Copeland, *Enfleshing*, 127.

it tragically becomes a ritual of exclusion in many churches.[86] For people with disabilities, architectural barriers, assumptions of the ability to stand or kneel, and reactions to nonconforming bodies such as staring make the Eucharist into a painful moment of exclusion.[87] Christ is not present when a group of people is segregated or excluded based on their bodily differences. The disabled God is incarnate in the Eucharist only when the sacramentality of bodies in all their diversity is celebrated.[88]

The Eucharist is only one example of the more general principle of sacramentality in Christianity by which the material becomes the visible sign of God's invisible grace, making the divine present in material form. This principle of sacramentality rests upon a more fundamental "principle of Incarnation" through which all bodies, in their particularity, can function as the visible, material signs of God's grace. Because Jesus is the exemplary sacrament of God, making God visible and present through the incarnation in one particular form, all bodies can be seen as sites of sacramental encounter, as extensions of the body of Christ in the world.[89] The principle of incarnation, by which flesh becomes the sign of divine grace, makes embodiment itself sacramental.[90]

Suffering

When white feminist theologians include women's bodies in their Christologies through the figure of divine Wisdom or through liberating and redemptive community, they tend to de-emphasize Christ's suffering and death on the cross. The crucifixion is often seen as a tragedy, as the forces of empire putting to death a radical ministry, but without redemptive or atoning significance in itself.[91] For many white feminists, redemption comes through Jesus' way of life, ministry, and resurrection, but not his death. Women participate

[86] Nancy L. Eiesland, *The Disabled God: Toward a Liberatory Theology of Disability* (Nashville, Tenn.: Abingdon, 1994), 107.

[87] Eiesland, *Disabled God*, 113.

[88] Eiesland, *Disabled God*, 114.

[89] Hannah Bacon, "A Very Particular Body: Assessing the Doctrine of Incarnation for Affirming the Sacramentality of Female Embodiment," in *Women and the Divine: Touching Transcendence*, ed. Gillian Howie and J'annine Jobling (New York: Palgrave Macmillan, 2009), 238.

[90] Bacon, "Particular Body," 238.

[91] For a critique of this perspective and argument for the feminist value of the crucifixion itself as a moment of self-shattering represented by the cross, see Kent L. Brintnall, *Ecce Homo: The Male-Body-in-Pain as Redemptive Figure* (Chicago: University of Chicago Press, 2012).

in the Christ by sharing in redemptive community, not by imitating his self-sacrifice or sharing in his suffering. The notion of participating in redemptive suffering is rejected as a dangerous burden assigned to women under patriarchy. In contrast, many *mujerista*/Latina/feminista and womanist theologians see the suffering of Christ as a place of shared incarnation with redemptive significance. That is, instead of being enjoined to suffer like Christ suffered, these theologians flip the narrative to claim that Christ participates in the suffering of women.

The encounter of Christ in suffering takes on incarnational significance in the writings of Latina theologians. Christ walks with those who suffer and empowers struggle, survival, and resistance through resurrection. Christ appears incarnate "hidden in, with, and under our suffering."[92] Jesus Christ did not suffer simply for the sake of suffering, nor do Latinas, according to Alicia Vargas, but their suffering gains meaning when it is understood through the framework of Christ's suffering. More precisely, his suffering is a way of identifying with and participating in *their* suffering, of offering it meaning and redemption. The common suffering shared by Christ and Latinas is a moment of incarnation, in which God embraces bodily pain, suffering, and oppression. In her elaboration of *mujerista* theology, Ada María Isasi-Díaz criticizes the traditional image of Christ proclaimed by the church as seeming "to float above human reality, nullifying the most precious meaning of the incarnation of God in Jesus of Nazareth,"[93] which, for her, is found in the daily struggles of ordinary women. Christ brings salvation through liberation in this world through solidarity, compassion, and the struggle against injustice.

Womanist theologian Jacqueline Grant likewise identifies Jesus as the divine cosufferer who meets and empowers African-Americans in the context of oppression.[94] Recognizing shared suffering with Christ locates his presence directly in the bodies of those who suffer. This gesture extends the incarnation to incorporate the oppressed through their suffering. It also lays the theological foundation for a new way of encountering and naming the Christ.[95] James Cone famously asserted that because Jesus identified with

---

[92] Alicia Vargas, "The Construction of Latina Christology: An Invitation to Dialogue," *Currents in Theology and Mission* 34, no. 4 (2007): 271–77, 273–74.

[93] Ada María Isasi-Díaz, *La Lucha Continues: Mujerista Theology* (Maryknoll, N.Y.: Orbis Books, 2004), 245.

[94] Shared suffering meant that Christian Black women "identified with Jesus because they believed that Jesus identified with them. As Jesus was persecuted and made to suffer undeservedly, so were they." Grant, *White Women's Christ*, 212.

[95] Grant describes how Black women affirm that "Jesus is the Christ, that is, God

the lowly, becoming incarnate as a poor Jew, we can affirm today that Christ *is* Black.[96] But in a womanist theological perspective, this logic can be taken further: "this Christ, found in the experiences of Black women, is a Black woman."[97] To name and depict Christ as a Black woman is not to limit our understanding of the incarnation to one particular group, much less to the particularity of Jesus' historical body. Instead, it opens up the incarnation in a universal direction through the shared categories of human suffering and oppression on account of particular differences.

Christ embraces all who suffer in his own body and proleptically unites the suffering bodies of others to his own body.[98] This embrace does not diminish, justify, or rationalize the pain and misery of human suffering. There is no directive to suffer like Christ, nor does Christ redeem tragic suffering, as if the suffering of slavery is ever deserved or willed by God. Like Christ's own crucifixion, much human suffering is innocent. In Christ's suffering the suffering of all who suffer undeservedly is made visible, particularly those who have been singled out because of their bodily markers of difference, their race, their disability, or their gender, and those who have challenged systems of domination. And in our own suffering, conversely, we can discover Christ's presence. Here the incarnation takes place through suffering: in becoming human, God takes on human suffering in all its particular forms in his own body;[99] in our suffering bodies, we discover the incarnate God. Just as Christ can paradigmatically be seen in the hungry, the thirsty, the stranger, the naked, the sick, and the imprisoned, Christ is incarnate in those who suffer.[100]

---

incarnate . . . as Jesus identified with the lowly of his day, he now identifies with the lowly of this day, who in the American context are Black people. The identification is so real that Jesus Christ in fact becomes Black." Grant, *White Women's Christ*, 215.

[96] James H. Cone, *God of the Oppressed*, rev. ed. (Maryknoll, N.Y.: Orbis, 1997), 134.

[97] Grant's particular interpretation of Christ includes an implied universality through which Black women's experience of racism is shared with Black men; their experience of sexism is shared with women of all races; their experience of class oppression is shared with the poor everywhere. Grant, *White Women's Christ*, 216–17.

[98] See Copeland's description of the crucifixion, which "neither diminishes nor empties, neither justifies nor obscures the horror and misery of black suffering. Rather, the proleptic embrace of the suffering Jesus, who is the Risen Lord, interrupts the abjection of black bodies and creates an horizon of hope." Copeland, *Enfleshing*, 6.

[99] Wendy Farley describes how God's knowledge of suffering is radicalized in the incarnation, where it is accompanied by transforming power, in *Tragic Vision and Divine Compassion: A Contemporary Theodicy* (Louisville, Ky.: Westminster John Knox, 1990), 112.

[100] Matt 25:31-46.

Mary and the Spirit

Not all womanists accept, however, the identification of Black women with Jesus through the category of shared suffering. Delores Williams rejects traditional atonement theologies for presenting redemption through an oppressive image of surrogacy.[101] For her, the cross is an image of violence and desecration; there is nothing redemptive about it. Instead, redemption is found in the life of Jesus, his incarnation, his ministry of righting relationships, and in his resurrection from the dead.[102] Human beings share in redemption by participating in his ministry and vision of right relations, not by sharing in his suffering or imitating his surrogacy. The point of the incarnation, in Williams' view, is the revelation of new life, new resources for survival, and right relationships, not an inevitable march to an atoning death on the cross. This revelation takes place through the body of a woman.

Incarnation is a continuum that both precedes and exceeds Jesus. Williams uses traditional West African religious language to describe this event as God's self-disclosure in a woman, Mary, so that one can say, "The Spirit mounted Mary."[103] The Word was made flesh in Mary's body through the Spirit. This initial location of the Spirit of God in Mary's body allows Williams to extend the incarnation from the particular male body of Jesus to the body of his mother, and from there to the wider Christian community. Incarnation is a continuum rather than a unique event; divine spirit manifests in Mary, in Jesus, and in the life of the church.[104] Mary's spirit-filled body and her Magnificat biblically echo Hagar's surrogate motherhood and struggle for survival in the wilderness. Both women name God out of their experience, and both women typify the experience of African-American women. Theological notions of incarnation and revelation therefore must be inclusive of the oppressed mother in whom both incarnation and revelation take root.

An African-centered engagement with womanist theology can take this expansive interpretation of the incarnation even further.[105] Examining the symbols of the cross and the incarnation in the African-derived religions of Jamaica, Dianne Stewart discovers a cross that is oriented toward the

---

[101] Delores Williams, *Sisters in the Wilderness: The Challenge of Womanist God-Talk* (Maryknoll, N.Y.: Orbis, 1993), 161–77.

[102] God did not intend the suffering of his son, nor did God will surrogacy roles or the defilement of black women's bodies. Williams, *Sisters in the Wilderness*, 166.

[103] Williams, *Sisters in the Wilderness*, 168.

[104] Williams, *Sisters in the Wilderness*, 168.

[105] Dianne M. Stewart, *Three Eyes for the Journey: African Dimensions of the Jamaican Religious Experience* (New York: Oxford University Press, 2005), 158–68.

well-being of the community and an inclusive, recurring incarnation. Neither symbol is particularly christocentric in the BaKongo groups of Africa
and their Jamaican descendents such as Kumina.[106] Instead incarnation indicates "the concrete embodiment of a Divinity or Ancestor for the benefit of
the human community," which takes place at the sign of the cross—that is,
the crossroads between human and divine, visible and invisible.[107] Instead of
a unique event associated with Jesus or his mother, incarnation is a recurring activity, the temporary and repeated embodiment of the divine/ancestor
through possession trance.[108]

Possession trance makes the human body the site of divine encounter. The body itself functions as a spiritual medium, and anyone, female or
male, young or old, abled or disabled, is a potential host of the divine when
mounted by the spirit. In this African-centered religious perspective, all people may be "participants in the event of incarnation."[109] The recurrent form
of incarnation implies an expansive and inclusive view of divine revelation.[110]
Just as incarnation extends far beyond the body of Jesus and even beyond
the bodies of Christians, so too does revelation take place in different times
and places and in a wide variety of bodies. Because these bodies are sites of
incarnation, they are also sites of revelation, oriented toward the well-being
of the community. Here the divine manifests in embodied form through the
work of the spirit(s), wherever it might appear.

There is a subterranean tradition in Christian history by which the Spirit
extends the incarnation to other bodies and, in particular, to female bodies
that are otherwise disparaged as unfitting representatives of Christ. This tradition includes heretical movements such as the thirteenth-century followers of Guglielma of Milan, who was revered as the incarnation of the Holy
Spirit,[111] as well as the nineteenth-century Shakers, who believed Mother

---

[106] The important exception is Rastafari, in which Haile Selassie is seen as the incarnation of God, the Black messiah who proclaims "the divinity of all African people." See
Stewart, *Three Eyes for the Journey*, 161.

[107] Stewart, *Three Eyes for the Journey*, 160.

[108] Enslaved Africans used these West African theological categories to filter Christian
ideas and symbols. The pneumatological emphasis and embodied spirituality that result have
shaped both the North American Black church and the African-derived religions of the
Caribbean and Latin America. Stewart, *Three Eyes for the Journey*, 160–61.

[109] Stewart, *Three Eyes for the Journey*, 160–61.

[110] Stewart, *Three Eyes for the Journey*, 165.

[111] See Stephen Wessley, "The Thirteenth-Century Guglielmites: Salvation through
Women," in *Medieval Women*, ed. Derek Baker (Oxford: Blackwell, 1978), 289–303; and
Barbara Newman, "The Heretic Saint: Guglielma of Bohemia, Milan, and Brunate," *Church
History* 74, no. 1 (2005): 1–38.

Ann Lee to be the second coming of Christ in the body of a woman through a new outpouring of the Spirit.[112] In both of these cases, the Holy Spirit was the source of a new female embodiment of God, a new incarnation in history in the form of a woman. Both groups linked this new incarnation with ideals of gender equity and communal life.[113] In both African and European religious traditions, the liberty of the Spirit extends the incarnation to the bodies of women.

Divinization

The incarnation can be interpreted from many different directions. Rather than approaching the incarnation "from above," as the Word or Wisdom made flesh, one powerful way of making it more inclusive is by thinking the incarnation "from below." In some Christian contexts, incarnation from below is a much more logical way of understanding Christ than through appeals to Greek metaphysics.[114] In the traditional West African perspective, rulers are regarded "as hedged by divinity," and so Christ's coincidence of humanity with divinity raises no metaphysical problems.[115] Likewise, in a Korean religious world in which it is not uncommon for human beings to be deified through their acts of love, suffering, and sacrifice, it makes sense to say that Jesus was elevated to become the Messiah and Savior through his sacrificial love.[116] In this model, Korean Christian women are invited to imitate Christ by elevating their own self-consciousness to the divine. "Korean women experience the mystery of incarnation and 'God-with-us' by becoming like Jesus," writes Chung Hyun Kyung. "For many Korean women, Jesus is not the objectified divine being whom people must worship. Rather, Jesus is the one we relive through our lives."[117] The indigenous Korean religious perspective expands the meaning of Immanuel; God is present in the human struggle for dignity as women experience the incarnation by becoming like Jesus.

[112] See Richard Francis, *Ann the Word: The Story of Ann Lee, Female Messiah, Mother of the Shakers, the Woman Clothed with the Sun* (New York: Arcade, 2000).

[113] Although frequently at the price of celibacy or a stereotypical androgyny. See Ruether, *Sexism and God-Talk*, 130–35.

[114] As Chung Hyun Kyung notes, "Many Asian women cherish the mystery of the incarnation through Jesus' person and work . . . Their understanding of Jesus' humanity and divinity, however, is very different from that of Nicene-Chalcedonian theological definitions stressing the son's relationship to the Father and the two natures of his person." Chung, *Struggle*, 59.

[115] Oduyoye, "Jesus Christ," 168.

[116] Lee Oo Chung, cited in Chung, *Struggle*, 61.

[117] Chung, *Struggle*, 61.

Chung's description of participation in the incarnation "from below" is similar to the ancient Christian understanding of divinization as it developed in the writings of the church fathers. Patristic writers such as Athanasius and Gregory of Nyssa identified the divinization of humanity as the primary effect of the incarnation of the Word, what is sometimes called the "divine exchange." Athanasius put it like this: "He, indeed, assumed humanity that we might become God."[118] As discussed in chapter 3, Angela of Foligno's words are even more vivid: "my God became flesh in order that he might make me God."[119] Divinization is the direct effect of the incarnation, and, as in the examples from Korea and West Africa, divinization is a powerful way of making the incarnation more inclusive by interpreting it from below. Charlene Burns also uses the traditional language of salvation as divinization to argue, following thinkers like Maximus and Schleiermacher, that "Christ differs from us in degree, not in kind."[120] An ontological understanding of incarnation is therefore possible, in her view, if we recognize that "as God continually incarnates the divine in and through humanity, human beings are enabled through the grace of God to become God."[121] Using similar traditional language of divinization to develop feminist philosophy of religion, Grace Jantzen argues that women are called to "become divine" as the full development of their subjectivity in relation to the incarnate divine, which, for her, takes the form not only of Christ but also of pantheism, God fully incarnate in the world.[122]

Feminist, womanist, and *mujerista* theologians, among others, have found a myriad and remarkable variety of ways to include women in their Christologies: whether through divine Sophia; the cosmic and ecological Christ; Jesus' prophetic message and liberating praxis; redemptive community, the church, and its sacraments; Jesus' suffering, death, and resurrection; the body of Mary and the movement of the Spirit. The creativity and richness of this vision extends the incarnation far beyond the historical body of Jesus, as women theologians translate the poet's claim that "Christ plays in ten thousand places,

---

[118] Athanasius, *On the Incarnation*, sec. 54.

[119] Angela of Foligno, *Il Libro della Beata Angela da Foligno*, ed. Ludger Their, O.F.M., and Abele Calufetti, O.F.M. (Grottaferrata [Rome]: Editiones Collegii S. Bonaventurae ad Claras Aquas, 1985), 714; the English translation is published as *Angela of Foligno: Complete Works*, trans. Paul Lachance, O.F.M. (New York: Paulist Press, 1993), 308.

[120] Burns, *Divine Becoming*, 56.

[121] Burns, *Divine Becoming*, 8.

[122] See Jantzen, *Becoming Divine*, 265–75.

Lovely in limbs, and lovely in eyes not his."[123] Out of these many fruitful approaches, the theological lens of divinization, thinking the incarnation from below, is particularly insightful for reconsidering the Johannine categories of word and flesh. As the writings of medieval women mystics make clear, the incarnation provides a path to the divine for female flesh. Because the Word was made flesh, flesh becomes word through practices of writing the body of Christ.

---

[123] Gerard Manley Hopkins, "As Kingfishers Catch Fire," in *Poems and Prose of Gerard Manley Hopkins*, ed. W. H. Gardner (Baltimore, Md.: Penguin Books, 1953), 51.

1

ATTENDING TO WORD AND FLESH

The wisdom recovered and developed by diverse feminist theologians makes it possible to interpret the incarnation inclusively, as extending beyond the historical body of Jesus. Christ is incarnate in a multiplicity of bodies, wherever the hungry are fed, justice is pursued, and love is shared. Careful attention must be given to the particularity of Jesus' historical body, including his maleness, but this particularity initiates a wider incarnation of Christ wherever liberation, justice, compassion, and Wisdom appear. Christ is present in diverse bodies today, always marked by the particularity of multiple differences. Feminist and womanist theologians have found a remarkable variety of creative ways to make Christology more inclusive of women, indeed, of all persons in their embodied differences.

Still, the poetic and traditional language of the incarnation in the prologue to the Gospel of John beckons: "the Word became flesh and lived among us." Both the language of *logos* and the language of *sarx* were shaped and received within a patriarchal and androcentric context, and so they must be handled with caution. That context has distorted Christian anthropology, theology, and especially Christology through an androcentric interpretation of both word and flesh. But instead of rejecting the traditional language of the incarnation, of "Word" and "flesh," in favor of more innovative gestures of inclusion, new interpretations of these key terms are both possible and necessary. Without careful attention to the evocative symbols of "Word" and "flesh," to the way they have functioned to exclude women, and to the inclusive possibilities latent within these very terms, we risk leaving a narrow incarnation intact. If we develop our inclusive Christologies too quickly in other directions, we risk conceding traditional language—that the word is indeed consubstantial with "the Father," for instance; or that Logos is ideally reflected in the perfect rationality and control of a male ruler; or that the male flesh of the historical body of Jesus is "more noble" than other flesh. Without attention to the Johannine language of word and flesh, and the possibilities for locating difference within these very terms, our understanding of the incarnation remains partial and incomplete. This language remains a powerful site for feminist intervention. It is worth contemplating, therefore, the Word who became flesh and lived among us.

Inclusive possibilities emerge from inhabiting the traditional language of Word and flesh. In the writings of the Hellenistic Jewish philosopher Philo, *logos* resonates with the philosophical terms of both *Sophia*-Wisdom and *Nous*-Mind, making the *logos* present to some degree in each person through creation and particularly through reason.[1] When *logos* is translated as "Word," it functions as a multivalent and suggestive symbol for Christians. It is the Word of God spoken at creation, incarnate in Jesus, written in scripture, proclaimed in the gospel, preached and interpreted by unfolding traditions. The Christian "Word" is ambiguously both a person and a text, and it encompasses both speech and writing.[2] As such, it carries a rich range of meaning. Of particular interest is the way in which Word can signify what we frequently name "the written word," or writing itself: in scripture and in the act and production of writing.

In Paul's writings, "flesh" (*sarx*) has the connotation of sinful human nature (Rom 8:4-8, Gal 5:16ff.), which has been the source of much suspicion of the body in Christian history. But in the prologue to John's gospel, flesh indicates the humanity assumed by the Word and positively connotes the goodness of the human body. Against docetic interpretations of Christ, John insists on the fleshiness of the divine Word. The Word was not transformed *into* flesh (so that it was no longer divine Word—that is, became mere flesh), but rather became human, *in* the flesh.[3] "Flesh" here functions metonymically to signify the entire human being, but with a particular emphasis on the goodness of Jesus' body as a fully embodied, fully human divine being. That embodiment included his male sex and sexuality, along with his other particular bodily characteristics of race, ethnicity, size, language, and so on.

---

[1] See Rosemary Radford Ruether, *Sexism and God-Talk: Toward a Feminist Theology* (Boston: Beacon, 1983), 124–26; and Elizabeth A. Johnson, *She Who Is: The Mystery of God in Feminist Theological Discourse* (New York: Crossroad, 1997), 97–99.

[2] See David Tracy, "Writing," in *Critical Terms for Religious Studies*, ed. Mark C. Taylor (Chicago: University of Chicago Press, 1998), 383–93.

[3] Paul W. Schmiedel, *The Johannine Writings*, trans. Maurice A. Canney (London: Adam & Charles Black, 1908), 152.

The message of "flesh" in the incarnation is, in Elizabeth Johnson's words, the insight of "the transcendent God's capacity for embodiment, divine passion for liberation, and the constitutive nature of relation."[4] The flesh of the incarnation is "not only a concession to our bodily life, but a vindication of it."[5] The doctrine of the incarnation resonates with the feminist value of embodiment: God fully participates in human bodiliness. And bodiliness connects the transcendent mystery of God to place, time, history, birth and death, pleasure and pain, joy and suffering.[6]

The problem for the traditional understanding of the incarnation, however, is that human flesh comes in *at least* two sexes, male and female.[7] Sexual dimorphism is what feminist theorists mean by the concept of sexual difference: the human species has evolved in at least two forms of being. When that ontological sexual difference is further marked by differences of race, ability, size, and sexuality, and interpreted through innumerable cultural and social systems, we can see that human flesh is irreducibly diverse, shaped by a multiplicity of differences that are the product of both evolution (sexual selection and genetic variation) and social construction. Our doctrine of incarnation, Word made flesh, ought to reflect the diversity of flesh.

Flesh is never just one thing assumed by the Word once and for all. In Laurel Schneider's sharp description, it is *promiscuous*. "Flesh is indiscriminate in its porous interconnection with everything, and it is never, at any level, absolutely unified. To insist upon a solitary incarnate moment is to betray the very fleshiness of flesh, its innate promiscuity, pesky shiftiness, and resilient interruptions of sense. A solitary incarnation is, in other words, not incarnation at all but a disembodiment: a denial of the flesh that in its very cellular structure of integration, disintegration, and passage is always re-forming, dispersing, and returning."[8] Jesus' own body was intermingled

---

[4] Johnson, *She Who Is*, 168.

[5] Mark D. Jordan, "God's Body," in *Queer Theology: Rethinking the Western Body*, ed. Gerard Loughlin (Oxford: Blackwell, 2007), 290.

[6] "She becomes flesh, choosing the very stuff of the cosmos as her own personal reality forever . . . human bodiliness is manifest as irreplaceable sacrament of mutual communion between heaven and earth, not only in Jesus' case but ontologically for all." Johnson, *She Who Is*, 168.

[7] I do not exclude the possibility of more; my point is that there are at minimum two, not one. See Thomas Laqueur's discussion of the "one-sex model" of humanity in *Making Sex: Body and Gender from the Greeks to Freud* (Cambridge, Mass.: Harvard University Press, 1990), 26–142.

[8] Laurel Schneider, "Promiscuous Incarnation," in *The Embrace of Eros: Bodies, Desires, and Sexuality in Christianity*, ed. Margaret D. Kamitsuka (Minneapolis: Fortress, 2010), 241–42.

with the flesh of his mother *in utero* and while breastfeeding; he incorporated the flesh of the animals he ate; his flesh mingled with the flesh of the people he touched, shared meals with, and healed, at times through the intimacy of his own spit. Human flesh, including the flesh of Jesus, is indiscriminate; it is inherently promiscuous.[9] From the perspective of flesh, the incarnation cannot be limited to the unique body of Jesus.

Nor can the Word be limited to the second person of the Trinity. In the histories of Hellenistic Jewish and Christian theologies, "Word" includes connotations of the divine figure of Wisdom-*Sophia* and Mind-*Nous*. The Word was with God in the beginning and is the principle of creation. The Word is incarnate in Christ, encountered in scripture, read, proclaimed, preached, and interpreted. It is both spoken and written. The Word is creative and productive; it is multiple, generative of other words. For this reason, Margaret Miles describes the history of Christianity as the story of incarnate words, of unfolding interpretations of the meaning of the incarnation for embodied religious beliefs and practices.[10]

Neither Word nor flesh can be contained or limited to the unique person of Jesus Christ. The symbol gives rise to thought: both terms push back against reduction, straining to multiply beyond their borders. The multiplicity contained within "Word" and "flesh"—their plurality and restiveness—hints at inclusive possibilities within the most traditional language of the incarnation. To approach the incarnation from the perspective of women, we have to return to these evocative terms, here where Word and flesh meet.

The biblical connection of divine Word with human flesh raises metaphysical questions, however, in the Greek philosophical system in which early Christian thought took shape. Human and divine, the material and the spiritual, were thought to be opposed and mutually exclusive in ways that make incarnation seem paradoxical and absurd. If God is conceived as an entity that is juxtaposed with another entity, the humanity of Jesus, it is difficult to make sense of the incarnation, which appears only as a scandal to reason. The problem arises from dualistic and essentialist thinking, a mental habit that conceives everything in terms of identity and opposition—subject

[9] "Promiscuity," Schneider concludes, "suggests intercourse and multiplicity, a posture of generosity toward change and of ambiguity toward identity, any of which goes a long way actually to describing the character of Jesus' interactions in the narratives of his life. Incarnation, as least as the stories of Jesus imply and as the long history of the church demonstrates, is neither pure nor unambiguously categorizable." Schneider, "Promiscuous Incarnation," 244.

[10] Margaret Miles, *The Word Made Flesh: A History of Christian Thought* (Oxford: Blackwell, 2005).

and object, same and other.[11] But this way of thinking is a category mistake when applied to divinity, which is characterized by self-giving love rather than being. Church councils tried to clarify the matter of the incarnation with increasing precision before settling on the hypostatic union described in the Chalcedonian definition. Jesus Christ is fully God and fully human, consubstantial with the Father with respect to his divinity and consubstantial with human beings with respect to his humanity, one person "recognized in two natures, without confusion, without change, without division, without separation" between the two. This technical theological definition hardly conveys the poetic language of the prologue, but it wisely refrains from answering the question of what is meant by divinity or, for that matter, humanity. Nor does it attempt to explain how these two are conjoined in Christ—merely that they must be.[12]

Taking the incarnation out of the context of dualistic and essentialist metaphysics and thinking it through the poetic terms of Word and flesh underscore the message of the Gospels, the good news of the embodiment of God and its salutary effect on human liberation. Looking at the incarnation this way, the story of Jesus is as much about the flesh becoming word as it is the Word made flesh. This perspective coincides with the development of feminist theologies, which emphasize experience and embodiment and see the body as the site of revelation.[13] Flesh speaks theologically as women's bodies gain sacramental significance.[14] A feminist interpretation of the incarnation begins by interrogating, not how Word became flesh, but how female flesh becomes divine word.

[11] Wendy Farley describes the problems that emerge from a dualistic theology of the incarnation in *Gathering Those Driven Away: A Theology of Incarnation* (Louisville, Ky.: Westminster John Knox, 2011), 89–90.

[12] See Sarah Coakley, "What Does Chalcedon Solve and What Does It Not? Some Reflections on the Status and Meaning of the Chalcedonian 'Definition,'" in *The Incarnation: An Interdisciplinary Symposium on the Incarnation of the Son of God*, ed. Stephen T. Davis, Daniel Kendall, S.J., and Gerald O'Collins, S.J. (Oxford: Oxford University Press, 2002), 143–63; and Oliver D. Crisp, *Divinity and Humanity: The Incarnation Reconsidered* (Cambridge: Cambridge University Press, 2007).

[13] Here I follow Lisa Isherwood's description of feminist liberation theology: "The flesh made word enables us to find a voice and to make our desires known." "The Embodiment of Feminist Liberation Theology: The Spiralling of Incarnation," *Feminist Theology* 12, no. 2 (2004): 148. See also Stephanie Paulsell, *Honoring the Body: Meditations on a Christian Practice* (San Francisco: Jossey-Bass, 2002).

[14] Tina Beattie points out the persistence of an attitude toward women's bodies as neither sacramental nor in the *imago Christi*, precisely because of their female flesh, in her article "Feminism, Vatican-Style," *The Tablet*, August 7, 2004, http://www.thetablet.co.uk/article/2190, accessed May 15, 2012.

Practicing the Incarnation

The incarnation is the heart of the Christian good news: God with us, incarnate in our world, our flesh. This good news overturns social hierarchies and founds a community based on love and the recognition of the divine image in each person: "we are all Christ."[15] Many contemporary feminists and womanists argue as much, but they were not the first women to do so. Looking back within the history of Christian theology, we can find precedent for this broad and inclusive interpretation of the incarnation in the writings of the medieval women mystics. These theologians provide an alternative source for a radically inclusive incarnation from within neglected strands of the Christian tradition. Medieval women mystics use traditional categories of "word" and "flesh" to describe the incarnation but they effortlessly extend it to other bodies, making it inclusive of women's flesh and boldly claiming their share in it. They thereby provide important resources for constructive feminist theology today.

The theme of incarnation in the writings of medieval women reveals how they interpreted it as authorization for their own spiritual writing practices. In their texts, the incarnation emerges as an inverted paradigm for their theological writing: because the Word of God became flesh for them, their flesh in turn becomes divine word through mystical writing and speech. Women such as Hadewijch of Brabant, Angela of Foligno, and Marguerite Porete extend the significance of the incarnation from Christ's body to other bodies: Mary's body, the bodies of poets and mystics, the "annihilated soul," and even their composed books. Their writings support an inclusive understanding of the incarnation: beginning with the embodiment of God in Jesus Christ, the incarnation extends to other bodies that live into the mystery of the incarnation through spiritual practices in which word and flesh meet.[16] Principal among these is the practice of writing undertaken by the medieval women theologians in which their flesh becomes word through writing and speech.

In what follows, an examination of the writings of three medieval women mystics supports the view that the incarnation is not a once and for all event

---

[15] Farley, *Gathering*, 14.

[16] On the role of spiritual practices as a way of orienting oneself toward reality and truth, see Wendy Farley, *Eros for the Other: Retaining Truth in a Pluralistic World* (University Park: Pennsylvania State University Press, 1996), 185–200; and idem, *The Wounding and Healing of Desire: Weaving Heaven and Earth* (Louisville, Ky.: Westminster John Knox, 2005), 115–65. See also Paulsell, *Honoring the Body*.

but an ongoing embodiment of the divine. The incarnation takes place in our bodies, our flesh, through our spiritual and ethical practices. Following the medieval women writers, the way we live into and accomplish our participation in the incarnation is through these practices and, paradigmatically, the practice of writing through which flesh becomes word. Considering the incarnation in terms of practices might help to escape some of the metaphysical difficulties that have made the doctrine so harmful to women's full representation within the church. More importantly, it returns us to the ethical and spiritual practices of Jesus' own historical body in his prophetic praxis and ministry. The spiritual practice of writing is a paradigmatic way of participating in the incarnation because of the visible way in which the traditional Johannine terms of "word" and "flesh" function within it. But more broadly conceived, all embodied ethical and spiritual practices that seek justice and the love of God and neighbor are ways of living into the incarnation of Christ. Through our practices we embody Christ in the world; they are the means of our own divinization, of our flesh reaching for its divine word.

The incarnation authorized the writing practices of medieval women mystics through a form of the divine exchange: God became flesh so that their flesh might become embodied divine word. Their texts anticipate the work of contemporary feminists in thinking the incarnation from below. Beginning from women's bodies becoming spoken and written word, the incarnation—the divine enfleshed—appears in their writings as multiple and fluid.[17] The significance of the incarnation can be seen as internally differing and deferring final meaning, always open to ongoing, further interpretations.[18] A feminist interpretation of the incarnation refuses a static sense of the Word having been made flesh once and for all in one particular male body; instead, the incarnation takes place in an unfolding process of becoming in multiple bodies.[19]

---

[17] On the metaphor of fluidity for the God-human relationship in the writings of Mechthild of Magdeburg (a contemporary of the women examined here), see Michelle Voss Roberts, *Dualities: A Theology of Difference* (Louisville, Ky.: Westminster John Knox, 2010); and Mechthild of Magdeburg, *The Flowing Light of the Godhead*, trans. Frank J. Tobin (New York: Paulist Press, 1998).

[18] On this point, see Gianni Vattimo's hermeneutical interpretation of the incarnation as secularization in *Belief*, trans. Luca D'Isanto and David Webb (Stanford, Calif.: Stanford University Press, 1999) and *After Christianity*, trans. Luca D'Isanto (New York: Columbia University Press, 2002).

[19] For a different approach to women's "becoming divine" in the field of philosophy of religion, see Grace Jantzen, *Becoming Divine: Towards a Feminist Philosophy of Religion* (Bloomington: Indiana University Press, 1999).

This expansion of the incarnation also entails that we rethink the task of theology as, in Hélène Cixous' description of feminine writing, "writing the body"—writing the body of Christ, to be sure, but also writing (and reading, and rewriting) other bodies in the history of Christianity, as well as writing our own bodies into that history. Embodied writing is the transmission of flesh into word. By participating in the incarnation through their spiritual practices, and in particular through their writing, medieval women mystics provide a helpful way forward today for those who have been excluded on the basis of a narrow Christology. We incarnate Christ through our embodied writing practices, and writing the body of Christ extends Christ's body in the world.

Medieval Writers

Hadewijch of Brabant, a Dutch beguine of the thirteenth century, wrote in a wide variety of genres: visions, letters, poems in stanzas, and poems in rhyming couplets. Angela of Foligno, an Italian Franciscan tertiary who died in 1309, created a collaborative text composed of the *Memorial*, written together with her confessor, and the *Instructions*, a collection of letters and teachings, written for her spiritual disciples. Marguerite Porete, a beguine from northern France, was executed as a relapsed heretic in Paris in 1310 for disseminating her book, *The Mirror of Simple Souls*. Hadewijch, Angela, and Porete each lived in a world in which female sanctity was recognized and admired. As Caroline Walker Bynum has shown, the popular female sanctity of the late Middle Ages was based on physical identification of women's bodies with Christ's suffering, bleeding, and nourishing humanity.[20] Each of these three writers recognizes that for the women of her time and place, their primary access to Christ's divinity is through his humanity. This perspective makes the incarnation central to salvation history and the spiritual life. But each of these writers takes her understanding of the incarnation further

[20] See Caroline Walker Bynum, *Jesus as Mother: Studies in the Spirituality of the High Middle Ages* (Berkeley: University of California Press, 1982), *Holy Feast and Holy Fast: The Religious Significance of Food to Medieval Women* (Berkeley: University of California Press, 1987), and *Fragmentation and Redemption: Essays on Gender and the Human Body in Medieval Religion* (New York: Zone Books, 1991). For additional perspectives on medieval women's mysticism, see also Karma Lochrie, *Margery Kempe and Translations of the Flesh* (Philadelphia: University of Pennsylvania Press, 1991); Laurie Finke, *Feminist Theory, Women's Writing: Reading Women Writing* (Ithaca, N.Y.: Cornell University Press, 1992); Ulrike Wiethaus, ed., *Maps of Flesh and Light: The Religious Experience of Medieval Women Mystics* (Syracuse, N.Y.: Syracuse University Press, 1993); and Elizabeth Petroff, *Body and Soul: Essays on Medieval Women and Mysticism* (New York: Oxford University Press, 1994).

and pushes beyond acts of bodily imitation—for example, that of shared suffering through penance or through miraculous feats of food multiplication.[21] Instead they each claim a share in Christ's divinity. This movement, from imitation of humanity to participation in divinity, takes place through their writing. In these three particular examples, women read and interpret the body of Christ in ways that make possible the divinization of their own bodies and their own writing, as their flesh becomes word in response to the Word made flesh.

What motivated and enabled these women to write of God was the way they experienced and appropriated the message of the incarnation. The tradition has often assumed incarnation to imply a top-down, hierarchical descent of a preexistent Word into the body of Jesus. This view, as already noted, creates problems of representation and exclusion for women, among others. But the women mystics do not worry about the metaphysics of incarnation. They are much more interested in its effects: on Mary, on women contemplatives, on the world, and on the radical reorientation to the world made possible through the soul's transformation in God's love experienced through Christ. In a time when women were denied official preaching and teaching authority and were frequently under suspicion for heresy, these thirteenth-century writers found a voice that persists in speaking to us today.

Hadewijch, as discussed in chapter 2, traces the incarnation to its origin in Mary's spiritual assent to what takes place in her body. Mary then becomes an exemplar for all Christians, not as our representative in her handmaid's *fiat*, but as a model of human potential to emulate. The spiritual life, for Hadewijch, reaches its pinnacle in conceiving and giving birth to love. Spiritual birthing corresponds, not incidentally, to Hadewijch's own production of texts as she negotiates the rhythms of language and the passage of "growing up" spiritually. A feminist theology of the incarnation recognizes the maternal origins of the incarnation in Mary's body and the ways in which the poet equally transmits the mother's body through language that becomes divine, rhythmic word.

Chapter 3 traces Angela of Foligno's remarkable spiritual journey from symptomatic flesh to articulate spiritual leader. This transition provides a concrete example of writing the body of Christ in her own body as she imitated Christ's actions, and in her own words as they are transmitted in

---

[21] Darby Kathleen Ray finds in medieval women's spiritual practices "a compelling resonance between these women's moral courage and liberative imagination and the redemptive ingenuity of the God they adored." See *Incarnation and Imagination: A Christian Ethic of Ingenuity* (Minneapolis: Fortress, 2008), 51–89, 87.

collaboration with her confessor. For Angela, the incarnation has personal significance for the divinization of her own flesh. She feels the word enter her body, and it erupts in her speech. While her experience, like all mystical experience, is ultimately beyond the capacity of language to convey, the incarnation serves as a kind of root metaphor for the divinity she finds in the world: the word became flesh to make Angela God; flesh becomes divine word as the world is pregnant with God. Angela insists on the personal significance of the incarnation for her own divinization, which issues in an experience of God that can only be conveyed through eruptions of speech that leave behind traces in her *Memorial*.

Marguerite Porete, the subject of the fourth chapter, is often singled out as unusual (for a woman mystic) for her detached, speculative language and the seeming lack of intimacy with Christ in contrast to her contemporaries. Unlike many of her contemporaries, she shows little interest in the body of Christ or his sufferings. Instead, in her book, Christ is the exemplar for the soul's annihilation of the will. Annihilation transforms the soul so that it becomes the place of love's incarnation in the world. Like Christ, the soul sacrifices her will in a kenotic gesture which transforms her, through detachment, into the place of divine love. This transformed soul, which Porete represents as the character Soul, sings (and writes) in her book from a place of spiritual detachment, as the *Mirror* puts it, "without a why," purely as the incarnation of God's love.

Hadewijch, Angela, and Porete together contribute a broad and inclusive interpretation of the incarnation. For each medieval woman, her encounter with the incarnation issues in writing; her flesh is made word in response to the mystery of word made flesh. These three women in particular permit us to understand one effect of the incarnation through writing practices in which flesh is transformed into word.

French Feminists

In reading the writings of these medieval women, juxtaposition with the theoretical writings of the so-called French feminists is advantageous. French feminist theorists help illuminate the question of how women's bodies enter language and particularly writing. When read together, one can see the broader significance of the rich incarnational symbols of flesh and word. Thus this study equally suggests a theological interpretation of French feminist theory.[22] The theoretical work of the French feminists opens a space

---

[22] The term "French feminist" should be kept in quotation marks, given the non-French

for broadening our understanding of the incarnation by interrogating how female flesh and desire signify within language and disrupt the paternal symbolic. Writing in French and about the French language, Hélène Cixous, Luce Irigaray, and Julia Kristeva share a concern with systems of representation and how the female body signifies within those systems. Each proposes a theory of embodied linguistic practice that recognizes the significance of women's bodies—that is, the way women's bodies *signify* in language. The respective theories discussed in the chapters to follow—Kristeva's maternal semiotic, Cixous' *écriture féminine* (feminine writing or writing as feminine), and Irigaray's *parler-femme* (speaking [as] woman)—have frequently been understood in terms of their psychoanalytic, linguistic, philosophical, and literary import. But these theories of language offer important theological resources as well. In light of their embodied linguistic theories, French feminists support contemporary feminist theological efforts to reconceive the incarnation beginning from women's bodies and their advent to language. In this regard, the French feminists offer at least three places to begin, three transformative suggestions[23] for a feminist interpretation of the incarnation.

First, along with other poststructuralist thinkers, the French feminists question the binary oppositions that have structured Western metaphysics, including much of Christian theology. Pairs such as active/passive, form/matter, intelligible/sensible, and transcendent/immanent all shape and inform received interpretations of the incarnation.[24] While recognizing that

---

origins of the most prominent "French feminists" (Irigaray is French but was born in Belgium, Monique Wittig was from Germany, Kristeva is from Bulgaria, and Cixous grew up in French Algeria) as well as their uneasy identification with feminism and the politics of identity. See Christine Delphy, "The Invention of French Feminism: An Essential Move," *Yale French Studies* 87 (1995): 190–221, for a scathing critique of the Anglo-American appropriation of "French feminism." Nevertheless, they all write in French and about the French language, and in different ways they are all contesting masculine and patriarchal norms for the construction of what counts as knowledge, meaning, and truth in order to open the possibility for other ways of thinking, speaking, and writing that might take account of sexual difference (see Elizabeth Grosz, *Sexual Subversions: Three French Feminists* [Sydney: Allen & Unwin, 1989]). In other words, their feminist intervention is not at the level of liberal economic or political access (though in general they support these efforts) but at the level of the symbolic organization of language, representation, knowledge, and meaning that makes political and economic systems possible.

[23] See Jantzen's use of this phrase to describe the function of therapeutic symbols in *Becoming Divine*, 129.

[24] One of the founding moments of Western metaphysics through binary opposites can be found in the Pythagorean table cited in Aristotle, *Metaphysics*, 986a. See also Jantzen, *Becoming Divine*, 266.

these opposed terms are not only gendered but also legislated and function to uphold a paternal symbolic order with God the Father (or his substitutes, the phallus or the Logos) at its center, the more important question is how to interrogate or deconstruct the oppositions without simply reinscribing them. We cannot simply reverse the valuation of Word and flesh. Nor can we simply step outside of these constitutive categories of Christian thought. Instead, the French feminists suggest that feminist theology must proceed carefully, through local interventions in particular theological texts rather than wholesale denunciations of "Western metaphysics." Irigaray's careful readings of the history of philosophy in *Speculum*, Kristeva's analyses in *Tales of Love*, and Cixous' flying/stealing (*voler*) through literature in *The Newly Born Woman* indicate some directions. Following their strategic suggestions makes it possible to identify the ways in which the incarnation is figured in particular theological texts without reinscribing the opposition between Word and flesh. After all, one of the effects of the incarnation is to reveal the artificiality of that opposition.

Second, these theorists suggest an interpretation of the biblical Logos as language, both spoken and written. Word as language (the French *langage* rather than *langue*) is spoken by particular sexed subjects of enunciation.[25] It is written in scripture, in an open-ended and productive manner that demands interpretation and endlessly defers final meaning.[26] It is preached and proclaimed. In this regard, the Word is both spoken and written. Word as language is conditioned by the materiality of what Kristeva calls the semiotic, the rhythms that make meaning possible and betray its mastery. And Word as language is marked by sexual difference in the feminine speaking/writing called for by Cixous and Irigaray. The Word that becomes flesh can consequently be understood as already material and fleshly, only ever given to us as structured by the rhythms of the body, the materiality of the text, and the breath that makes speech possible.[27] Rather than conceiving the Word of God as transcendent, immaterial, wholly disembodied, and atemporal, we can meet the theological Word as spoken and written, gendered and embodied.[28]

---

[25] See Margaret Whitford, *Luce Irigaray: Philosophy in the Feminine* (New York: Routledge, 1991), 41–49.

[26] The patristic theologians read scripture in this manner; see especially Origen, *On First Principles*, trans. G. W. Butterworth (New York: Harper & Row, 1966) and my discussion ahead.

[27] See Luce Irigaray, *I Love to You: Sketch of a Possible Felicity in History*, trans. Alison Martin (New York: Routledge, 1996).

[28] See Rebecca S. Chopp, *The Power to Speak: Feminism, Language, God* (New York: Crossroad, 1989).

Third, the French feminists also suggest that the flesh that is the "stuff" of the incarnation be interpreted in terms of sexually (and otherwise) different bodies that enter language differently and might be represented differently within language. The flesh of the incarnation cannot be restricted to a particular male body, Jesus of Nazareth, nor to the material substance taken from his mother Mary. Instead it indicates the flesh of human beings that is always marked by multiple differences. The flesh of human bodies is never prelinguistic, waiting for the Word to give it meaning, but already signifies, always carries meaning with it.[29] Reconceiving flesh in this way entails that it can no longer be understood as an empty category, mute flesh, but as multiply signifying in particular bodies that are constituted by differences.[30] These varied instances of flesh challenge the ability of one paternal Word to speak for them theologically.

Writing as a Spiritual Practice

The focus of the French feminists on language and particularly on writing brings to light the importance of writing within the Christian theological and spiritual tradition. In her contribution to a collection of essays on the vocation of the theological teacher, Stephanie Paulsell makes the case for writing as a spiritual discipline.[31] Her model for the contemporary writing and teaching theologian is the medieval mystic Marguerite d'Oingt, who with trepidation takes up her pen for the first time carefully to inscribe her experience of God. Paulsell's evocative description establishes the link between Marguerite's experience of God and her act of writing: "But the God known by this woman is a God who writes, an author whose chosen parchment is the human heart. Her own heart is now congested with God's writing and overburdened with the response to it that is taking shape within her."[32] Writing was a spiritual discipline for Marguerite d'Oingt through which she sought to understand God and to communicate with others, to "preach with her hands," like her fellow Carthusians.

---

[29] On this point, see Elizabeth Grosz, *Volatile Bodies: Toward a Corporeal Feminism* (Bloomington: Indiana University Press, 1994). In many ways, a feminist theology of the incarnation follows Grosz' "möbius strip" model, borrowed from Lacan: follow the Word and one discovers flesh in sexual difference; follow flesh, and one reaches the Word/language.

[30] That is, we have no access to the body per se prior to or outside language; see esp. Judith Butler, *Bodies that Matter: On the Discursive Limits of "Sex"* (New York: Routledge, 1993).

[31] Stephanie Paulsell, "Writing as a Spiritual Discipline," in *The Scope of Our Art: The Vocation of the Theological Teacher*, ed. L. Gregory Jones and Stephanie Paulsell (Grand Rapids: Eerdmans, 2002), 17–31.

[32] Paulsell, "Writing," 8.

So, too, argues Paulsell, can writing be a spiritual discipline for the contemporary theologian. Against the academic commodification of writing on the one hand and the facile opposition of writing to teaching on the other, Paulsell seeks a way of understanding writing "as part of our spiritual formation and the formation of our students . . . as a creative, meditative, intellective activity that might gradually change our lives . . . a discipline within which we might meet God."[33] To that end, she identifies the paired writing virtues of audacity and humility ("Audacity, for attempting to write anything of God at all; humility, because all one's attempts will have to be revised") and cites Simone Weil's essay on the capacity of study to increase our attention, and thereby to increase our capacity for prayer and the love of God.[34] Through careful consideration of both sources and audience, writing becomes "a kind of reading, a kind of thinking. A way of receiving and considering the work of others, a way of discovering what we think about particular questions . . . in a way that invites others into the process of reading, thinking, and articulating."[35] The inevitable need for revision demands a combination of "loving attention with detachment" as we consider our own failures and mistakes.[36] Undertaken daily, the practice of writing both demands and cultivates virtues of humility, audacity, faith, hope, and charity, as it forms us in attention to God and others.[37]

This approach to writing as a spiritual practice has a long history in Christianity, but it is rarely made so explicit. Paulsell has a predecessor, for instance, in Origen of Alexandria, for whom exegetical writing about scripture—inseparable from reading scripture—was a spiritual practice. For Origen, the ideal exegete of scripture directly encounters the pedagogical role of the Logos through both the letter and the spirit of the text.[38] Like other philosophical schools of late antiquity, Origen's Christianity offered

[33] Paulsell, "Writing," 21.

[34] Simone Weil, "Reflections on the Right Use of School Studies with a View to the Love of God," *The Simone Weil Reader*, ed. George A. Panichas (New York: David McKay, 1977).

[35] Paulsell, "Writing," 24.

[36] Paulsell, "Writing," 25.

[37] See Paulsell, "Writing," 26: "Like any spiritual discipline, we must practice it regularly in order for it to do its work on us, to form us in attention, to draw us more deeply into the life of the world;" and 30: "Writing is too difficult, and too potentially transformative, for us to write out of motives other than love and generosity. This does not mean that we should not write critically, or polemically, or prophetically. But it means we should write in a way that betrays what we care most deeply about, a way that betrays our love."

[38] See Karen Torjesen, *Hermeneutical Procedure and Theological Method in Origen's Exegesis* (Berlin: De Gruyter, 1986).

a particular way of life and a set of spiritual exercises through which the mind could be disciplined, the self examined, and the individual connected to the divine.[39] Origen's hermeneutical method aimed to inculcate spiritual practices of reading, writing, and interpretation in his fellow Christians that transform the reader.[40]

This practice depends on a particular theological understanding of scripture not only as inspired but also as the direct teaching of the Logos himself.[41] Scripture is the body of Christ incarnate in writing; Origen's famous threefold meaning corresponds to Christ's human body, soul, and divine nature. Human beings have access to divine teaching through the words of scripture. Those words, however, demand certain techniques, skills, and practices; in short, they require *habits* of reading, writing, and interpretation to make available their spiritual meaning. Reading is a transformative spiritual practice that allows the reader to enter into a relationship with Christ by means of the text of scripture.[42] Since, for Origen, scripture is analogous to the incarnation, the body (including Christ's body, the body of the cosmos, the reader's body, and the text itself) is the site of the reader's spiritual transformation. If scripture is the Word of God, then the text of scripture is nothing other than Christ the Logos, whose body is written in the letter of the text. By entering the text, the reader, in a sense, becomes the page on which the saving doctrine is written directly by the Spirit. The reader is assimilated to Christ in that he or she, too, becomes the bodily material upon which the doctrine is inscribed: just as the words of scripture incarnate Christ, according to Origen, so too does the reader imitate Christ, as the spiritual teaching is written upon his or her soul.[43]

As with devotional reading, so too with writing. Origen provides a model and precedent for seeing writing as an incarnational spiritual practice, but

[39] See Pierre Hadot, *Philosophy as a Way of Life: Spiritual Exercises from Socrates to Foucault*, trans. Michael Chase (Oxford: Blackwell, 1995), 186; and Rowan Williams, "Origen: Between Heresy and Orthodoxy," in *Origeniana Septima*, ed. W. A. Bienert and U. Kühneweg (Leuven: Leuven University Press, 1999), 14.

[40] Williams, "Origen," 14.

[41] Origen's hermeneutical principle is summarized in his famous description of the threefold method in *De princ.* 4.2.4.

[42] Origen, *Hom. in Lev.* 1.1 (quoted in Torjesen, *Hermeneutical Procedure*, 110): "For just as he is cloaked by the flesh, so also he is clothed with the garment of these words, so that the words are that which is seen, just as the flesh is seen, but hidden within (the words) the spiritual sense is perceived, just as the flesh is seen and the divinity perceived."

[43] See Ronald Heine, "Reading the Bible with Origen," in *The Bible in Greek Christian Antiquity*, ed. Paul M. Blowers (Notre Dame, Ind.: University of Notre Dame Press, 1997), 142.

the medieval women writers examined here go further. All three are writing "after" scripture. Scripture serves as both their precedent and their model of writing, allowing them to assert their place in the "proper context" of the Logos' scriptural pedagogy. Whereas Origen was concerned with the practice of exegesis and the profound spiritual transformation available to the exegete (and through him, the church), exegesis in this technical sense was not permitted to medieval women. These writers take a more direct and radical approach in their exegetical writings. Instead of interpreting scripture as the body of Christ, they undertook to write the body of Christ for themselves. Hadewijch, Angela, and Porete, along with Mechthild of Magdeburg, each presented their writings as directly inspired by God, prompting Bernard McGinn to dub them "the four female evangelists of the thirteenth century."[44]

Although rarely recognized as such in Christian history, writing is a powerful spiritual practice. Writing (and reading) are habituated and embodied activities that require patience, attention, and the particular writing virtues of humility, audacity, faith (in the word), hope (that one's own words might be read), and charity (toward sources, audience, and, not least, oneself). Origen's description of the way in which the exegete encounters Christ while reading the words of scripture illustrates what Paulsell means by the potential of writing as "a discipline within which we might meet God."[45] The medieval women mystics take their writing seriously as a spiritual practice, a way of practicing the incarnation, a discipline through which flesh is made word and in which they meet Christ. What these examples highlight is the transformation of the flesh into the divine through practices that are spiritual in their intention, attention, and effect. Not all writing is of the body of Christ. But a certain practice of mystical writing conveys the incarnation in both content and form, through the work of the flesh of both writer and text, the corporeal presence of signs and images, and the open-ended, unforeseen play of the word(s).

In her essay, "The Redemption of Women," Luce Irigaray reflects on what she has retained from her Roman Catholic heritage. Choosing the spirit over the letter, Irigaray summarizes the essence of Christianity in two key principles: "an incarnational relationship between the body and the word, [and]

---

[44] Bernard McGinn, "The Four Female Evangelists of the Thirteenth Century: The Invention of Authority," in *Deutsche Mystik im abendländischen Zusammenhang*, ed. Walter Haug and Wolfram Schneider-Lastin (Tübingen: Niemeyer, 2000), 175–94.

[45] Paulsell, "Writing," 21. See also Kathryn Tanner's discussion of practices in *Theories of Culture: A New Agenda for Theology* (Minneapolis: Fortress, 1997), 120–55.

a philosophy and a morality of love."[46] Within a framework of sexual difference, these principles are equally relevant for men and women. But in order to
"live a theology of incarnation in a free and responsible way" in a culture and
tradition in which women have been silenced, she argues that "women have
to discover their word(s), be faithful to it and, interweaving it with their bodies, make it a living and spiritual flesh."[47] The mystics recognized this effect
of the incarnation on their own bodies and their own texts. By identifying
with the bleeding, broken, and birthing body of Christ (who identified with
them by becoming human), and yet by further transforming that identification into speech, interpretation, and written text, they write their bodies into
the unfolding Christian tradition. Their interpretations of the incarnation
proceed through spiritual practices, and particularly through their practice
of writing, with its contemplative aims and active effects on their community
of readers. The incarnation of God in Jesus the Christ showed them the way,
so that the production of their texts took place in response to the Word made
flesh. And they, in turn, show us the way to live a theology of incarnation, by
writing the body of Christ along with their own bodies, transforming flesh
into writing subjects.

An Inclusive Incarnation

The incarnation provided a path for the mystical writings of medieval women,
and one way to practice the incarnation today is through spiritual practices
of writing. By approaching the incarnation from the side of female flesh that
becomes incarnate word, this interpretation through writing widens the
incarnation for all. The medieval women here considered were seeking their
divine words. The incarnation meant seeing themselves as having capacities
for creativity beyond the bodily reproduction of labor and children. Deliberately seeking the expression of their flesh in words demonstrates their faith-
fulness to the idea of incarnation and to the message of the Gospels.[48] The
incarnation is an invitation to express the divine word, and for women in
particular, who have been relegated to the realm of flesh and materiality, this
invitation is ennobling. But that invitation is extended to all who live out the
incarnation through their embodied spiritual and ethical practices.

This route to the incarnation supports the inclusive Christology identified by feminist and womanist theologians in which the incarnation takes

---

[46] Luce Irigaray, "The Redemption of Women," in *Key Writings* (London: Continuum,
2004), 150.

[47] Irigaray, "Redemption," 151.

[48] See Irigaray, "Redemption," 151.

place at multiple levels: in Wisdom and in the body of Mary, in the church and its sacraments, in redemptive community, in the cosmos, in suffering, in Christ, and in the bodies of men and women who imitate him in their acts of love and justice. Through our spiritual and ethical practices, we share in the incarnation: we become divine. Divinization makes us not less embodied, much less impassible, but more embodied, more present, more open to the world. Nor is becoming divine incarnate, in this view, to become other than what we are. Rather, we become divine as we become more fully ourselves: in the words of Hopkins' oft-quoted poem, "the just man justices; keeps grace: that keeps all his goings graces."[49] To incarnate the divine is to become like Christ, through whom we know God: the incarnation of love, fully embodied in the world. In this view, Jesus Christ can be understood as an exemplar (among others) of human possibility.[50] Spiritual practices of divinization, such as reading and writing, are ways of participating in this mystery through increasing conformity to Christ, to use traditional Christian language. Women's mystical writings participate in the mystery of incarnation through these practices of flesh becoming word.

The theological definition of "incarnation" takes on increasingly nuanced significance. In its root sense, it refers to the movement of descent by which the Word became flesh and lived among us. The medieval writers discussed here accept this basic Nicene-Chalcedonian definition of the incarnation. But they have little interest in the metaphysics of the incarnation or even in its soteriological justification, at least in the narrow sense by which the incarnation led directly to Jesus' atoning death. They are much more interested in the implications of the incarnation for human divinization.

The term "incarnation" functions most broadly as "a compelling paradigm for divine presence."[51] Although the term has been too frequently narrowed through technical theological argument, scripture provides ample resource for this broader understanding of incarnation as the distinctive way in which God is present in the world. The writings of the Christian

---

[49] Gerard Manley Hopkins, "As Kingfishers Catch Fire," in *Poems and Prose of Gerard Manley Hopkins*, ed. W. H. Gardner (Baltimore: Penguin Books, 1953), 51.

[50] Such as the possibility of God-consciousness communicated through Jesus' ideality and exemplarity (making him both redeemer and the communication of redemption) as described by Friedrich Schleiermacher in *The Christian Faith* (1830; New York: T&T Clark, 1999); see also R. R. Niebuhr, *Schleiermacher on Christ and Religion* (New York: Scribner, 1964).

[51] Wendy Farley, *Tragic Vision and Divine Compassion: A Contemporary Theodicy* (Louisville, Ky.: Westminster John Knox, 1990), 112.

Testament contain ample evidence of this incarnate presence; among others, through the poor and hungry and naked, the "least of these" of Matthew 25; in the resurrection appearances and in the breaking of bread; wherever two or three are gathered; through abiding in God's love and in love for one another.[52] In these moments, we encounter the incarnate God; through our spiritual and ethical practices God is incarnate in the world. Interpreting the incarnation through embodied practices (such as writing) affirms this more extensive vision of God's presence in the world found in scripture and in the inclusive Christologies of womanist and feminist theology.

Following these sources, we might understand the term "incarnation" in the following ways. First, all uses refer back to the Nicene-Chalcedonian definition and its precedent in the prologue to the fourth gospel: Word became flesh, God became human, in the person of Jesus of Nazareth. Second, the incarnation can refer to the embodiment of God more generally—that is, it is the characteristic way that God is present in the world. This way naturally includes the body of Jesus through his birth, his life and ministry, his suffering, death, and resurrection, as well as the body of Christ in the church and its sacraments, in redemptive community more broadly, and as extended to the body of creation in the form of the cosmic Christ. Anytime we encounter Christ's body in any form, we brush up against the mystery of the incarnation. Third, the incarnation has real effects on the human beings who encounter that mystery; these are the effects explored by women mystics through the spiritual life, mystical theology, and the process of divinization. Finally, the definition of the incarnation stretches to encompass the relationship between word and flesh expressed in mystical speech and writing, and in embodied spiritual and ethical practices more generally. It is in this sense that these medieval women writers come to understand the effect of the embodiment of Christ on their lives and their texts. In writing the body of Christ, they each convey 1) the word become flesh in Jesus of Nazareth; 2) the body of Christ in the diversity of forms in which he is met; 3) divinization through the transformation of the spiritual life; and 4) their own flesh become word through their writing practices. The Word made flesh invites all flesh to become divine word.

In the late medieval period, the incarnation of God in the male body of Jesus occasioned ecstatic symptoms and miracles on the bodies of numerous holy women who identified with Christ, who identified with them by

---

[52] Farley concludes her description by noting that "it is these acts of love and compassion that continue to incarnate God in history." See *Tragic Vision*, 112–14.

becoming a bleeding, suffering, and nourishing body.[53] Some have called this manifestation a type of writing—a performative writing *on* the bodies of women through gestures and miraculous symptoms.[54] But the incarnation did, and does, more than identify women more firmly with their bodies. It also effects their divinization by authorizing women's writings, in which their particular female flesh issues in embodied divine word(s). By writing the body of Christ, his followers participate in the incarnation through a spiritual practice in which word and flesh meet. This practice is not only salutary for women, but also especially empowering for all those who have been relegated to the margins of Christian history and theology on account of their bodily differences. Through writing, they register their bodies and their words in the written Christian tradition.[55] Their story becomes part of the unfolding narrative of the word made flesh. They claim a place for themselves in the humanity—and the divinity—of Christ. By writing, they leave a legacy that establishes the possibility of a "female train of thought,"[56] a genealogy and heritage that, however broken and incomplete, support the theological writings of contemporary women. These texts provide ample resource for feminist efforts in constructing more inclusive Christologies. In the writings of medieval women, the incarnation grows and expands from a unique, special revelation in a particular male body to a more general theological feature of the relationship between word and flesh, matter and spirit, manifested in a multiplicity of bodies and texts marked by difference and desire, pleasure and pain, transcendence and limitation, possibility and loss.

[53] See Caroline Walker Bynum among others.

[54] See Cristina Mazzoni, *Saint Hysteria: Neurosis, Mysticism, and Gender in European Culture* (Ithaca, N.Y.: Cornell University Press, 1996).

[55] See Emily A. Holmes and Wendy Farley, eds., *Women, Writing, Theology: Transforming a Tradition of Exclusion* (Waco, Tex.: Baylor University Press, 2011).

[56] See Emily Culpepper, "Philosophia: Feminist Methodology for Constructing a Female Train of Thought," *Journal of Feminist Studies in Religion* 3, no. 2 (1987): 7–16.

2

Hadewijch of Brabant and the Mother of Love

Hadewijch was a woman in love with love. The love of love permeates her writings across a variety of genres, both poetry and prose.[1] Love (*Minne* in Hadewijch's native Dutch language) is both subject and object, noun and verb, lover and beloved, and the love that unites the two. Her written ode to love that takes so many different forms finds one of its finest expressions in poem 15 of her *Mengeldichten*. Greeting her beloved, the poet describes the desire that draws her to love:

> I greet that which I love
> With my heart's blood
> My senses wither
> In love's primeval rage.[2]

---

[1] Hadewijch wrote in four different genres: visions, stanzaic poems, letters, and poems in couplets (or "poems in mixed forms"). All quotations are taken from the critical editions edited by Jozef van Mierlo, S.J.: *Hadewijch: Visionen*, 2 vols. (Louvain: Vlaamsch Boekenhalle, 1924, 1925), hereafter cited as *Visions* by chapter and line; *Hadewijch: Strophische Gedichten*, 2 vols. (Antwerp: Standaard, 1942), hereafter cited as *Stanzaic Poems* by number and line; *Hadewijch: Brieven*, 2 vols. (Antwerp: Standaard, 1947), hereafter cited as *Letters* by number and line; and *Hadewijch: Mengeldichten* (Antwerp: Standaard, 1952), hereafter cited as *Poems in Couplets* by number and line. The English translation is by Mother Columba Hart, O.S.B., from *Hadewijch: The Complete Works* (Mahwah, N.J.: Paulist Press, 1980), hereafter cited as CW, with modifications where noted.

[2] Ic groete dat ic minne
Met miere herten bloet
Mi dorren mine sinne
Inder minnen oerwoet. (*Poems in Couplets*, 15; translation modified)

The poet's courtly greeting barely masks the "primeval rage" (*oerwoet* or *ore-woet*)³ that bubbles the heart's blood, withering her senses with passion, both suffering and love. The word evokes an ambivalent and overwhelming feeling of attachment to the one who is loved, a passion older even than the "I" who greets her beloved in this poem.

Over the course of the next seven stanzas, Hadewijch describes the raging desire that inspires her to love in a variety of ways, each addressed to a manifestation of love: "Oh, dear sweet love," "Oh, lord most dear," "Oh, nature most sweet," "Oh, dear maiden."⁴ She returns to the first person "I" of her opening stanza with a series of internally rhyming lines: "I yearn, I watch, I taste," "I am good, I endeavor for the heights," "I tremble, I cling, I give."⁵ By the end of the poem, the syntax disintegrates into something resembling infantile babble, a rhythmic repetition of sounds recalling the primeval feelings of passion and rage (*oerwoet*), prior to organized language, with which the poem began. In the final stanzas, Hadewijch addresses love through the intimate form of *lief*, personified as lover or beloved, before invoking the overwhelming power of *Minne*:

> Oh beloved, have I love a love
> Be love my love
> Who gave love for love
> So that love could lift up love
>
> Oh love were I love
> And with love loved you love
> Oh love for love give that love
> Which love fully knows as love⁶

---

³ For a discussion of *oerwoet* (or *oerwort*), see Paul Mommaers, *Hadewijch: Writer, Beguine, Love Mystic*, trans. Elisabeth Dutton (Leuven: Peeters, 2004), 98–101.

⁴ "Ay hertelike suete minne" (15.5), "Ay here ouer kare" (15.9), "Ay ouer suete natuere" (15.17), "Ay hertelike ioffrouwe" (15.21). Love is transgendered in Hadewijch's writings, sometimes addressed as a lord and sometimes as a lady.

⁵ "Jc hake, ic wake, ic smake" (15.33), "Jc doge, ic poghe omt hoghe" (15.37), "Jc beue, ic cleue, ic geue" (15.41).

⁶ Ay, lief, hebbic lief een lief,
Sidi lief mijn lief,
Die lief gauet omme lief,
Daer lief lief mede verhief.

Ay, minne, ware ic minne
Ende met minnen minne v minne!
Ay, minne, om minne gheuet dat minne
Die minne al minne volkinne (*Poems in Couplets*, 15).

Here the repetition of words and the rhythm of sounds threaten to over-whelm any semantic content, just as love overwhelms the poet's senses with ancient rage and passion. In this poem, the materiality of language conveys love through the resonance and reverberation of sounds that overpower language's meaning. Love, Hadewijch seems to say, is a force that transforms our ordinary ways of speaking. Love's origin can be discerned in the rhythms of language, which the poet's desire touches upon and offers to her audience. The poet's skill with words expresses the love that is embodied, rhythmic word from the beginning.

———

Love is a complex and multivalent word in Hadewijch's writings. Among other significations, it is Hadewijch's preferred name for Christ, who is Love incarnate. In writing of divine love, Hadewijch makes the poet and writer the instrument of the incarnation, the one whose flesh becomes word and through whom word becomes flesh. Her poetry proclaims the origins of the incarnation in the maternal body of Mary, who provides a model for spiritual growth through both suffering and delight. Hadewijch likens the poet's role to that of Mary in conveying the divine Word: in both the poet and in the mother of God, word and flesh meet. When Hadewijch writes the body of Christ, she extends our understanding of the incarnation from Jesus' body to the body of his mother to the flesh of the writers and poets whose embodied words sing of divine love. Writing in multiple genres and poetic forms becomes, in Hadewijch's hands, a way of practicing the incarnation, a way of expanding its significance through the diversity of word and flesh.

Little is known about Hadewijch, a Dutch woman of the middle of the thirteenth century.[7] From her writings, she was clearly well educated in rhetoric, numerology, astronomy, and music, and therefore likely studied the liberal arts. Her familiarity with courtly love literature and the poetry of the *trouvères* speaks to an upper-class, if not necessarily noble, background. She knew scripture well, along with the writings of the church fathers, especially Augustine, as well as the theology of the Victorines and the Cistercians. Although she wrote in Middle Dutch, she was also familiar with Latin and French, frequently introducing Latin phrases and French words into her texts.

———

[7] For biographical material, see the introduction to Hart's translation of *The Complete Works*, 2–6. See also Mommaers' chapter "In Pursuit of the Historical Hadewijch," in *Hadewijch: Writer*, 8–12, for the very little that can be definitively known of Hadewijch's life. His subsequent chapters supplement this information with a discussion of Hadewijch's fellow beguines and her likely role as spiritual leader of her community.

Hadewijch was a beguine and therefore part of the popular women's religious movement that spread through the Low Countries and northern Europe in the twelfth and thirteenth centuries.[8] Unlike nuns, beguines lived a communal life of poverty and prayer without entering a cloister or taking vows. Most were economically self-sufficient, often through the cloth industries. Beguines did not obey a particular rule, and, although they received the sacraments from sympathetic clerics,[9] they were largely independent of male authority. Based on her writings, Hadewijch either founded or joined a group of beguine women and served as their mistress and spiritual director. At some point, her authority was opposed and it seems she was exiled from her community. The pain of this separation from her sisters colors much of her writing.

Hadewijch directs her writings to a group of young beguines, instructing them in the knowledge of love.[10] Her writings fall into four different genres, collected in books of letters, stanzaic poems, visions, and poems in couplets.[11] *Visions* conveys spiritual guidance and insight, authenticated by the divine revelations she received.[12] *Letters* and *Poems in Couplets* are didactic in character, written after separation from her community, and *Stanzaic Poems* contains songs to be sung by the women, who, some suggest, may also

---

[8] For the history of the beguines, see Walter Simons, *Cities of Ladies: Beguine Communities in the Medieval Low Countries, 1200–1565* (Philadelphia: University of Pennsylvania Press, 2001).

[9] See Simons, *Cities of Ladies*, 38–39 and 47.

[10] For Hadewijch's writing as a leader of a beguine community, see Mommaers, *Hadewijch: Writer*, 45–57.

[11] These texts deeply influenced the fourteenth-century Flemish mystic John Ruusbroec (1293–1381) before they were lost to history, rediscovered in Brussels only in 1838. See Jessica A. Boon, "Trinitarian Love Mysticism: Ruusbroec, Hadewijch, and the Gendered Experience of the Divine," *Church History* 72, no. 3 (2003): 484–503.

[12] Whether Hadewijch describes her own mystical and visionary experience in her visions or adopts a narrative persona is debated. Mommaers makes a distinction between the extratextual experience and its literary expression in *Hadewijch: Writer*, 58. Caroline Walker Bynum (*Holy Feast and Holy Fast: The Religious Significance of Food to Medieval Women* [Berkeley: University of California Press, 1987]), John G. Milhaven (*Hadewijch and Her Sisters: Other Ways of Loving and Knowing* [Albany: SUNY Press, 1993]), and Elizabeth Dreyer (*Passionate Spirituality: Hildegard of Bingen and Hadewijch of Brabant* [Mahwah, N.J.: Paulist Press, 2005]) all take Hadewijch's writings to be in some way directly indicative of her own experience. Barbara Newman (*From Virile Woman to WomanChrist: Studies in Medieval Religion and Literature* [Philadelphia: University of Pennsylvania Press, 1995]) and Gordon Rudy (*Mystical Language of Sensation in the Later Middle Ages* [New York: Routledge, 2002]), in contrast, focus on the textual appearance of a narrative persona.

have danced while singing.[13] Both the prose texts and the poems were written for a beguine audience that received them as a ritual community. According to Veerle Fraeters, Hadewijch's writings "were received in a ritual, collective setting, in which declamation and jubilant song alternated."[14] Beguines sang the stanzaic poems in a liturgical or paraliturgical manner and read aloud from the letters and visions in a religious setting that was part of an essentially oral culture.[15]

Hadewijch is unique among medieval women writers not only for the diversity of genres in which she wrote, but also for her complex model of the spiritual life, by which she instructed her fellow beguines to achieve "full-grownness" in love. While Hadewijch is frequently read (and sometimes dismissed) as an exemplar of erotic bridal mysticism,[16] in this chapter I examine the neglected theme of maternality in her writings as it intersects with her understanding of the incarnation. According to Hadewijch, beguines grow spiritually by imitating Christ in both his divinity and his humanity as well as his mother in conceiving and giving birth to Love. Hadewijch's poetry, and the spirituality of the incarnation it expresses, further resonates with what theorist Julia Kristeva calls the "maternal semiotic": the material rhythms of language that convey and disrupt meaning.

In her groundbreaking *Revolution in Poetic Language*, Kristeva examines the way meaning is conveyed by language through signs. All signification, she argues, depends on two modalities of the same signifying process:

---

[13] Paul Mommaers, *The Riddle of Christian Mystical Experience: The Role of the Humanity of Jesus* (Leuven: Peeters, 2003), 168.

[14] Veerle Fraeters, forward to Mommaers, *Hadewijch: Writer*, x. Fraeters cites recent Dutch scholarship on Hadewijch by Louis P. Grijp ("De zingende Hadewijch," in *Een zoet akkoord: Middeleeuwse lyriek in de Lage Landen*, ed. Frank Willaert [Amsterdam: Prometheus, 1992], 72–93) and Anikó Daróczi (*Hadewijch: Ende hieromme swighic sachte* [Amsterdam-Antwerp: Atlas, 2002]). Prior to this more recent scholarship, Tanis M. Guest, *Some Aspects of Hadewijch's Poetic Form in the "Strophische Gedichten"* (The Hague: Martinus Nijhoff, 1975), examines the musicality of Hadewijch's stanzaic poems in her chapter on "Sound and Music," 62–91.

[15] "It seems, in sharp contrast to the transmission of religious texts in schools, communal reading aloud and interpretation of texts was preferred over quiet, individual reading." Mommaers, *Hadewijch: Writer*, 30.

[16] See, for instance, Jacques Lacan, "Dieu et la jouissance de La Femme" ("God and the Jouissance of The Woman—A Love Letter," trans. by Jacqueline Rose in *Feminine Sexuality: Jacques Lacan and the école freudienne*, ed. Juliet Mitchell and Jacqueline Rose [London: Macmillan, 1982], 137–48). See also Amy Hollywood's discussion of Lacan in *Sensible Ecstasy: Mysticism, Sexual Difference, and the Demands of History* (Chicago: University of Chicago Press, 2002), 146–70.

the semiotic and the symbolic.[17] The symbolic order of language organizes meaning through the rules of syntax. It is associated by French theorists with the "law of the father," the patriarchal social system that governs the organization of law, religion, and economics. Every language user enters into this symbolic order, which preexists the individual. This paternal, symbolic order of language, however, rests upon an earlier material reality that is prior to language, but which nevertheless conveys meaning. Kristeva names this mode of signification the semiotic, and she associates it with the body of the mother. The rhythms and drives of the maternal body allow an infant to enter into the symbolic order and become a language user. These maternal rhythms are not forgotten but in some sense are always present; they reappear in the embodied and material dimensions of language, such as rhythm. Whereas the symbolic is abstract and impersonal, the semiotic is intimate and embodied. Both modalities are necessary for signification—that is, for meaning to operate through language, although the symbolic order tends to erase its reliance on the semiotic, material, and maternal dimension of language. Kristeva identifies the semiotic in psychoanalytic speech as well as in the rhythms of art, music, and poetry, and her privileged examples come from literature. The theory of the semiotic points to the origins and foundation of language in the maternal body. The symbolic order of language, Kristeva argues, is subject to disruption by the rhythms of the semiotic. Such disruption brings the potential for social and symbolic revolution through an influx of the semiotic into the symbolic, of the rhythms of the body into language.

Hadewijch's poetic language reveals the presence of the semiotic in a form strikingly similar to that described by Kristeva. Hadewijch's repetition of words and sounds through assonance and alliteration, her use of paradox and wordplay to convey additional levels of meaning, and her understanding of the interplay between what she calls "song and melody" all reveal an awareness of the semiotic modality of language, which is often suppressed in the scholastic and didactic theology of her thirteenth-century contemporaries. Hadewijch's poetic playfulness with the material dimension of language adeptly conveys the rhythms and drives of the semiotic. This influx of the semiotic into Hadewijch's writing, in turn, provides a material support and vehicle for her conception of the spiritual life as incarnate in form, both human and divine.

---

[17] Julia Kristeva, *La Révolution du langage poetique* (Paris: Éditions du Seuil, 1974). I have primarily used the 1984 English translation by Margaret Waller: Julia Kristeva, *Revolution in Poetic Language* (New York: Columbia University Press, 1984).

According to Kristeva, the semiotic is the source of artistic creativity, inspiration, and revolution in language and thought. This effect of the semiotic is demonstrated by Hadewijch's prolific writings and by her theological insights. After examining Hadewijch's model of spiritual growth and the presence of the semiotic in her poetry, I turn to her most insightful theological contribution. Hadewijch approaches the incarnation from the perspective of Mary's experience of conception, pregnancy, and birth. By interpreting Mary's biological experience in spiritual and allegorical terms, Hadewijch effectively extends the incarnation to all others, male or female, whose spiritual practices similarly give birth to love in imitation of both Christ and Mary. The legacy of Hadewijch's own spiritual practice is found in her poetic writings, which convey the maternal semiotic, her Marian and incarnate model of spirituality, and her own flesh made word.[18] Hadewijch's striking understanding of the incarnation as the birth of love within the soul supports her own creative generation of texts written for love of God and love of her fellow beguines.

The Soul's Growth in Love

Hadewijch's overriding theological concern is the soul's relation to love (*Minne*): "I constantly wished to know, and kept thinking of it, and repeated ceaselessly: 'What is love? And who is Love? (*wat es minne ende wie es minne*)."[19] *Minne* functions as a name for God, for Christ, and for the soul in relation to these. It is also a dynamic term, a verb performed by God and

---

[18] One way in which Hadewijch transforms her flesh into word is through somatic language that is continuous with the body. According to Rudy (*Mystical Language of Sensation*, 67–100), her writing is neither a precise transcript of bodily experience on the one hand, nor spiritualized allegory on the other. Rather, because the human being is both body and soul, Hadewijch describes the encounter with the incarnate Christ by using language of touch and taste that is at once spiritual and somatic.

[19] *Visions*, 2.20 (CW, 271). Hadewijch's interest in love began, like some other mystics, in the time between late childhood and early adolescence, which she describes in a rare autobiographical passage: "Since I was ten years old I have been so overwhelmed by intense love that I should have died, during the first two years when I began this, if God had not given me other forms of strength than people ordinarily receive, and if he had not renewed my nature with his own Being . . . Sometimes Love so enlightens me that I know what is wanting in me—that I do not content my Beloved according to his sublimity; and sometimes the sweet nature of Love blinds me to such a degree that when I can taste and feel her it is enough for me; and sometimes I feel so rich in her presence that I myself acknowledge she contents me." *Letters*, 11.10 (CW, 69). Mechthild of Magdeburg similarly reports that she was first "greeted" by the Holy Spirit at age twelve (*The Flowing Light of the Godhead*, trans. Frank J. Tobin [New York: Paulist Press, 1998]).

the soul, and the divine power or source of all existence. It is both the intra-Trinitarian bonds of love and the expression of these in the incarnation.[20] In Hadewijch's writings, *Minne* is frequently personified and addressed as Lady or Queen, following the conventions of the *trouvère* poets, especially in her stanzaic poems. But *Minne* also refers to the intimate relationship Hadewijch advocates with Christ in his humanity and his divinity. *Minne* is both the satisfaction of desire and unending longing. Consequently it is both unbearably painful and exquisitely pleasurable. The complexity, richness, and specificity of Hadewijch's deployment of *Minne*-language make generalizations about her theological teachings difficult.[21] Nevertheless, several themes can be identified.

Hadewijch's writings primarily serve a pedagogical function: to teach her fellow beguines the mysteries of *Minne*. Love of Love makes the soul vacillate between two poles, the heights of passionate ecstasy and the pain and frustration of disappointment in love. These two poles, however, are not sequential, but instead are two aspects or moments of one single relationship to Love as union with God. Paul Mommaers has noted Hadewijch's consistent use of the contrast between *ghebruken* and *ghebreken*.[22] *Ghebruken* (or *ghebrukelecheit*) is translated by Mother Columba Hart as "fruition," although "enjoyment," "satisfaction," or, in French, "jouissance," are better translations.[23]

---

[20] On Hadewijch's use of "minne" and its interpretation, see Guest, *Some Aspects of Hadewijch's Poetic Form*, 4–14; Joris Reynaert, "Hadewijch: Mystic Poetry and Courtly Love," in *Medieval Dutch Literature in Its European Context*, ed. Erik Kooper (Cambridge: Cambridge University Press, 1994), 208–25, esp. 210–15; and Bernard McGinn, *The Flowering of Mysticism: Men and Women in the New Mysticism (1200–1350)*, vol. 3 of *The Presence of God: A History of Western Christian Mysticism* (New York: Crossroad, 1998), 201–11.

[21] Guest (*Some Aspects of Hadewijch's Poetic Form*, 7) takes the example of letter 25, in which Hadewijch writes that "De Minne es al!": "In a context of instruction to others, this might mean: 'The only thing you can do, must do, is to give all the loving devoted service of which you are capable.' As a description of personal experience, it might mean: 'To give love, and be loved in return, is the most wonderful thing in the world.' Both these readings, however, seem to restrict a phrase which by its placing seems to demand an absolute meaning, without qualification; a poor interpretation might be: 'The One I love—whom we should all love—is literally everything, limitless and without bounds; all we are and all we experience is part of him; he it is that draws our love and service to himself, and he that gives us the love and support we need; when we suffer, that too comes from him; outside him there is nothing; worse, there is nothingness.' This in four words; can language be more compressed?"

[22] Mommaers, *Riddle*, 170–83.

[23] Mary A. Suydam, "The Touch of Satisfaction: Visions and the Religious Experience According to Hadewijch of Antwerp," *Journal of Feminist Studies in Religion* 12, no. 2 (1996): 5–27, 14. See also Milhaven, *Hadewijch and Her Sisters*, 29.

Ghebreken, by contrast, signifies "to fail" or "to lack."[24] Mommaers identifies these terms as two intrinsic and inseparable moments of Hadewijch's understanding of mystical union.[25] The similarity in sounds between the two terms verbally echo one another in her writings. But her use of *ghebruken/ghebreken* is more than simple wordplay. Coming to accept the necessity of *ghebreken* in the spiritual life, rather than desiring to remain forever in the enjoyment of *ghebruken*, is part of fully growing up (*volwassen*)—one of Hadewijch's three basic metaphors for the soul's relation to Love.

Hadewijch instructs her fellow beguines in the ways of spiritual growth.[26] Her own spirituality appears to have matured through a difficult process, through which she attempts to guide her sisters. Although her initial desire, described in her first vision, was "to be one with God in fruition (*om een te sine ghebrukelike met gode*)," she immediately qualifies it: "For this I was still too childish and too little grown-up (*te kinsch toe ende te onghewassen*)."[27] Hadewijch's desire is fulfilled in the encounter with Christ that follows,[28] but she gradually comes to realize the childishness of her wish to enjoy God without suffering or failure (*ghebreken*). And so she comes to instruct her beguines in the necessity of growing up as well. "You are still young (*Ghi sijt noch ionc*)," she writes, "and you must grow a good deal (*ende behoeft sere te*

---

[24] Jacques Lacan also links these two terms in courtly literature and in mysticism with reference to Hadewijch in his provocative "Dieu et la jouissance de ła Femme."

[25] "However strong and permanent the contrast between *ghebruken* and *ghebreken*, they complement each other intrinsically. Far from indicating a succession of exaltation and depression, or a construction made up of loose component elements, these opposites appear as interacting elements of an organic unity. For Hadewijch there can be no 'enjoying' independent of 'failing,' and 'failing' is essentially connected with 'enjoying.' Moreover, these two contrary feelings intensify each other within the mystic's single experience of the being-one. And so radical is this interrelation that the distinguishing mark of the accomplished mystic—of the 'grown-up,' as she puts it—is precisely her being enabled to sense these contrary feelings 'at once': 'Consolation and ill treatment both at once, / this is the essence of the taste of Love.'" Mommaers, *Riddle*, 171–72, quoting *Stanzaic Poems*, 31.25–26.

[26] See Barbara Newman, *From Virile Woman*, 147; Sheila Carney, "Exemplarism in Hadewijch: The Quest for Full-Grownness," *Downside Review* 103, no. 353 (1985): 276–95; and Elona K. Lucas, "Psychological and Spiritual Growth in Hadewijch and Julian of Norwich," *Studia Mystica* 9, no. 3 (1986): 3–20.

[27] *Visions*, 1.7–10 (CW, 263).

[28] She introduces her eucharistic vision, given to fulfill her initial desire, as follows: "When I had received our Lord, he then received me to him, so that he withdrew my senses from every remembrance of alien things to enable me to have joy in him in inward togetherness with him." (*Doen ic onsen here ontfaen hadde, doen ontfinc hi mi te heme, Soe dat hi mi op nam alle mine sinne buten alle ghedinckenisse van vremder saken omme sijns te ghebrukene in enecheiden.*) *Visions*, 1.15–18 (CW, 263).

wassen), and it is much better for you, if you wish to walk the way of Love, that you seek difficulty and that you suffer for the honor of Love, rather than wish to feel love."[29] A mature relationship to love entails more than ecstatic pleasure, more than adolescent romance. Service and suffering for the sake of love are required in order to understand what love is. The promise of spiritual maturity is the effect of selfless service to love: "For if you abandon yourself to Love, you will soon attain full growth (*want wildi v ter Minnen verlaten, soe suldi saen volwassen*)."[30]

Growing up requires acceptance of failure (*ghebreken*) as an inseparable part of enjoyment (*ghebruken*). Hadewijch's basic metaphor of spiritual growth is further extended in two strikingly different directions. The first is related to her innovative use of the courtly love lyric for her stanzaic poems.[31] According to this genre of poetry, the poet-knight's true love for his lady is expressed in his selfless and long-suffering service to her. His desire can never be satisfied, for *fin'amor* (noble or courtly love) is always *amor de lonh* (love from afar).[32] Hadewijch adopts the *trouvère*'s voice in her stanzaic poems to describe the soul's relationship to *Minne* in terms of *ghebreken* (failure or suffering). The promised and desired enjoyment (*ghebruken*) is impossible because the soul cannot do enough to satisfy or content (*ghenoegh doen*) her Lady, nor will she (as poet-knight) ever be enough or be content (*ghenoegh sine*) with the satisfaction of her desire. The stanzaic poems paint a picture of love as a cruel mistress; her desires are excessively demanding, and the poet complains of poor treatment as s/he suffers her wounds.[33]

---

[29] *Letters*, 2.66–69 (CW, 50). It seems evident that her disciples are not young in years but immature in spiritual experience and expectations.

[30] *Letters*, 6.45–46 (CW, 57).

[31] Hadewijch invents a new genre, what Newman describes as "la mystique courtoise" (*From Virile Woman*, 137–67) and Mommaers calls the mystical love lyric (*Riddle*, 168). Reynaert ("Hadewijch: Mystic Poetry," 208–25), however, situates Hadewijch more precisely within the literary tradition of the religious use of courtly literature motifs and explains her religious use of courtly imagery in terms of her beguine status, situated in the world, and thus competing with worldly culture: "We should also take into account that the language of courtly mystic poetry, which she seemingly initiated, in fact already existed or was coming into existence in her cultural milieu (beguine or otherwise) and that she could make use of it quite naturally, not necessarily manifesting herself as an imitator of the worldly poets, but on the contrary stepping forward as a representative of a certain conception of 'divine love' and as a member of the spiritual 'community' which was founded on it." 221.

[32] And the desire of the "amie" is denied or invisible. Lacan's discussion of the failure of all sexual relations speaks to this aspect of courtly love in "Dieu et la jouissance."

[33] For a feminist critique of the commixture of violence with erotic language in Hadewijch's writings (among others), see Julie B. Miller, "Eroticized Violence in Medieval

By adopting the voice of the male poet-knight in love with his lady Love to express the relationship of *ghebreken* (failure or suffering), the female poet Hadewijch transgresses gender norms in order to convey her theological and didactic message.[34] According to Karma Lochrie and Amy Hollywood, she thereby queers the presumptively heterosexual relations of courtly love and creates a mystical discourse in which gender, sex, and the erotic are excessively deployed. The changing gender identity of the poet reminds the reader of its fictional status as metaphor, pointing to the ineffable relationship of the soul to love. Hadewijch's literary transvestism is but one literary and theological strategy that expresses the relativity and failure of all human images to adequately convey the transcendent divine love.[35]

Hadewijch adapts the poetic genre of the *trouvères* to convey the inability to satisfy or be satisfied by love. Desire (*begherte*) is insatiable due to the transcendence of the beloved and the failure (*ghebreken*) of human attempts to sustain enjoyment (*ghebruken*). The soul's relationship to love, according to the stanzaic poems, is essentially composed of failure, absence of the Beloved, suffering, and the frustration of desire. Acceptance of what Hadewijch describes as *ghebreken* is part of growing up, and so the voice of the poet-knight represents a stage along life's way of spiritual growth. Mommaers argues that Hadewijch gradually came to understand *ghebreken* as a necessary and intrinsic part of mystical union by learning to identify suffering and failure with the humanity of Christ.[36] What initially appears in negative

---

Women's Mystical Literature: A Call for a Feminist Critique," *Journal of Feminist Studies in Religion* 15, no. 2 (1999): 25–48.

[34] See Karma Lochrie, "Mystical Acts, Queer Tendencies," in *Constructing Medieval Sexuality*, ed. Karma Lochrie, Peggy McCracken, and James A. Schultz (Minneapolis: University of Minnesota Press, 1997), 180–200; Amy Hollywood, "Sexual Desire, Divine Desire; Or, Queering the Beguines," in *Queer Theology: New Perspectives on Sex and Gender*, ed. Gerard Loughlin (Oxford: Blackwell, 2006), reprinted in *Toward a Theology of Eros: Transfiguring Passion at the Limits of Discipline*, ed. Virginia Burrus and Catherine Keller (New York: Fordham University Press, 2006), 119–33.

[35] This transgendering continues as the "maternal" source of the incarnation is unmoored from bodies, so that male readers and poets can also become mothers in the semiotic production of text. See Kitty Scoular Datta, "Female Heterologies: Women's Mysticism, Gender-Mixing and the Apophatic," in *Self/Same/Other: Re-visioning the Subject in Literature and Theology*, ed. Heather Walton and Andrew W. Hass (Sheffield, U.K.: Sheffield Academic, 2000), 125–36. See also Michael Sells on the "unsaying" of gender through excessive language in the cases of Marguerite Porete and Meister Eckhart in *Mystical Languages of Unsaying* (Chicago: University of Chicago Press, 1994), 180–205.

[36] "As we have seen in her general account of mystic union, Hadewijch was granted the gratifying feeling of *ghebruken* ('to enjoy') coupled at once with the frustration of *ghebreken*

terms as a failure of love is thus reinterpreted by Hadewijch as a form of participation in Christ's suffering in solidarity with his humanity and therefore
with all humanity—the essence of Christian love.[37]

Hadewijch's second basic metaphor for the soul's maturing relationship with love is motherhood.[38] Part of growing up entails that the soul, like
Mary, become the mother of love, which in this case signifies both the person
Christ and the Christian virtue of love. Mary thus provides an image for
the spiritual life of all Christians who, too, can become the mother of love.[39]
This metaphor is repeated in all four of Hadewijch's genres and provides a
counterpoint to her model of the soul as poet-knight in service of Lady Love,
thereby relativizing the gender identity of each.

The theme of the mystic's soul as mother of love first appears in a letter
to a young beguine. Hadewijch advises, "You, however, must keep yourself so
naked before God, and so despoiled of all repose outside of him, that nothing
can ever satisfy you but God alone. And if this is not the case, you should feel
as much pain for his sake as a woman who cannot bring her child into the
world (*alse ene vrouwe die haers kints niet en can ghenesen*)."[40] Hadewijch here

---

('to fail'). The sense of failure was brought home to her mainly in two ways: by her impotence
to 'content' Love and by her suffering at the absence of Love. There is ample evidence in her
writings that Hadewijch found it a real struggle to recognize the 'failing' as part and parcel
of mystic union. . . . It now becomes clear that Hadewijch was able to accept 'failing' with
all her heart only by understanding it as part of her being tangibly united with Jesus. This
perception of the Humanity seems to have dawned on her in two stages. First, she saw that
Christ had lived through the same experience of distress: in fact, he was the one who suffered complete 'failing.' But she also came to realize that for herself and kindred souls to feel
their 'failing' was precisely their being actually 'like him in the Humanity' (*gheliken inder
menscheit*)." Mommaers, *Riddle*, 179–80.

[37] On the value of suffering in solidarity with others, see also Amy Hollywood's discussion of Georges Bataille in *Sensible Ecstasy: Mysticism, Sexual Difference, and the Demands of
History* (Chicago: University of Chicago Press, 2002).

[38] Newman interprets the "motherhood" imagery of Hadewijch in terms of the bridal
subject position, taken from the tradition of Song of Songs exegesis. But "motherhood" in
Hadewijch's writings is much more nuanced than merely the consequence of becoming a
bride of Christ. Nevertheless, Newman makes a helpful distinction between the contrast-
ing, but not exclusive, subject positions of bride, *fin amant*, and *amie* in *From Virile Woman*,
143–45.

[39] The emphasis on motherhood may reflect Cistercian influence, as Hadewijch was
familiar with and cites the writings of Bernard of Clairvaux. For a discussion of Cistercian
spirituality in which both Jesus and abbot are described as mother, see Caroline Walker
Bynum, *Jesus as Mother: Studies in the Spirituality of the High Middle Ages* (Berkeley: University of California Press, 1982).

[40] *Letters*, 21.14–20 (CW, 93).

likens the frustration of erotic desire for God to the pain of laboring unto birth, associating two realms of signification—pain and suffering on the one hand with maternality on the other—that at first glance appear distinct.[41] Suffering coincides with enjoyment in the process of giving birth, again associating failure (*ghebreken*) with fruition (*ghebruken*). The theme of the soul as the mother of Christ appears again in a second letter in which Hadewijch chastises the spiritual failure of her beguines: "Therefore we do not carry God's Son maternally (*en draghen wi den gods sone niet moederleke*) or suckle him with exercises of love (*Noch en soghene niet met oefeninghen van Minnen*). We have too much self-will, and we want too much repose, and we seek too much ease and peace."[42] These passages and others like them presuppose a model of the spiritual life that is Marian in form, that entails both suffering and pleasure, and that culminates in the soul giving birth to love and becoming, like Mary, the mother of God.

In *Visions*, Hadewijch reiterates this maternal spirituality. On Christmas night, she has a vision of an abyss containing all beings. While listening to the music of David's harp, Hadewijch then "perceived an Infant being born in the souls who love in secret (*doe uerkindic kint gheboren werdende in die uerhoelne minnende gheeste*), the souls hidden from their own eyes in the deep abyss of which I speak, and to whom nothing is lacking but that they should lose themselves in it."[43] The nativity occasions the birth of the Infant in all souls who love, and who thereby become the mother of Love. But the maternal spirituality Hadewijch invokes is not merely the joy of Christmas. In vision 13, Hadewijch indicates that *ghebreken*, failure and suffering, is equally a part of becoming the mother of Love:

> And one Seraph cried with a loud voice and said: "See here the new secret heaven, which is closed to all those who never were God's mother with perfect motherhood (*al die ghene die nie moeder gods der volcomenre dracht en waren*), who never

---

[41] Karma Lochrie, Richard Rambuss, and Amy Hollywood all critique Bynum's tendency to read the feminized body of Christ in maternal terms of fertility and nourishment, and not, *therefore*, as erotic, denying any conjunction of the erotic with the maternal and downplaying or translating the homoeroticism of the texts. See Lochrie, "Mystical Acts," 187–88; Richard Rambuss, *Closet Devotions* (Durham, N.C.: Duke University Press, 1998), 48–58; Hollywood, "Sexual Desire," 121–23. The same holds true for the mystic's relationship to Christ's body: if the mystic is infantilized in relation to the maternal Christ, that relationship is frequently illegible in erotic terms. In the medieval context, however, eros was not limited to genital sexuality, but had a much wider scope, including, in the Platonic tradition, the soul's desire for the divine.

[42] *Letters*, 30.200–205 (CW, 119).

[43] *Visions*, 11.18–22 (CW, 289).

wandered with him in Egypt or on all the ways, who never presented him where
the sword of prophecy pierced their soul, who never reared that Child to manhood and who, at the end, were not at his grave: for them it shall remain eternally
hidden!"[44]

Mary provides the model of the highest Christian life, but Mary is also the
mater dolorosa who suffered with her son. Becoming God's mother with perfect motherhood condenses the process of growing up, wandering in Egypt,
raising a child, and standing at his grave. In her visions and letters, Hadewijch teaches her fellow beguines that becoming the *moeder gods* entails suffering as well as joy, *ghebreken* along with *ghebruken*. Two poems explore this
theme at length and link it to the incarnation.[45]

In stanzaic poem 29, Hadewijch praises Mary, her humility, and her
desire as the cause of the incarnation and explores her crucial role in God
becoming human. She compares Mary to a great line of prophets,[46] but
asserts that Mary was greater:

No matter what benefits God ever conferred on us
There was no one who could
Understand veritable Love
Until Mary, in her flawlessness,
With deep humility,
Had received Love.
Love first was wild and then was tame;
Mary gave us for the Lion a Lamb.
She illuminated the darkness.[47]

In a later verse, lest we misinterpret Mary's humility as passivity, Hadewijch emphasizes Mary's deep and active desire for Love:

---

[44] *Visions*, 13.15–23 (CW, 297).

[45] See also *Letters*, 12, and *Poems in Couplets*, 2 and 3.

[46] Indeed, Mary's "Magnificat" is in the genre of prophetic speech that recalls Hannah's
hymn in praise of Yahweh in 1 Sam 2:1-10.

[47] Wat so ons god ye onste
En werdt nieman, die conste
Gherechte minne verstaen.
    Eer dat maria, die goede
    Met diepen oetmoede,
Die minne hadde gheuaen.
Tierst was si wilt, doen werdt si tam;
Si gaf ons vore den leeu een lam;
Si maecte die deemsterheit claer (*Stanzaic Poems*, 29.31–39 [CW, 208–9]).

It was by deep longing
That this mystery happened to her,
That this noble Love was released
To this noble woman
Of high praise
In overflowing measure;
Because she wished nothing else and owned nothing else,
She wholly possessed him of whom each had read.
Thus she became the conduit
Open to every humble heart.[48]

Wanting and having nothing but love recalls the nakedness of desire described in letter 21. Hadewijch concludes her poem by applying the lesson to all who seek God and exhorting them, too, to give up everything else:

Forsake and give up everything.
Then your hearts will become wide and deep;
Then shall come to you that conduit which flowed
To Mary without measure.
Pray lofty Fidelity to let it flow to you.[49]

For Hadewijch, the significance of the incarnation of God, born from Mary, is inclusive. All souls, like Mary, can become the "mother of Love" and

---

[48] Dat was bi diepen niede
Dat hare dat grote ghesciede,
Dat die edel minne wt wert ghelaten
        Dien edelen wiue van hoghen prise
        Met oueruloedegher maten:
Want si el ne woude, noch haerre el ne was,
So hadse al daer elc af las
Dus heeftse dat conduut gheleit,
Dat elker oetmoedegher herten es ghereit (*Stanzaic Poems*, 29.81–90 [CW, 210–11]; translation modified).

[49] Vertijt alles ende begheuet.
So wert v herte wijt ende diep;
So sal v comen dat conduut dat liep
Marien sonder mate.
Bidt der hogher trouwen dat sijt v vloyen late (*Stanzaic Poems*, 29.116–20 [CW, 212]).

Meister Eckhart includes similar themes in his German sermons—for example, sermon 22: *Ave gratia plena*, in which he preaches that all souls must, like Mary, conceive and give birth to God in the ground of the soul, although in much more explicitly neo-Platonic terms than Hadewijch's Minne-mysticism. See Meister Eckhart, *The Essential Sermons, Commentaries, Treatises, and Defense*, trans. Edmund Colledge and Bernard McGinn (Mahwah, N.J.: Paulist Press, 1981). It is tempting to speculate but difficult to demonstrate influence of the beguine on Eckhart; see Bernard McGinn, ed., *Meister Eckhart and the Beguine Mystics: Hadewijch of Brabant, Mechthild of Magdeburg, and Marguerite Porete* (New York: Continuum, 1994).

incarnate Christ by keeping themselves naked before God, by receiving love, and by giving birth in turn through both suffering and enjoyment.[50]

Hadewijch's maternal and Marian model for the spiritual life is most fully developed in poem 14 of *Poems in Couplets*. This poem describes a traditional ladder of progressive spiritual steps, but it is innovatively written as an allegory of Love's growth through the nine months of pregnancy. As in stanzaic poem 29, the conception and birth of love begin with Mary's humility; similar humility in Hadewijch's reader will equally lead to the birth of love:

> Greatness of love will come by this means.
> If you were willing to fall thus and to bow in all things,
> You would obtain perfect Love.
> For that brought God down into Mary,
> And he would yet acknowledge the same in one
> Who could hold himself so humble in love:
> He could not refuse his sublimity to him,
> But such a one would receive him and carry him for as long
> As a child grows within its mother.[51]

The spiritual steps (or months) that follow are faithful fear (through obedience as the *ancilla domini*), joyful suffering in patience, knowledge and adherence to scripture, a state of sweetness that nourishes Love, a secret sweet burden, confidence, justice, wisdom, and power. Most of these months indicate the progressive spiritual practices undertaken by the beguines in community. They symbolize the experience of growing closer to God in both

---

[50] Compare similar lines from other stanzaic poems. From poem 31 (CW, 216): "For she . . . so enlarges my heart That I have given myself over to her completely, To obtain within me the birth of her high being"; and from poem 42 (CW, 250): "For nothing less shall content [the soul] Than the upsurge of the birth of Love, And the great and wonderful things without number That lead to the mutual merging In which Love never conceals love from the loving soul." In vision 13, the theme of soul as mother reappears when a seraph address Hadewijch herself as "mother of Love" (CW, 299).

[51] Sal groetheit der minnen comen daer in.
Wildi dus vallen ende in allen nighen.
So suldi volmaecte minne ghecrighen.
Want dat haelde gode neder in marien.
Ende mettien seluen soude hi noch lien,
Die hem so neder in minne const hebben:
Hine mocht hem sine hoecheit niet ontsegghen,
Hi soudene ontfaen ende draghen tghetal
Also een kint in zijnre moeder volwassen sal (*Poems in Couplets*, 14.38–46 [CW, 346]). Mechthild of Magdeburg and Marguerite Porete explore similar themes of utter humility (even debasement and abjection in the case of Mechthild) as the path of divinization. Hadewijch gives this theme a characteristically Marian and pronatal emphasis.

ghebruken and *ghebreken*. The last two months, however, are worth considering in detail.[52]

Hadewijch describes the final stages of Love's gestation and birth as follows:

> The ninth month is as if wisdom engulfs
> All that it loves in love.
> Then Love's moment of power comes
> And continually assaults wisdom.
> As man with all that man is
> Contents Love and is conformed to Love,
> So in the ninth month is born
> The Child that lowliness had chosen.
> Then humility has its wish
> By which it satisfies itself.
> Between these two is brought to term that Child
> Which has lain in that great place:
> In the depths of lowliness, in the heights of love,
> Where with all, in every way,
> The soul lives for God with all power,
> In new love, day and night.
> So its whole life becomes divinized.[53]

[52] And not least because of feminist theoretical discussions of the (constrained) wisdom and power of maternity in the classic examples of, among others, Adrienne Rich, *Of Woman Born: Motherhood as Experience and Institution* (New York: Norton, 1986) and Sara Ruddick, *Maternal Thinking: Toward a Politics of Peace* (Boston: Beacon, 1989).

[53] Die neghende maent es alse wijsheit slint
Al dat si in minnen mint.
Dan comt ter minnen gheweldeghe tijt
Ende stormt alle vren op wijsheit.
Als men met allen dat men es
Ghenoech es der minnen ende ghetes
So werdt ter neghender maent gheboren
Dat kint dat oetmoet hadde vercoren.
Dan heeft oetmoedicheit haer gheuoech
Daer si hare seluen es mede ghenoech
Tusschen hen tween es dat kint voldreghen
Dat in di grote stat heuet gheleghen:
Jnt diepste van oetmoede, int hoechste der minnen,
Daer men met allen in allen sinnen
Gode dus leeft met alre macht.
Jn nuwe minne, dach ende nacht.
So werdet god al datmen leuet (*Poems in Couplets*, 14.133–49 [CW, 349]).

According to Hadewijch's extended metaphor, pregnancy begins in humility but leads to a "moment of power" in the birth of love.[54] The growth of love within the soul satisfies divine Love, unleashing a power that surpasses even the engulfing maternal wisdom (*wijsheit*). The growth of this power leads to divinization. That is, becoming the mother of love makes the soul increasingly divine.

This poem is not merely a literary description of Mary's *particular* experience of the incarnation taking place in her body. Rather, Hadewijch offers an interpretation of the incarnation as the spiritual path for *all* Christians, who, like Mary, might conceive and give birth to God through love. Moreover, while obviously not a literal exhortation to biological motherhood, Hadewijch's choice of imagery valorizes the theological significance of pregnancy, birth, and mothering. These uniquely female biological experiences are potentially empowering and revelatory, full of spiritual significance and insight.

Hadewijch's maternal model of the spiritual life thus supplements and complicates her image of the soul as Lady Love's poet-knight. The question remains of the relation between these two models of spiritual life in the process of "growing up" (*volwassen*). Hadewijch takes the usual biological sequence of heterosexual reproduction—sexual desire culminates in conception and eventually birth—and queers it by unmooring gender from particular sexed bodies and by juxtaposing two realms of signification, erotic desire and motherhood. The woman poet Hadewijch represents the feminine soul variously as the (masculine) poet-knight who desires his Lady Love and the (feminine) mother who conceives and gives birth to Love out of love. Such birth results from the erotic union or fruition (*ghebruken*) of the woman mystic with divine Love, which is always gendered feminine, even when context indicates a reference to Christ or God. Hadewijch's two spiritual and erotic models of desire and birth each culminate in production, but enjoyment also includes the failure, lack, and suffering of *ghebreken*. What is "produced" or

---

[54] Hadewijch crucially reinterprets humility in ways conducive to the spiritual progress of her beguines. Instead of indicating passivity or self-abasement, according to Ulrike Wiethaus, humility indicates a transition that is ultimately empowering, especially for women: "Humility, because it is explored in a way that is saturated with feminine metaphors of strength, paradoxically affirms the female identity and self-worth of both teacher and audience, and yet functions as a way of separating the neophytes from their previous identity (humility as a necessary letting go of social identities and norms)." "Learning as Experiencing: Hadewijch's Model of Spiritual Growth," in *Faith Seeking Understanding: Learning and the Catholic Tradition*, ed. George C. Berthold (Manchester, N.H.: Saint Anselm College Press, 1991), 89–106, 101.

"reproduced" through both suffering and enjoyment is the poetic and mystical text, inspired by love and written for other women, the "sweet beloveds" (*suete minne*) to whom Hadewijch addresses her writings.

At a deeper and perhaps more transgressive level of the text, Hadewijch implicitly ascribes erotic desire to the presumably anerotic virgin mother Mary. As the idealized woman-mother, Mary is frequently the object of desire in the medieval world but any hint of her own desire is denied by emphatic affirmation of her miraculous conception and virgin birth.[55] Hadewijch juxtaposes eros with maternity without apology or embarrassment, as in stanzaic poem 29, discussed earlier, in which Mary actively desires to conceive love. Her desire is what makes her a mother, enabling her to give birth to God.

Spiritual growth, as Hadewijch presents it, is not a straightforward movement. Her writings draw upon imagery known to her contemporaries but complicate and nuance these models theologically. While she begins her own narrative as a desiring lover who enjoys fruition or union in love above all else, she accepts the frustration of desire by identifying it with the humanity and suffering of Christ. At the same time, she transforms that desire into divinization by becoming, like Mary, the mother of God incarnate. Hadewijch provocatively brings together erotic desire and motherhood in her metaphor for spiritual growth, and she does it in terms that transgress and contest normative heterosexuality and reproduction. By depicting the soul as simultaneously the desiring poet-knight—that is, the lover who pursues (and writes of) his Lady Love—and the mother who conceives and gives birth to divine Love out of her desire for love, Hadewijch implicitly encourages her fellow beguines to confront their own desire for the feminine divine and to take the place of the mother by giving birth in turn without denying the desire or the suffering it entails.

In *Visions*, Hadewijch herself is addressed as both "mother of Love" (*moeder der minnen*) who can recognize the attributes of love in Love's own face[56] and the "strongest of all warriors" (*starkeste alre wighe*) who alone understands the mystery of the incarnation.[57] These epithets indicate the two models of spiritual growth, both mother and poet-knight, that Hadewijch taught

---

[55] See Marina Warner, *Alone of All Her Sex: The Myth and the Cult of the Virgin Mary* (New York: Knopf, 1976). Warner describes, and Kristeva reiterates, how devotion to Mary is evident not only in texts but also in the cathedrals dedicated to her, statues, paintings, music, etc.

[56] *Visions*, 13.111 (CW, 299).

[57] *Visions*, 14.171 (CW, 305).

to others; each further corresponds to Hadewijch's literary writings and her voice as poet.[58] The soul as poet-knight dominates the voice of the courtly love lyric adopted for Hadewijch's stanzaic poems.[59] This genre demands a masculine first-person narrator, who sings of his lady, the object and frustration of his desire, from afar. Much more subtle is the correspondence between the maternal model of the spiritual life and Hadewijch's innovative poetic language. Hadewijch works with the semiotic, material, and rhythmic dimension of language in ways that deepen and enrich her description of the spiritual life and the incarnation. Her focus on Mary as the mother of love parallels Julia Kristeva's twentieth-century psychoanalytic and literary fascination with the mother as *fons amoris*, the source of love.

The Maternal Semiotic

Kristeva's earliest theoretical writings analyze the material dimensions of language and the role of the maternal body in the process of becoming a speaking subject. In *Revolution in Poetic Language*,[60] Kristeva considers the formation of the speaking subject and the subject's production of signification through speech. In this book, she is primarily interested in the conditions of linguistic representation—that is, what allows the subject to speak and produce meaning. Kristeva criticizes the field of linguistics for considering language only as a formal object, abstracted from any particular, embodied subject of enunciation; as a discipline, it has forgotten the body. But psychoanalysis demonstrates how unconscious drives and primary processes (condensation and displacement) signify in speech, particularly in the context of the analytic session. Thus, she argues, the relation between the signifier and signified

---

[58] Or what Rudy calls her "narrative persona." *Mystical Language of Sensation*, 69–76.

[59] Although it appears elsewhere, e.g., *Visions*, 14. See also *Letters*, 12: "Think at all hours of God's goodness, and regret that it is so untouched by us, while he has full fruition of it; and that we are exiled far from it, while he and his friends, in mutual interpenetration, enjoy such blissful fruition, and are flowing into his goodness and flowing out again in all good. Oh, he is God, whom none of us can know by any sort of effort unless veritable Love comes to our aid! Love brings him down to us and makes us feel so tenderly who he is; in this way we can know from him who he is. This is an unspeakably delightful bliss but, God knows, in the bliss there always remains woe. For the heart of the courtly lover, however, that is the law of chivalry: The only rest of such a heart is to do its utmost for the sake of its Beloved and to render him love and honor in view of his sublimity; and to offer him noble service as a gift—not for pay in the hand, but because Love herself at all times is satisfaction and pay enough." CW, 7.

[60] Julia Kristeva, *La Révolution du langage poetique* (Paris: Éditions du Seuil, 1974). Subsequent citations refer to Julia Kristeva, *Revolution in Poetic Language*, trans. Margaret Waller (New York: Columbia University Press, 1984).

is not always arbitrary (the formalism of Saussurean linguistics), but in some cases is determined by the unconscious drive, which is indirectly articulated in the spoken context of analysis.[61] Psychoanalysis (along with trends in phenomenology such as recognition of intersubjectivity) allows Kristeva to consider how the body signifies in certain contexts of speech.

Kristeva distinguishes two modalities of the same signifying process, the semiotic and the symbolic.[62] The "symbolic" indicates the formal system of language that preexists the individual, who becomes a subject as such only by entering into it. The symbolic orders and conveys meaning. It is governed, according to psychoanalysis, by the law of the father. In distinction from the "symbolic," Kristeva introduces the term "semiotic" by linking its Greek etymology (as distinctive mark, trace, precursory sign, or imprint) with a Freudian understanding of the structure of drives in the infant:

> Discrete quantities of energy move through the body of the subject who is not yet constituted as such and, in the course of his development, they are arranged according to the various constraints imposed on this body—always already involved in a semiotic process—by family and social structures. In this way the drives, which are "energy" charges as well as "psychical" marks, articulate what we call a chora: a non-expressive totality formed by the drives and their stases in a motility that is as full of movement as it is regulated.[63]

According to Kristeva, there is no body prior to signification. Long before the child learns to speak, the infant is born into a semiotic process. Caregivers ascribe significance to the infant's energetic bodily movements, assigning meaning to the body's drives. These drives or movements of energy are organized by social reinforcement along particular erogenous zones of the body and directed to family members. What they "articulate," according to Kristeva, is the "chora."

In Plato's *Timaeus*, the chora refers to the receptacle, matrix, nurse, or place from which the elements of matter arise and in which the eternal forms beget their simulacra. The chora is essentially formless, so that it may receive all forms; it is volatile, in constant motility and flux. This movement allows discrete elements to appear.[64] Plato explicitly likens the origin/form, the place of generation (chora), and the thing generated to a father, mother, and child.

---

[61] Kristeva, *Revolution*, 21–22; Ferdinand de Saussure, *Course in General Linguistics*, trans. Wade Baskin (1959; New York: Columbia University Press, 2011).

[62] Kristeva, *Revolution*, 23–24.

[63] Kristeva, *Revolution*, 25.

[64] Plato, *Timaeus* 49b–50b (*The Collected Dialogues of Plato*, ed. Edith Hamilton and Huntington Cairns [Princeton, N.J.: Princeton University Press, 1961]).

Kristeva follows him in this analogy by applying the "chora" to the undifferentiated body of the mother and infant in the pre-Oedipal relationship. One can describe the chora, Kristeva contends, only from the perspective of the symbolic (post-Oedipal) order of language. But the symbolic presupposes the chora, which, "as rupture and articulations (rhythm), precedes evidence, verisimilitude, spatiality and temporality. Our discourse—all discourse— moves with and against the chora in the sense that it simultaneously depends upon and refuses it."[65]

The chora is the site where semiotic movement takes place. This maternal and somatic place is indistinguishable from the infant's libidinal drives, which are later ordered and organized into meaning along zones and axes of relationship by the paternal symbolic. The drives and processes of the semiotic chora precede the acquisition of language. However, they can be identified "diachronically within the process of the constitution of the subject precisely because *they function synchronically within the signifying process of the subject himself.*"[66] That is, evidence of the semiotic dimension of language and its emergence from the chora is all around us, but we are already located in the symbolic order of language, and therefore usually blind to its presence. Speech in the context of psychoanalysis, however, unveils the effects of unconscious drives, and the semiotic is especially found in the rhythms of the stylized genres of art, music, and poetry.[67] These cases identify the synchronic function and presence of the semiotic; through them the theorist can look back to the function of the semiotic diachronically, in the constitution of the subject and the origin of meaning.[68]

Between the semiotic chora and the realm of the symbolic lies the rupture of what Kristeva calls the "thetic," a break in the signifying process that makes a distinction between subject and object, enunciation and denotation, as well as the difference between signifier and signified. According to Kristeva, the thetic is figured psychoanalytically by the mirror stage and by entry into the symbolic through castration. It also marks a threshold between the semiotic and the symbolic.[69] This threshold, however, is not

---

[65] Kristeva, *Revolution*, 26. See also Judith Butler's critique of Kristeva in *Gender Trouble: Feminism and the Subversion of Identity* (New York: Routledge, 1990), esp. 79–91.

[66] Kristeva, *Revolution*, 29. Emphasis in original.

[67] Wonhee Anne Joh finds a semiotic rupture in the power of the cross, which includes both the horror of abjection and the power of *jeong. Heart of the Cross: A Postcolonial Christology* (Louisville, Ky.: Westminster John Knox, 2006), 113.

[68] Kristeva herself goes on to explore the disruptive emergence of the semiotic in the avant-garde poetry of Mallarmé and Lautréamont in the second part of *Revolution in Poetic Language.*

[69] Kristeva, *Revolution*, 48.

impermeable; the semiotic constantly threatens to cross over that boundary and engulf the speaking subject, who experiences the semiotic as a danger to the stability of his identity. It also threatens the linguistic and symbolic order that gives him a stable sense of meaning.[70] Poetic mimesis in particular puts the subject in process/on trial (*le sujet-en-procès*) and disrupts meaning by knowingly and willfully transgressing the thetic boundary between the symbolic and the semiotic, between the subject and the other.[71]

All discourse, according to Kristeva, ultimately depends on the maternal semiotic chora, but certain authoritative discourses aspire to being what she calls "theological." In these forms of speech or writing, the author claims access to truth that is objectively perceived and expressed through transparent and self-evident language. In Kristeva's terms, these forms of discourse take the thetic break as their origin. They ignore and disavow the semiotic material processes that make their discourse, and all discourse, possible. But poetic mimesis, the artist's imitation of reality through fiction, intentionally plays with the thetic boundary between subject and object, enunciation and denotation, semiotic and symbolic. Mimesis thereby undermines the "theological" pretensions of the speaking subject to be his own origin, to perceive truth, and to know objectively.[72]

The subversive effects of poetic mimesis lead Kristeva to link it with the possibility of revolution. By mobilizing the semiotic—what Kristeva calls the "enemy within"—poetic language and mimesis "may also set in motion what dogma represses. . . . And thus, its complexity unfolded by its practices, the signifying process joins social revolution."[73] Poetic language has the power of revolution because, unlike authoritative forms of discourse, it self-consciously plays with the thetic boundary through mimesis. The thetic break is necessary, and mimesis can operate only from the side of the symbolic order of

[70] For example, Marie Cardinal (*The Words to Say It: An Autobiographical Novel*, trans. Pat Goodheart [Cambridge, Mass.: Van Vactor & Goodheart, 1983]) describes listening to jazz music, which precipitates a near-psychotic break prior to the commencement of her psychoanalysis. The unpredictability of improvised jazz, which carries meaning apart from the imposed order of the symbolic (in the form of lyrics or a predictable theme or refrain), is a good depiction of what Kristeva means by the semiotic.

[71] Kristeva, *Revolution*, 57–58.

[72] Kristeva, *Revolution*, 58–59: "Mimesis and the poetic language inseparable from it tend, rather, to prevent the thetic from becoming theological; in other words, they prevent the imposition of the thetic from hiding the semiotic process that produces it, and they bar it from inducing the subject, reified as a transcendental ego, to function solely within the systems of science and monotheistic religion."

[73] Kristeva, *Revolution*, 61.

language. But by repositing the thetic on its own fictional terms (imitating the production of truth through literary meaning and creating new systems of signification), poetic language undermines the pretensions of the thetic ever to be fixed once and for all as absolute, "theological" origin. The resultant influx of the semiotic is the source of creativity and transformation of the symbolic—in short, revolution.[74]

Remarkably, Hadewijch exemplifies Kristeva's insights into poetic language in her own thirteenth-century Dutch writings, and so Kristeva's theories lead us back to reread Hadewijch more attentively. Hadewijch's understanding of the maternal and material origins of the incarnation in Mary's body correlates directly with her own use of poetic language to convey her spiritual teachings. Her maternal model of the spiritual life, which is so striking when coupled with her model of the soul as poet-knight, leads to a closer examination of her language and the ways in which the semiotic functions within it. Hadewijch's poetic language, in turn, deepens an appreciation of her revolutionary interpretation of the incarnation as maternal flesh made word.

Hadewijch's Poetic Language

Like all mystics, Hadewijch is caught between the necessity and impossibility of speaking and writing. Her letters and visions frequently refer to the difficulty of conveying her spiritual insights in prose. "For earth," she writes, "cannot understand heavenly wisdom. Words enough and Dutch enough can be found for all things on earth, but I do not know any Dutch or any words that answer my purpose. Although I can express everything insofar as this is possible for a human being, no Dutch can be found for all I have said to you, since none exists to express these things, so far as I know."[75] Despite

---

[74] Kristeva, *Revolution*, 62: "Though absolutely necessary, the thetic is not exclusive: the semiotic, which also precedes it, constantly tears it open, and this transgression brings about all the various transformations of the signifying practice that are called 'creation.' . . . what remodels the symbolic order is always the influx of the semiotic. This is particularly evident in poetic language since, for there to be a transgression of the symbolic, there must be an irruption of the drives in the universal signifying order."

[75] "Want hemelsche redene en mach ertrike niet verstaen; want van allen dien dat in ertrike es, mach men redene ende dietsch ghenoech venden; Mer hier toe en weet ic gheen dietsch noch ghene redene. Nochtan dat ic alle redene can van sinne alsoe mensche connen mach, al dat ic v gheseghet hebbe, dat en es alse gheen dietsch daer toe: want daer en hoert gheen toe dat ic weet." *Letters*, 17.114–22 (CW, 84). Cf. her description of union: "What a marvel takes place then—when such great dissimilarity attains evenness and becomes wholly one without elevation! Oh, I dare write no more here about this; I must always keep

the challenge of teaching "heavenly wisdom," Hadewijch matter-of-factly acknowledges her facility with her native Dutch. Indeed, she is recognized as one of the most gifted poets of the Middle Dutch language.[76] Her innovations in poetic form, translating the French courtly love lyric into a new mystical genre, can be traced to the sheer pleasure she takes in speaking and writing of Love. She writes to one of her fellow beguines: "You must gladly speak of God. This is a criterion of Love, that the name of the Beloved is found sweet. (*Dat es een teken van Minnen, dat lieues name suete es.*) Saint Bernard speaks of this: 'Jesus is honey in the mouth.' To speak of the Beloved is exceedingly sweet (*Het es ouer soete omme lief te sprekene*); it awakens Love immeasurably, and it lends ardor to works."[77]

The sweetness of speech is matched by the apparent delight Hadewijch takes in wordplay. We have already seen how *ghebruken* and *ghebreken* echo each other verbally to convey the relationship between spiritual suffering and delight. The use of *minne* (love) in all its rich variety is another case in point. In poem in couplets 15, to take the example with which this chapter began, *minne* is repeated to the point that it threatens to overwhelm the semantic content of the poem, just as the poet's senses are overwhelmed by her primeval rage for love. In Kristeva's terms, the semiotic dimension of language in this poem overpowers the symbolic's attempts to control and contain meaning. In both examples, *minne* and *ghebruken/ghebreken*, Hadewijch demonstrates the pleasure she takes in the material sounds of words and deploys these sounds to convey additional layers of meaning.[78]

---

silence about the best (*Ay ic en dar hier af nummer scriuen; ic moet emmer vanden besten meest swighen*), because of my sad lot, and besides no one can truly reproach himself because he knows nothing about God. People think the mystery is easy enough; and if they hear anything they do not understand, they doubt immediately." *Letters,* 22.72–80 (CW, 96).

[76] In addition to her innovations in translating the courtly love lyric into Dutch, "Hadewijch's visions display an unusually high level of linguistic creativity, abounding with metaphors, new compounds, familiar words used in unusual contexts, and new abstractions," according to Colette M. van Kerckvoorde, *An Introduction to Middle Dutch* (New York: de Gruyter, 1993), 189. For a critical discussion of Hadewijch's place in the history of Western literature, see Reynaert, "Hadewijch: Mystic Poetry," 208–25.

[77] *Letters,* 15.109–14 (CW, 79).

[78] Guest's study of the stanzaic poems (*Some Aspects of Hadewijch's Poetic Form*) focuses in great detail on Hadewijch's technical skill as poet of the *trouvère* form through the elements of stanza, rhyme, alliteration and assonance, repetition, paradox and contrast, and imagery. A second Hadewijch scholar writing in English, Saskia M. Murk-Jansen (*The Measure of Mystic Thought: A Study of Hadewijch's Mengeldichten,* Gèoppinger Arbeiten Zur Germanistik 536 [Gèoppingen: Kèummerle, 1991] has examined precisely the material, semiotic dimensions of Hadewijch's language in all of her genres in order to argue that the remaining

Hadewijch's facility with the semiotic dimension of language can be most strikingly seen in stanzaic poem 31. She opens with the theme that recurs throughout her work: the birth of love within the soul.

> For she, with her infinite strength,
> Makes my nature so wide
> That I have given all my being,
> To the high birth of her lineage.[79]

Hadewijch continues with her frequent pairing of the concepts of *ghebruken* and *ghebreken* and the suffering undergone by the poet in Love's service: "consolation and ill treatment both at once, This is the essence of the taste of Love (*Troest ende meslone in enen persone, Dats wesen vander minnen smake*)." But this paradoxical relationship to love invites a new response on the part of the poet:

> I pray and invite Love
> That she may incite noble hearts
> To sing in tune the true melody of Love
> In humble anxiety and high hope.[80]

The poet who sings invites Love to enjoin others in the song, which is the true melody of love. This song expresses the paradoxes of Love beyond the grasp of reason ("Wise Solomon, were he still living, Could not interpret such an enigma. We are not fully enlightened on the subject in any sermon"),[81] and thus Hadewijch exclaims: "The song surpasses every melody (*Die sanc verhoghet alle toen*)!" including the poet's own human melody. But

---

thirteen *Mengeldichten* should be attributed to her, instead of the disciple sometimes known as Hadewijch II. Rather than focusing on the content or topics of the poems that are in dispute, Murk-Jansen employs a statistical analysis of the repetition of words, assonance, alliteration, collocation, paradox, wordplay, juxtaposition of words, poetic figures, and the use of form (rhyme pattern) to make her case. All of these indicate a strong similarity in the poetic language deployed by the two poets.

[79] Want si mi met harer groter crachte
   Mine nature maect so wijt,
   Dat ic mijn wesen al verpachte
   Jn die hoghe gheboert van haren gheslachte (*Stanzaic Poems*, 31.3–6 [CW, 21]; translation modified).

[80] Der minnen biddic ende mane,
   Dat si die edele herten spane
   Dat si in minnen toene dus bleuen
   Jn nederen twiuele, in hoghen wane (*Stanzaic Poems*, 31.21–24 [CW, 216]).

[81] *Stanzaic Poems*, 31.27–29 (CW, 217).

in the following stanza, she reverses the terms to indicate her union with Love "above comprehension (*een wesen bouen all sinne*)." Now, she writes, "the melody surpasses every song (*Die toen verhoghet alle sanghe*)!" Hadewijch explains, "When I speak of the melody that surpasses every song, What I mean is Love in her might (*Die toen die alle sanghe verhoghet, Die meinic: minne in hare ghewout*)." Love is the melody that both carries and transcends every song, including the song of Love that the poet sings.

In Kristevan terms, the melody that surpasses every song indicates the semiotic dimensions of language: its materiality, music, and rhythm. Hadewijch uses the figure of the interplay between melody and song to indicate the incomprehensibility and transcendence of Love above reason; indeed, she directly identifies the melody with "Love in her might." But human beings are encouraged to sing the "melody of Love" and thereby dip into the semiotic by participating in love's song.[82] Here we can see the way in which Hadewijch's melody, her poetic song that so delights in the play of the semiotic, expresses something of Love's own power in and through the symbolic dimensions of language. Kristeva might identify this expression of what Hadewijch calls "Love in her might (*minne in hare ghewout*)" with the maternal body as chora. For Kristeva, the mother is the source of love for every subject,[83] and traces and echoes of the mother's body can be found in the semiotic dimensions of language. But for Hadewijch, the semiotic dimensions of her poetry have additional theological significance: the melody that surpasses every song is nothing other than Love in her might—that is, Christ, in material, melodic, incarnate form. Love is incarnate in the melody: both immanent and transcendent, both intimately embodied and beyond comprehension.

Excursus
Powers of Horror and the Terror of *Minne*

Kristeva examines another dimension of the maternal in *Powers of Horror*, a book subtitled "an essay on abjection."[84] This side of the maternal is related to the semiotic chora and merits a brief diversion for its resonance with aspects of Hadewijch's presentation of Love. "Abjection" attempts to name

---

[82] In Kristevan terms, we have no choice: try as they might, subjects can never fully keep the semiotic, or for that matter, the abject, at bay. Hadewijch delights in eruptions of the semiotic.

[83] See especially the first chapter of Kristeva's *Tales of Love*, trans. Leon S. Roudiez (New York: Columbia University Press, 1987).

[84] Julia Kristeva, *Powers of Horror: An Essay on Abjection*, trans. Leon S. Roudiez (New York: Columbia University Press, 1982).

an encounter with the unnamable, in which meaning collapses and annihilation threatens the subject. Such an encounter is not unlike the unspeakability registered by mystical writing. The abject, however, is not found at the upper limits of language, at the end of the ascent of the soul toward union with God. On the contrary, the abject, like the semiotic, provides the unspeakable condition for language, prior to the symbolic order, prior even to the subject who speaks.

The abject, according to Kristeva, is excluded by the nascent "I" who attempts to separate himself from his mother even before the intervention of the Oedipal father. As such, the abject can be traced back to the maternal body and the incest taboo. The fascination and repulsion the abject exerts over the infant (and later, the speaking subject) are codified by the law of the father into distinctions between clean and unclean, pure and impure, sacred and taboo. The difference on which these distinctions rest is the separation between the infant and the mother. Not yet a speaking subject, the child is already separate from the maternal body. But reabsorption into that body always threatens; the infant, faced with annihilation, rejects what is offered; it abjects. In so doing, according to Kristeva, the infant both asserts and abjects itself:

> Not me. Not that. But not nothing, either. A 'something' that I do not recognize as a thing. A weight of meaninglessness, about which there is nothing insignificant, and which crushes me. On the edge of non-existence and hallucination, of a reality that, if I acknowledge it, annihilates me. There, abject and abjection are my safeguards. The primers of my culture.[85]

Abjection is a condition for the possibility of language, of culture, of meaning. As condition, the abject itself remains on the edges of language. Kristeva, consequently, cannot tell us directly what the abject "is"; it can be approached only indirectly: phenomenologically, psychoanalytically, and through its traces in literature and in religious systems of meaning and difference. In her writing, Kristeva attempts to give glimpses of the abject—horror and repulsion—through fractured syntax and disrupted signifiers.

Kristeva notes how utter exclusion of the abject from symbolic, legal, or religious systems fails, although such systems attempt to regulate it by creating a separate domain of the unclean, impure, and abominable. She points to the hidden role of the abject that persists within the sacred. Where the sacred is established by Freud's murderous horde, the abject is regulated by

---

[85] Kristeva, *Powers of Horror*, 2.

the incest taboo.[86] "Could the sacred be, whatever its variants, a two-sided formation?" Kristeva asks, suggesting two aspects:

> One aspect founded by murder and the social bond made up of murder's guilt-ridden atonement, with all the projective mechanisms and obsessive rituals that accompany it; and another aspect, like a lining, more secret still and invisible, non-representable, oriented toward those uncertain spaces of unstable identity, toward the fragility—both threatening and fusional—of the archaic dyad, toward the non-separation of subject/object, on which language has no hold but one woven of fright and repulsion?[87]

Kristeva's language breaks down in an effort to describe the lining of the sacred. The lining is secret, invisible, nonrepresentable, and oriented in a particular direction: toward unstable identity and fragility. The lining discloses the archaic dyad, mother/child, subject/object, at a moment or place in which they are not fully separate. Hence the lining both threatens the unstable, not-yet identity of the subject, and fuses it back into its origins. Prior to subject/object, language cannot speak this lining; its hold, if it has one, consists in fright and repulsion. Language cannot speak the lining of the sacred; it does, however, disclose it, in fear and disgust, as abject.

The limit-terms of ineffability Kristeva uses for the abject are similar to those the mystical tradition, including Hadewijch, invokes for union with God. Language has no hold. The divine escapes representation. Identity is unstable. The soul is threatened with annihilation. Subject and object merge in confusion. Mystical theology finds familiar territory in Kristeva's evocation of the abject, where language falls apart in its attempt to unveil the secret lining of the sacred. Both God and the abject are accessible only through the symbolic order, in slippages of language, and disruptions of writing.

The abject, however, indicates the threat of an *archaic* relationship with the pre-Oedipal maternal-feminine. The God of the mystical tradition asserts itself as masculine, unitary, phallic. As the Name of the Father, even in mystical union it secures the symbolic order. Language may fail in both directions, when "coming face to face with an unnamable otherness," whether abject or transcendent, but that which escapes description is not the same. The abject maternal-feminine provides the hidden conditions for the symbolic order, the lining of the sacred; it itself is not sacred, but abominable. Separation

---

[86] Kristeva's reference is to Sigmund Freud, *Totem and Taboo; Some Points of Agreement between the Mental Lives of Savages and Neurotics*, trans. James Strachey (New York: Norton, 1950).
[87] Kristeva, *Powers*, 57–58.

from the maternal-feminine, the "'other' without a name,"[88] allows the subject to ascend toward knowledge of an Other beyond names. Although the language of mystical theology shares remarkable similarities with Kristeva's language for the unnamable (m)other,[89] the abject marks one limit of language, the divine, the other. In mystical theology, the soul attempts to leave the abject maternal behind and steadily progress toward identity with the Father God. The abject maternal-feminine, however, is never repressed once and for all; it persists, and it threatens, as the hidden lining of the sacred. And it frequently returns with a vengeance in the writings of some (primarily female) mystics, who embrace the abject as a privileged path to union with God through participation in the abjection of his Son.[90]

In Christianity, abjection appears as sin, which is absorbed into speech through confession.[91] Kristeva calls the interiorization of the abject (as sin) a reconciliation with the maternal. The abject is no longer thrust away in disgust, but it is incorporated as part of subjectivity. The continual necessity of confession simultaneously confirms the subject in his abjection and relieves him of that abjection through the remission of sins. Kristeva claims that Christianity accepts sin as part of the human condition. Rather than being rejected as unclean or abominable, the maternal abject is incorporated into subjectivity, and thereby "reconciled" to the speaking subject through sublation. Abjection is no longer the hidden condition for subjection to the symbolic; in confession, it becomes the privileged *content* of symbolic speech. By confessing sin, speaking subjects acknowledge their own abjection.[92] By partaking of the Eucharist, speaking subjects are reconciled with the devouring and nourishing pre-Oedipal maternal.[93]

[88] Kristeva, *Powers*, 58.

[89] Wendy Wiseman, "In the Beginning: Kristeva, Cixous, and the Abject Mother of Metaphysics" (paper presented at the annual meeting of the American Academy of Religion, Philadelphia, Pa., November 21, 2005).

[90] E.g., Angela of Foligno's ingestion of the leper's scale, discussed in chapter 3.

[91] Kristeva, *Powers*, 113.

[92] This reconciliation through confession is not necessarily good news for women. In Christianity, the "maternal principle, reconciled with the subject, is not for that matter revalorized, rehabilitated. Of its nourishing as much as threatening heterogeneity, later texts, and even more so theological posterity, will keep only the idea of sinning flesh." Kristeva, *Powers*, 117.

[93] In Kristeva's words, "By surreptitiously mingling the theme of 'devouring' with that of 'satiating,' that narrative [of the Eucharist] is a way of taming cannibalism. It invites a removal of guilt from the archaic relation to the first pre-object (ab-ject) of need: the mother." *Powers*, 118. For a Kristevan analysis of why the Eucharist, despite its pre-Oedipal

Hadewijch embraces abjection through the twinned themes of failure (*ghebreken*) and enjoyment (*ghebruken*), and she links these to both fear and fascination with the maternal.[94] Glimpses of the abjected maternal are found in Hadewijch's frequent description of *Minne* as a terrifying, capricious mistress, who has the power to destroy her lover. This version of love merits the name "Hell" in poem 16 of the *Mengeldicten*:

> As Hell turns everything to ruin,
> In Love nothing else is acquired
> But disquiet and torture without pity;
> Forever to be in unrest,
> Forever assault and new persecution;
> To be wholly devoured and engulfed
> In her unfathomable essence.[95]

In passages such as this, an eroticized violence operates to reduce the speaking subject to abjection through painful, suffering love. Failure (*ghebreken*), pain, and suffering are an intrinsic part of enjoyment (*ghebruken*) for Hadewijch. Although this linkage can (and should) be subjected to feminist critique, Hadewijch is after something other than domestic violence in a context of romantic relationships,[96] for she interprets pain, suffering, and failure theologically by identifying *ghebreken* with the suffering of Christ's humanity,[97] and she seemingly endorses abjection as a form of imitation of

---

connotations and reconciling functions, remains the domain of male priests, see Kelley A. Raab, *When Women Become Priests: The Catholic Women's Ordination Debate* (New York: Columbia University Press, 2000).

[94] Embracing abjection can also be seen in her profoundly eucharistic spirituality, with themes of eating and being eaten by Christ. For instance: "As he who is Love itself showed us When he gave us himself to eat. . . . By this he made known to us That love's most intimate union Is through eating, tasting, and seeing interiorly." *Poems in Couplets*, 16.33–38. Hadewijch's eucharistic spirituality is discussed by Caroline Walker Bynum in *Holy Feast and Holy Fast*, 153–65. See also Donald Duclow, "The Hungers of Hadewijch and Eckhart," *Journal of Religion* 80 (2000): 421–41, who discusses Hadewijch's theme of unending hunger in relation to Gregory of Nyssa's *epektasis*.

[95] *Poems in Couplets*, 16.155–61 (CW, 356).

[96] But if we misread her description as a model for romantic relationships it would seemingly support real acts of violence and/or female masochism. See Miller, "Eroticized Violence in Medieval Women's Mystical Literature."

[97] Mary Suydam mentions Karma Lochrie's reading of the transgressions of women mystics in Kristevan terms but does not elaborate or give examples of Hadewijch's embrace of abjection. However, with respect to the mystic's own body, Suydam writes, "In order to experience God 'in his humanity' the body serves as the connection to divinity, and divinity itself is somehow human (through the enfleshed god, Christ). By making the body, particularly the open, female body, the site of rupture in which mystical union is performed,

Christ, who experienced utter abjection and failure in crucifixion.[98] Abjection in identification with Christ's suffering humanity, accepting and even embracing "assault" and being "devoured" by love, is a direct path to the abjected maternal body. This maternal body haunts Hadewijch's writings in the form of both semiotic rhythm and terrifying, capricious, even violent love. The coincidence of suffering with birth, failure with fruition, can be seen in Hadewijch's inclusive interpretation of the incarnation.

Hadewijch's Incarnation

Hadewijch's remarkable ability to mobilize the semiotic aspect of language in her writing has the effect of setting "in motion what dogma represses,"[99] as Kristeva claims for the source of poetic revolution. And what dogma has too frequently repressed is the role of the maternal body in the incarnation of Christ. As Delores Williams and other feminist and womanist theologians have argued, incarnation takes place in the body of a woman.[100] In order to concede that Mary contributed the matter and the place for the Word of God to become human, dogma has purified her flesh of the taint of lust and original sin through the virgin birth and her own immaculate conception.[101]

Hadewijch (and other medieval female writers) created a new discourse of mysticism." "The Touch of Satisfaction," 15. Suydam refers to Karma Lochrie, "The Language of Transgression: Body, Flesh and Word in Mystical Discourse," in *Speaking Two Languages: Traditional Disciplines and Contemporary Theory in Medieval Studies*, ed. Allen J. Frantzen (Albany: SUNY Press, 1991), 124–29.

[98] See Hollywood, *Sensible Ecstasy*, and Kent L. Brintnall, *Ecce Homo: The Male-Body-in-Pain as Redemptive Figure* (Chicago: University of Chicago Press, 2012).

[99] Kristeva, *Revolution*, 61.

[100] Delores Williams, *Sisters in the Wilderness: The Challenge of Womanist God-Talk* (Maryknoll, N.Y.: Orbis, 1993), 168.

[101] Traditional theology also interprets Mary's role as both an appropriate guarantee of her Son's humanity and a model for women so that they are not "despised." For an account of the fifth-century christological debates that began from the dispute over the title "theotokos," see the primary sources collected in Richard A. Norris, Jr., trans. and ed., *The Christological Controversy* (Philadelphia: Fortress, 1980). See also Thomas Aquinas, *Summa Theologica* 3.31.4, "Whether the Matter of Christ's Body Should Have Been Taken from a Woman." Thomas (and his authorities) offer a number of affirmative reasons: to ennoble all of human nature (not just the male part); to demonstrate the truth of the incarnation (Christ born as a human); and to demonstrate the variety of ways God can create human beings (Adam from the earth, Eve from a man without a woman, human beings from a man and a woman, and finally Christ from a woman without a man). His reply to objection 1 cites Augustine: "The male sex is more noble than the female, and for this reason He took human nature in the male sex. But lest the female sex should be despised, it was fitting that He should take flesh of a woman. Hence Augustine says (*De Agone Christ.* xi): 'Men, despise

The association of woman with matter, flesh, and place, so clearly visible in Mary's traditional role, is conventional in the Western philosophical and theological tradition and hardly liberating for women (nor has Mariology prevented women from being "despised," as Augustine claimed—on the contrary). However crucial Mary's official role in salvation-history, she has been denied her own incarnation, her own flesh becoming word in the encounter between humanity and God.

Hadewijch taps into an undercurrent of official theology by focusing on the maternal origins of the incarnation in Mary's flesh.[102] This insight—setting in motion what dogma represses—takes place in her work not because she is a woman or a mother, but because of her poetic facility with language. Like all writing, Hadewijch's texts depend on linguistic materiality, but she draws explicit attention to this materiality by emphasizing the semiotic dimension of language in her writing. The deliberateness of semiotic intensity seen in Hadewijch's ability to convey the body of Christ as Love in the material form, melody and song, of her poetic language reflects her theological attention to Mary's role in the incarnation (as seen especially in stanzaic poem 29, discussed earlier).[103] Contributing the matter or flesh to the incarnation of God, Mary appears as an image of the poet, who weaves symbolic word out of semiotic material sounds. With reference to the incarnation, the materiality of language itself becomes redemptive, as the poet gives birth to the texts that exhort her community to love, not least through their communal reception and performance.

---

not yourselves: the Son of God became a man: despise not yourselves, women; the Son of God was born of a woman.'"

[102] Hadewijch's writings also include a eucharistic focus on eating and being eaten as the way to know Christ's body. See, for example: "By this he made known to us That love's most intimate union Is through eating, tasting, and seeing interiorly. He eats us; we think we eat him, And we do eat him, of this we can be certain. . . . But let him who is held captive by these chains Not cease to eat his fill, If he wishes to know and taste beyond his dreams The Godhead and the Manhood!" *Poems in Couplets*, 16 (CW, 353). Passages like this link the Eucharist to the pre-Oedipal relation to the mother's body as primarily oral in nature. Behind the consumption of Christ's body in the Eucharist lie his origins in Mary's body: the body of the Mother.

[103] Elizabeth Petroff identifies stanzaic poem 29 as the central poem of the series and thus the incarnational focal point of Hadewijch's spirituality: "Poem 29 reveals the secret the soul needs to grow—the incarnation, with the transcendent paradox of the God Man. It would seem that Hadewijch deliberately structured her collection of poems to lead irrevocably to this point." *Body and Soul: Essays on Medieval Women and Mysticism* (New York: Oxford University Press, 1994), 196.

The incarnation depends on a divine Word that preexists Mary's flesh and Jesus' humanity. Hadewijch recognizes the role of the symbolic order as Word and the way in which it orders the maternal semiotic with her discussion of names:

> The Father poured out his name and gave us the Son . . . The Son poured out his name when he was born Jesus, when with this name he wished to make all our virginity fruitful (*woude vet maken al onse magherheit*) and to save all who wished to be saved. The Son poured out his name when he was baptized Jesus Christ. Thereby he imparted Christian fruitfulness (*kerstenne vetheit*) to us who are called after his name, and who are fed with his name and with his Body (*met sinen name ende met sinen lichame*), yes, and who partake of him and consume him as eagerly, and fruitfully, and deliciously (*alsoe beghereleke ende also vetteleke ende also smakeleke*) as we ourselves wish.[104]

The name, indicative of the symbolic order, makes us fruitful as we give birth to Love like Mary. Just as we consume the body of Christ, we equally are fed by his name. Becoming fruitful in response to the incarnation is equated with consuming Christ's name, and therefore with entering into the symbolic order (the name that is poured out) through an oral and maternal (pre-Oedipal) metaphor of eating. Christian fruitfulness, giving birth to Love, is akin to the poet's practice of transforming flesh into word and interweaving the semiotic with the symbolic, the body with the name.

In Hadewijch's reflections, the primary effect of the incarnation is divinization, described through the metaphors of "growing up" and "giving birth to love." This process, like birth, is not without suffering or, as she puts it, failure. As the union of humanity with God, the incarnation becomes a paradigm for the mystical union of human beings with Love through divinization. For instance, in letter 28, Hadewijch writes, "I saw God was God, and humanity was human; and then it did not astonish me that God was God, and that humanity was human. Then I saw God was human, and I saw humanity was divine. Then it did not astonish me that humanity was blissful with God."[105] Divinization toward union with God is the effect of the incarnation, which overcomes the gulf between God and humanity. In

---

[104] *Letters*, 22.279, 285–94 (CW, 100); translation modified. The theme of the fruitful virgin is found in other beguine writings and in Eckhart; see Amy M. Hollywood, *The Soul as Virgin Wife: Mechthild of Magdeburg, Marguerite Porete, and Meister Eckhart* (Notre Dame, Ind.: University of Notre Dame Press, 1995).

[105] "Jc sach gode god ende den mensche mensche. Ende doe en wonderde mi niet, dat god god was, ende dat de mensche mensche was. Doen saghic gode mensche, Ende ic sach den mensche godlec. Doen en wonderde mi niet dattie mensche verweent was met gode." *Letters*, 28.231–36 (CW, 113); translation modified.

Hadewijch's interpretation, this growth toward God takes place as the soul becomes the mother of Love and as the poet sings Love's true melody—both of which incarnate and give birth to Love in both joy and pain.

Hadewijch's understanding of the mystery of the incarnation is powerfully conveyed by her emphasis on *imitatio Christi*, or as she puts it, being human with his Humanity: "We all indeed wish to be God with God, but God knows there are few of us who want to live as men with his Humanity (*die mensche met siere minscheit wille leuen*), or want to carry his cross with him, or want to hang on the cross with him and pay humanity's debt to the full."[106] Divinization, even union with God, means giving birth to Love, which entails the pain of labor or suffering with the Humanity. Hadewijch's spiritual life was transformed when she came to understand *ghebreken* (failing) as an integral part of union as enjoyment (*ghebruken*). When she began to associate failing with the Humanity of Jesus Christ, the one who suffered complete failure, she transformed *ghebreken* into *gheliken*—that is, becoming *like* Jesus' Humanity in imitation of Christ.[107] Union with God then takes place on the model of the incarnation: enjoying God's divinity by becoming like the Humanity of Jesus.[108] Imitation of Christ involves suffering and failure as well as giving birth to love, in imitation of Mary, which the poet accomplishes through her written transformation of the semiotic in her poetry, as well as through other spiritual practices, such as works of justice.[109]

---

[106] *Letters*, 6.230–35 (CW, 61).

[107] Quoting vision 1, in which Christ teaches Hadewijch, "If you wish to be like me in my Humanity (*mi gheliken inder menscheit*), as you desire to possess me wholly in my Divinity (*inder gotheit als te ghebrukene van mi*), you shall desire to be poor," Mommaers writes, "It is significant that the basic contrast already familiar from Hadewijch's general phenomenology—'to have joy in' / 'to fail'—reappears here, but with two alterations. On the one hand, 'to fail' (*ghebreken*) is replaced by 'to be like' (*gheliken*), and on the other, this 'to be like' is connected with Christ's 'Humanity,' while 'to have joy in' (*ghebruken*) is linked to Christ's 'Divinity.' To fully appreciate Hadewijch's mystic view of the Humanity it is important to notice that 'to be like' replaces 'to fail.' This semantic shift illustrates how the real human Humanity of Christ is given its rightful place in the mystic's experience of being united with God." Mommaers, *Riddle*, 179.

[108] See also *Letters*, 6.117–21: "With the Humanity of God (*metter menscheit gods*) you must live here on earth, in the labors and sorrow of exile, while within your soul you love and rejoice with the omnipotent and eternal Divinity in sweet abandonment. For the truth of both is one single fruition (*een enich ghebruken*)" (CW, 59).

[109] "The greatest radiance anyone can have on earth is truth in works of justice performed in imitation of the Son (*ghewaricheit in ieghenwordeghen werken van gherechticheden*), and to practice the truth with regard to all that exists, for the glory of the noble love that God is (*edelre minnen die god es*)." *Letters*, 1.8–12 (CW, 47).

Works of justice and songs of love are ways of practicing the incarnation as it took place in the bodies of both Mary and Jesus, and as it takes place in other bodies, such as the young beguines to whom Hadewijch writes.[110]

The Mother of Love

In her essay "Stabat Mater,"[111] Kristeva explores and performs the interdependence of the two modalities of language discussed earlier, the symbolic and the semiotic. The right-hand, "symbolic" side of the text is a reflection on motherhood as it is represented in the Christian West by the Virgin Mary. The left-hand column is a poetic meditation on Kristeva's own experience of pregnancy, birth, and motherhood. This column is written as an eruption of the semiotic into the symbolic text. As a meditation on the experience of motherhood, it is written without distinction between subject and object; these two poles only gradually emerge in the semiotic text as they do between mother and child. In contrast, the symbolic right-hand column gradually dissolves into the semiotic music of "Stabat Mater."

Kristeva's essay is important for her reflections on the cultural significance of the maternal figure as she calls for a distinction between "the mother" (a fantasy and idealization of the relationship that attaches both women and men to her as first Other) and the new understandings of femininity emerging in feminism. She also calls for new images of motherhood, without which Western culture is left with the impossible model of the virgin mother. But the essay is equally significant for Kristeva's attempt to perform the disruption of the semiotic associated with the maternal body within the text itself. This disruption explains the appeal to heresy at the end of the essay: crossing back and forth between the thetic break in the text (between semiotic and symbolic, mother and child), the reader realizes the possibility for different conceptions of motherhood that do not take the cultural fantasy of the virgin mother as absolute, "theological" origin. The influx of the semiotic is thus explicitly a-theological and "herethical": it crosses the thetic break

---

[110] Hadewijch's vision of the Countenance of Love—that is, the face of Christ—earns her the title "mother of Love" (*Visions*, 13) and her understanding of the incarnation grants her the title "warrior": "The Voice said to me: 'O strongest of all warriors! You have conquered everything and opened the closed totality, which never was opened by creatures who did not know, with painfully won and distressed Love, how I am God and Man! O heroine, since you are so heroic, and since you never yield, you are called the greatest heroine! It is right, therefore, that you should know me perfectly!'" *Visions*, 14 (CW, 305).

[111] First published in 1976; reprinted in Julia Kristeva, *Histoires d'amour* (Paris: Denoël, 1983), 295–327; published in English as *Tales of Love*, trans. Leon S. Roudiez (New York: Columbia University Press, 1987).

and denies that this break has the last word (or the first Word). But Kristeva's essay equally recognizes that it is only from the side of the symbolic—that is, from contemporary cultural figures of motherhood (which are still largely those of medieval Christianity)—that one can unleash the semiotic creativity of new images. Thus the text practices the heretical ethics it invokes at its end by figuring a new relationship to the other/mother, while at the same time reinscribing the figure of the mother—this time as the semiotic chora—as *fons amoris*.

Feminists might wonder whether Kristeva is offering a new mystification of motherhood and woman as mother. Of the most well-known "French feminists," Kristeva offers the most ambiguously feminist project, given her disidentification with the uses of "woman" by the Mouvement de libération des femmes (MLF) and her relentless focus on the biological mother.[112] More directly than other theorists, Kristeva insists on the diachronic and synchronic presence of the maternal body in language and the discernable disruption of the symbolic by the material, maternal semiotic. That is, she approaches the maternal as a material reality, as the traces of the physical body of the mother that persists even though repressed by the symbolic order. At best, Kristeva's preoccupation with the theoretical significance of the mother's body is a call to distinguish women as subjects from their conflation with the mother, to give the denied and disavowed maternal access to the symbolic in new cultural significations, and to make room in the symbolic order for an influx of the semiotic in new images of motherhood, so that one, fantasied virgin mother no longer governs the Christian religious imaginary.[113] These effects would equally deny orthodox theology its attempts to capture and contain the semiotic chora for its own dogmatic purposes (in religious art, music, and liturgical language) and thereby "set in motion what dogma represses" through the revolution of *héréthique d'amour*.

In contrast, Hadewijch seems primarily interested in the maternal as a metaphor for spiritual life. Whereas Kristeva's reinscription of the mother figure risks a conservative conflation of women with mothers, Hadewijch proceeds in the opposite direction and resists any implicit essentialism. Instead of reducing women (such as her sister beguines) to the biological mother, Hadewijch uses the metaphorical concept of motherhood to interpret the

---

[112] See, for example, Kristeva's interview with "Psych et Po" reprinted in *New French Feminisms: An Anthology*, ed. Elaine Marks and Isabelle de Courtivron (New York: Schocken Books, 1980), 137–41. See also Judith Butler's critique in *Gender Trouble*, 79–91.

[113] Kristeva, "Stabat Mater," *Histoires*, 327: "Écoutons donc encore le *Stabat Mater*, et la musique, toute la musique . . . elle engloutit les déesses et en dérobe la nécessité."

incarnation and to teach spiritual practices.[114] By describing the incarnation and divinization as the birth of love in the soul, Hadewijch unmoors maternal imagery from biology. Motherhood provides a metaphor for the spiritual life available to anyone who engages in spiritual practices—such as writing poetry, or acts of justice—that give birth to love, in both joy and pain, within the soul and in the community. Hadewijch's own poetic writings reflect her approach to motherhood through language: if author, reader, love, and God can be transgendered, if genres can be transgressed and reconfigured, if anyone can be Mary, and if the beguines themselves eschewed biological motherhood in favor of spiritual pursuits, then Hadewijch's use of the maternal model is primarily poetic.

That said, the material reality at the heart of language is at the heart of the message of the incarnation, and in this sense, maternality is not merely a metaphor. If Mary's motherhood is only metaphorical, then the body, the material, the flesh of the incarnation is meaningless. For those who would share in the incarnation, their practices of divinization must equally be embodied. Hadewijch's recognition of the materiality of the incarnation and its origin in the maternal is evident not only in her use of the maternal metaphor but also in her delight in the semiotic, material, and rhythmic aspects of language. This dimension of language is associated, on Kristeva's account, with the maternal body, but in Hadewijch's skillful hands, this material reality is again extended beyond biological mothers. Her writings open up and expand, rather than restrict through any form of essentialism, how women and men might practice the incarnation in imitation of both Christ and Mary. Any Christian can become the mother of love and so incarnate Christ, just as any poet can become Mary by making flesh into word, weaving the semiotic into the symbolic. Motherhood is a metaphor for Hadewijch, but because of the fleshy materiality of the incarnation, it is not merely one.

Hadewijch writes the body of Christ in each of her different genres. Her attraction to the humanity of Christ acknowledges that suffering is an inseparable part of the enjoyment of his divinity; the failure to sustain union in love is transformed into suffering in solidarity with all those who suffer in their humanity. By drawing our attention to the maternal origins of the incarnation in the body of Mary, she extends the incarnation first to the body of Christ's mother, whose flesh and desire become the place of divinity. This theological focus makes Mary the model for the spiritual life. But Hadewijch does more

---

[114] See Marcia W. Mount Shoop, "Embodying Theology: Motherhood as Metaphor/Method," in *Women, Writing, Theology: Transforming a Tradition of Exclusion*, ed. Emily A. Holmes and Wendy Farley (Waco, Tex.: Baylor University Press, 2011), 233–52.

than that: she extends the significance of the incarnation itself from one particular male body to the spiritual life of pregnancy and birth potentially lived by anyone, but particularly addressed to her young beguines in their spiritual practices. One of the most important of these spiritual practices of the incarnation, for Hadewijch, is her own writing, which takes place in a variety of texts based on her reading of scripture, patristic and high medieval theology, and the secular poetry of the *trouvères*. Following Kristeva, one can interpret Hadewijch's poetic language as a transformation of the symbolic order through an influx of the semiotic, setting in motion what dogma represses as she presents the incarnation as the embodiment of Love. Her poetic writing is both the product and the practice of that love, love for God and love for her beguines as she sings the true melody of Love.

Hadewijch makes important theological contributions to a feminist interpretation of the incarnation through both the content and the form of her writing. In considering the incarnation by weaving her own material sounds into words, Hadewijch gives a clear direction in the figure of the poet, whose embodied, spiritual writing practices weave materiality into language. Mary figures the poet in whom word becomes incarnate, and whose flesh issues in words, but Hadewijch is not interested in constraining women's roles through reduction to biology. Instead, the poet's writing practices take place through a wide variety of genres, including letters and visions along with verse, which are mimicked in the wide diversity of flesh in which word takes root and is expressed. This way of participating in the incarnation extends it to other bodies in all their differences: the bodies of Mary, Hadewijch, and her fellow beguines, along with her readers today who share her desire to write the body of Christ.

3

Angela of Foligno Writing
the Body of Christ

In Angela of Foligno's final instruction to her disciples,[1] she describes the vision she has received of the preparation for her death. Her soul was washed in the blood of Christ and clothed in colorful royal garments. Her divine spouse favorably compared her to a bride in preparation for her wedding. And then she received a vision of "the Word":

> Then God showed me the Word, so that now I would understand what is meant by the Word and what it is to speak the Word (*quid est Verbum et quid est dicere Verbum*). And he said to me: "This is the Word who wished to incarnate himself for you" (*Hoc est Verbum quid voluit incarnari pro te*). At that very moment the Word came to me and went all through me, touched all of me, and embraced me (*Et tunc etiam transitum fecit per me, et totam me tetigit et amplexatus est me*).[2]

Angela's spirituality—so focused on the suffering God-man—reaches its consummation on her deathbed as the Word made flesh was incarnate in her own dying body. Here at last she understands directly in her own flesh what is meant by the Word and what it means for her to speak that Word. Her readers do not know exactly what she saw or what she felt on that death/

---

[1] Angela's *Memoriale* and *Instructiones* are published in the critical edition edited by Ludger Their, O.F.M., and Abele Calufetti, O.F.M., *Il Libro della Beata Angela da Foligno* (Grottaferrata [Rome]: Editiones Collegii S. Bonaventurae ad Claras Aquas, 1985), hereafter cited as *Il Libro*. English quotations are from *Angela of Foligno: Complete Works*, trans. Paul Lachance, O.F.M. (New York: Paulist Press, 1993), hereafter cited as *Complete Works*, with modifications where noted.

[2] *Il Libro*, 734 (*Complete Works*, 315). One might also translate *amplexatus est me* as "copulated with me," indicating, as the passage suggests, the most intimate union with the Word.

bridal bed. But her words describe an intimate experience of incarnation, of the external Word touching and entering her own body, "all" of her, as she says. This experience of incarnation revealed to her the significance of the "Word": when touched and embraced by the divine Word, her dying flesh issued forth in words of instruction and consolation spoken to her gathered disciples and transmitted to her readers.[3]

———

In the popular women's piety of the Middle Ages, women were identified with the suffering humanity of Christ. Historian Caroline Walker Bynum has shown how Christ's suffering humanity and sacramental presence mirrored the social and biological roles of women by suffering, bleeding, birthing, feeding, and comforting. Medieval women identified with Christ, Bynum argues, because Christ, by becoming wounded flesh that is broken and eaten, was thought to have identified in a special way with them.[4] The incarnation, the passion, and the Eucharist became the focus of women's piety, and their bodies became the locus where God was manifest through extraordinary and miraculous phenomena. The somatic miracles of holy women described in hagiographies—visions, locutions, healings, radical asceticism such as inedia, as well as food multiplication and charity or miraculous lactation— reflect the depth of assimilation between women's bodies and the body of Christ. Women saints were widely admired for their extreme feats of suffering in imitation of Christ and their food miracles, such as their own inability to eat or their miraculous feeding of others.

But medieval women *writers*, as Amy Hollywood has shown, often eschewed bodily identification with Christ and his suffering in their own treatises. Beatrice of Nazareth's thirteenth-century *Seven Manners of Loving God*, for example, describes the soul's love for God using metaphors of wounding and suffering. Her hagiographer, however, literalizes, personalizes, and somatizes these metaphors as her own bodily experience—and adds paramystical phenomena attesting to her sanctity—in his *Life of Beatrice*. He

---

[3] *Instruction* XXXVI was likely composed by a scribe after Angela's death and based on her remembered words, but Paul Lachance thinks her deathbed visions and teachings are authentic. See his introduction to the complicated history of the *Instructions'* redaction in *Complete Works*, 81–84.

[4] Caroline Walker Bynum, *Holy Feast and Holy Fast: The Religious Significance of Food to Medieval Women* (Berkeley: University of California Press, 1987); and idem, *Fragmentation and Redemption: Essays on Gender and the Human Body in Medieval Religion* (New York: Zone Books, 1991). For a more theoretical reflection on the same primary historical material, see Martha J. Reineke, "'This Is My Body': Reflections on Abjection, Anorexia, and Medieval Women Mystics," *Journal of the American Academy of Religion* 58, no. 2 (1990): 245–65.

takes what she describes as inner spiritual experience and turns it into external and visible bodily signs in a way that she herself refuses.[5] Like Beatrice, Hadewijch writes using sensual language and she freely deploys physical metaphors of hunger and satiety, of enjoyment and suffering, of growing up and giving birth. But she rarely refers to her own experience, much less her own bodily experience of suffering or miraculous phenomena. As an accomplished writer and theologian, Hadewijch is much more interested in examining the maternal origins of the incarnation, its implications for the spiritual life, and the material dimension of poetic language itself than the miraculous feats, signs, or symptoms of holy women. As a teacher, Hadewijch's primary concern is with the pedagogical application of poetic metaphors for her audience's spiritual growth. While she uses the theological paradigm of the incarnation and the materiality of language itself, Hadewijch resists the hagiographical restriction of women to identification with Christ's suffering flesh. Instead, flesh ever reaches for divine word through participation in the incarnation, through becoming the spiritual mother of love, and through the poet's words. In works written by their own hands, medieval women are remarkably uninterested in the bodily miracles and feats of suffering that preoccupied male hagiographers of women saints. Instead, these writers aim to understand, and to teach, the spiritual and theological significance of the mystical life.

What we know of the life of Angela of Foligno places her somewhere between the two descriptive categories of medieval women—call them "saints" and "writers"—as we see them today. Because Angela's *Book* is cowritten with her confessor, it includes features of both hagiography and her own theological reflections, which come to us mediated through him. Her story indicates how a woman might have fallen under suspicion on account of the extraordinary experiences that first attract the attention of her confessor, as well as how those suspicions were transformed into the recognition of spiritual authority through the act and product of writing. What makes Angela ultimately more a "writer" than a "saint" is the depth of her theological reflections that shine through her confessor's astonishment and the control she exerts over the production of her *Book*. Angela of Foligno's spiritual journey demonstrates the transformative effect of the incarnation

---

[5] Amy Hollywood, "Inside Out: Beatrice of Nazareth and Her Hagiographer," in *Gendered Voices: Medieval Saints and Their Interpreters*, ed. Catherine M. Mooney (Philadelphia: University of Pennsylvania Press, 1999), 78–98; and idem, *Sensible Ecstasy: Mysticism, Sexual Difference, and the Demands of History* (Chicago: University of Chicago Press, 2002), 241–66.

on women's bodies and women's words. In Angela's *Book*, we see the way in which such a transformation might take place: from suspect to saint, from holy woman to theologian, from writing on one's own body through signs, symptoms, and miracles to writing the body of Christ with authority.

Angela of Foligno demonstrates how female flesh becomes divine word through the paradigm of Christ's incarnation. For Angela, the incarnation is not limited to the historical body of Jesus; she encounters Christ's body in multiple forms—in the host, in the body of the leper, in the world—and she experiences the incarnation in her own body. Angela interprets the significance of the incarnation inclusively; Christ appears in multiple forms, including, she claims, in our own bodies. Because her interpretation is mediated through her book, as it is cowritten with her confessor, writing becomes the vehicle of her self-understanding. Writing, as a record of Angela's divine words and in the production of her *Book*, assists the process of becoming divine.

Compared to many medieval women writers, a number of biographical details are known about the life of Angela of Foligno (c.1248–1309). She was born outside Assisi, married at age twenty, and in 1288 her husband, mother, and sons all died suddenly. What modern readers would view as traumatic, Angela describes as an opportunity to pursue a religious vocation to which she had been increasingly drawn.[6] Living in Umbria, her spiritual life was greatly influenced by the Franciscans, and in 1291 she entered the Third Order of Penance. After an extraordinary pilgrimage to Assisi that same year in which Angela was found screaming on the floor of the church of St. Francis, she began to narrate her spiritual journey to her relative and confessor Brother Arnaldo.[7]

The Book of Blessed Angela that resulted from that narration and Arnaldo's subsequent redaction contains two parts. The *Memorial* was written by Brother Arnaldo as Angela dictated in her Umbrian dialect and he translated on the spot into Latin. After the *Memorial* was completed by Arnaldo, Angela lived for thirteen more years until her death in 1309. Her *Instructions* cover this period in her life and reflect her role as spiritual mother and

---

[6] *Il Libro*, 138 (*Complete Works*, 126). Although in this passage she claims to have "prayed to God for their death" (*rogaverum Deum quod morerentur*), later in the text she claims, in a period of suffering, that "to live was a source of greater pain than that caused by the death of her mother and sons" (*vivere erat mihi poena super dolorem mortis matris et filiorum*). *Il Libro*, 186 (*Complete Works*, 143). In the second passage, she does not mention her husband, who may have been an obstacle to her religious life.

[7] Angela's scribe is identified in the text only as a "trustworthy Friar Minor." The name "Arnaldo" came from a later Franciscan tradition but has generally been adopted by Angela scholars. See Lachance's introduction, *Complete Works*, 47–54.

teacher. They include a collection of letters, teachings, and anecdotes transmitted to her "sons and daughters," a group of Franciscan disciples that gathered around her as her fame as a holy woman grew. Many of these were written after the death of Brother Arnaldo and some after Angela's own death.[8] Due to the complex evolution of these texts, the role of Brother Arnaldo as scribe, and the subsequent redactions of the material, discerning "Angela's voice" is a difficult endeavor, especially in comparison to the writings of Hadewijch and Marguerite Porete. It is not, however, impossible. Her own interpretation of her experience is evident especially in those moments in which Brother Arnaldo himself seems puzzled by her words, and in her short and memorable episodes (such as screaming in the church of St. Francis) that seem to have taken everyone by surprise. In the first, we can identify her words because they are astonishing; in the second, we have Angela's actions, even though the words in which the event is described may not always be hers.

Angela of Foligno offers a concrete and visceral example of the Franciscan practice of *imitatio Christi*. Her spiritual itinerary, as outlined in her *Memorial*, begins with her conversion and proceeds through acts of penance and extraordinary displays of paramystical phenomena in which she "writes the body" in a way that resonates with the nineteenth-century hysteric, whose physical symptoms manifest what cannot be spoken. What cannot be spoken by Angela is the ineffability of the God-human encounter that she receives in her revelations. Through her sessions with Brother Arnaldo, her physical symptoms appear to recede gradually as she begins to interpret her experience and speak her desire. Her transmission of what she calls her "secreta divina" begins under obedience to her confessor but continues as she gains confidence in her spiritual authority.[9] In both parts of Angela's book, the incarnation is central, culminating in the experience of the Word within her own flesh that occurs on her deathbed. The incarnation, which overcomes the unknowability of God by humanity through the union of

[8] See Lachance's introduction, *Complete Works*, 81–84.

[9] While most readings of Angela's *Book* focus on the extraordinary experiences of her spiritual journey, she and Brother Arnaldo are primarily interested in the theological knowledge those experiences convey. Gillian Ahlgren argues against a disjuncture between "experience" and "theology" because "'extraordinary' experiences are meant to be revelatory and invitational, that is, they reveal to humanity something about God's nature and, concurrently, they invite all humanity into deeper relationship with God." "Teresa of Avila and Angela of Foligno: Ecstatic Sisters," *Magistra: A Journal of Women's Spirituality in History* 10, no. 1 (2004): 88–116, 94. Indeed, Angela was early accorded the title of "Magistra Theologorum"; see Paul Lachance, *The Spiritual Journey of the Blessed Angela of Foligno according to the Memorial of Frater A* (Rome: Pontificium Athenaeum Antonianum, 1984), 404.

word and flesh, thus becomes the exemplar for Angela, who finds the words to speak her experience and translate her desire.

The impact of the incarnation on Angela's theology can be seen from the perspective of the production of her text. Angela's *Book* depicts the translation of writing *on* the body through paramystical symptoms to writing the body of Christ through speech, interpretation, and writing. The concept of "writing the body" is affiliated with Hélène Cixous' theory and practice of *écriture féminine*, feminine writing or writing as feminine.[10] In a number of essays reflecting on women's writing and her own writing process, Cixous, a contemporary French Algerian writer, closely associates women's writing with the disruptive effect of women's bodies in a patriarchal social and symbolic order. "Writing the body," according to Cixous, has the effect of transforming the symbolic order, but only insofar as women claim the written word as contiguous with their bodies, histories, and desires. Before turning to these themes, and the larger question of their intersection with a theology of incarnation, we must examine Angela's relationship to the book written in her name.

Angela and the Question of Authorship

To speak of Angela as writer is difficult for a number of reasons. In her *Memorial*, she dictated her spiritual insights to her confessor-scribe, Brother Arnaldo, who hastily translated from her Umbrian dialect into Latin. The chronological order of Angela's spiritual journey does not precisely correspond to the order of events that originated her text, much less to the order in which these events were narrated. It is equally problematic to speak of Angela as "author" of *The Book of Blessed Angela*.[11] She is its subject, to be sure, and

---

[10] Elizabeth Petroff and Karma Lochrie also read Angela of Foligno in light of the writings of Hélène Cixous. Petroff (*Body and Soul: Essays on Medieval Women and Mysticism* [New York: Oxford University Press, 1994], 204–24) describes Angela's bodily imitation of Christ as a kind of "writing the body" that gives her wholeness and narrative subjectivity. Lochrie (*Margery Kempe and Translations of the Flesh* [Philadelphia: University of Pennsylvania Press, 1991], 44–47) reads Angela's words and her vision of the Word as a language of the body with subversive potential. My approach benefits enormously from their work, but differs from both in seeing the incarnation as the central point of connection between Angela's transformation through writing and Cixous' theoretical writings. That is, I read both Angela and Cixous with an eye toward the implications of their writings for a constructive contemporary feminist theology of incarnation.

[11] On the problem of authorship generally, see Roland Barthes' distinction between writer and author in "The Death of the Author," in *Image-Music-Text*, trans. Stephen Heath (New York: Hill & Wang, 1977), 142–48; and Michel Foucault, "What Is an Author?" in *The Foucault Reader*, trans. Josué V. Harari (New York: Pantheon Books, 1984), 101–20.

the objective genitive in the title registers this: the book is "about" her—that is, Angela is the topic of the book. But is she its subject in the sense indicated by the subjective genitive: is she the origin or author of her book?

One way of answering the question of authorship in Angela's favor is by emphasizing the book's orality. Because the book was dictated, Angela's readers frequently remark on the oral character of the language. The operative assumption here is that if the oral dictation was directly and faithfully recorded, the proximity of writing to speech likewise indicates a proximity of the text to Angela's words. In her essay, "Angela or Concerning Friendship," Romana Guarnieri describes the oral nature of the part of the book known as the *Memorial* in particular:

> It is neither a didactic-expository treatise, nor a literary text, in poetic or customary prose form, obedient to a formal and linguistic code. Nor is it a collection of letters, more or less paraenetic, intended more to teach, to persuade, and to guide, or, ultimately, to convert, rather than simply to narrate. Rather, what we have here, precisely recorded, though in a rather disorganized and often highly emotional way, is the simple, bare, oral narrative, exact to the point of scrupulosity (at least if the numerous affirmations in the text in this regard are given the credit they seem to deserve), of a mystical text in the pure state, very rich in the extraordinary variety of its visionary phenomena, some recalled, others recorded as they were taking place.

Guarnieri concludes that even if the book "does not come directly from Angela's hand," at least as far as the *Memorial* is concerned, it is "a true and authentic 'author's text,' no more nor less than the writings of a Hadewijch or a Porete, who did not make use of any secretaries: sole authors of their own writings, and such authors! What more can I say?"[12]

Indeed, Guarnieri's compelling description conveys something of the power of Angela's *Book*, and of the *Memorial* in particular, which is striking in its oral character and vivid narrative style. She is right to compare the power of the words recorded to those of Hadewijch and Porete, who did not use secretaries; we might also point to someone like Thomas Aquinas, who did make use of multiple secretaries, and whose authorship is never questioned. But Guarnieri's assessment of the orality of the text as an indication of authorship avoids the issue of Arnaldo's influence in his composition of the *Memorial*.[13] Surely he is more than Angela's secretary, just as writing is

---

[12] Romana Guarnieri, preface to *Complete Works*, 6–7.

[13] Most scholars have no choice but to trust Arnaldo's repeated affirmations of his scrupulosity as scribe. Lachance summarizes Arnaldo's role as follows: "When [Arnaldo] would reread his notes to Angela, she would carefully point out that there were many weaknesses in

more than the simple transcription of speech, and particularly in this case, in which Arnaldo had a stated interest as Angela's confessor in the material he recorded. Speech, like writing, has its formal constraints, especially for those like Angela, speaking in obedience to her confessor. Arnaldo's presence, perspective, and interests are never far from the surface of the narrative; indeed, they guide its structure and composition.[14] Instead of appealing to the orality of the text to affirm Angela as an author in the traditional sense, that orality can instead be read as an indication of Angela's physical presence in the scene of transcription—the way in which she "writes" through her body and her words the "visionary phenomena . . . recorded as they were taking place," as Guarnieri puts it. Angela is the writer of her text in multiple senses: through her imitation of Christ she writes his passion on her own body; through her words to Arnaldo, she transmits her spiritual insights; through her encounter with the incarnation, she secures God's own approval of the writing that results.

The place to begin to untangle these questions of writing is at the boundaries of the text, in its openings and closings. The *Memorial* itself begins with its approbation. Whoever added the approbation claims that it was "written with utmost care and devotion by a certain trustworthy Friar Minor to whom it was dictated by a certain follower of Christ," and refers to numerous authorities who read the book, "none of [whom] saw any sign of false teachings in this book—on the contrary, they treat it with a humble reverence, and cherish it most dearly, like a holy book."[15] In the prologue that follows, the Friar Minor himself, identified by tradition as Brother Arnaldo, introduces the text by quoting the "Incarnate Word of Life," who promised in the gospel of John to reveal himself to those who love him.[16] The scribe explains

his redaction but nothing 'false or superfluous.' Arnaldo felt these weaknesses keenly. Some ten times he asserts that what he had written was a short and defective version of what he had heard. He compares himself to a 'sieve or sifter which does not retain the precious and refined flour but only the most coarse.' Of the sublime words, he was able to note only the meanest part. One time when he reread his text to Angela, she, on her part, protested that 'she did not recognize it'; that what he had written was 'dry and without any savor' and did not convey the meaning she intended." *Complete Works*, 48–49. For an excellent discussion of Arnaldo's influence on the composition of Angela's book, see Catherine M. Mooney, "The Authorial Role of Brother A. in the Composition of Angela of Foligno's Revelations," in *Creative Women in Medieval and Modern Italy*, ed. E. Ann Matter and John Coakley (Philadelphia: University of Pennsylvania Press, 1994), 34–63.

[14] See Mooney, "Authorial Role of Brother A."

[15] *Il Libro*, 126–28 (*Complete Works*, 123).

[16] This is one of the few references to scripture in the entire book. *Il Libro*, 128 (*Complete Works*, 123).

that God has recently "in some way shown this experience and this teaching, through one of his faithful, to increase the devotion of his people."[17] The showings or revelations of the book are not given to Angela alone; they merely pass *through* her, for the greater purpose of increasing devotion. The purpose of the book was not to make a record of an extraordinary mystical life, but to increase devotion through Angela's example and teachings.

While the friar repeatedly affirms the essential truth of his record, he immediately makes the reader doubtful of its accuracy: "In the pages that follow, there is an incomplete, very weak and abridged (*minus plene et multum diminute et detruncate*) but nonetheless true description of [the revelation]." He identifies himself as "unworthy scribe" (*ego indignus scriptor*) and defers an explanation of how he "was compelled to write" (*coactus . . . fuerim ad scribendum*) and how the servant was "compelled to speak" (*coacta fuerit ad dicendum*) until its proper place in the narrative. Instead of explaining the origin of the book, he begins with Angela's own description of thirty steps of the soul on the way of penance, relayed initially to her companion Masazuola. The narrative thus began before the friar entered the scene, but he interpolates himself as Angela's pupil in identification with her companion.[18]

Six years passed between Angela's initial conversion and the beginning of the redaction of her *Memorial*.[19] At what point she began to organize her experience into thirty successive steps is unclear (if, indeed, this was her own typology and not Arnaldo's attempt to impose order on her narrative).[20] In retrospect, and midway through her journey (but prior to her meetings with Arnaldo), Angela began to reflect on her experience for the purpose of sharing it with others.[21] She describes her spiritual journey beginning with her conversion, in which she or, more universally, "the soul" becomes aware of her sinfulness, fears damnation, and weeps bitterly. Steps one through seven are primarily purgative: Angela is purified through suffering, stripped of her possessions, and increasingly related to Christ through his crucifixion. Steps seven through seventeen intensify her visions of the Crucified, through which she is conformed to him. These visions are focused on intimate physical

---

[17] "per aliquam suorum fidelium ad devotionem suorum praedictam experientiam et doctrinam fecit aliqualiter indicare." *Il Libro*, 128 (*Complete Works*, 123); translation modified.

[18] On Angela's companion Masazuola, see Lachance's introduction, *Complete Works*, 23.

[19] See *Complete Works*, 48.

[20] On Angela's numerologically significant division of steps, see Lachance, *Spiritual Journey*, 127.

[21] I have generally followed Lachance's condensation of Angela's typology through the categories provided in *Instruction* II; see *Complete Works*, 57ff.

relationship to Christ expressed in strikingly somatic language[22] and best
exemplified by her vision of placing her mouth on the wound in Christ's side
and drinking his blood.[23] Steps seventeen through nineteen indicate a turning point, as Angela receives further consolations that manifest themselves
both spiritually and somatically. As she is absorbed into God, she experiences
a hypersensitivity of the senses that causes her to forget to eat, to scream when
she hears the name of God, to fall ill with a fever upon seeing a depiction of
the passion, and to lose her power of speech.[24] Contemplating the divinity
and humanity of Christ only increases her desire as she prays, "I do not want
anything else but you."[25] She then receives assurance that the "whole Trinity"
will soon come into her (*tota Trinitas veniet in te*).[26]

It is at this point that Arnaldo enters Angela's life and interrupts his
narration to reassert himself in the text.[27] Arnaldo's role in Angela's journey
began in the midst of the twentieth step with their encounter in Assisi (this
crucial step is discussed ahead). He then condensed the remaining ten steps
into "seven supplementary steps," which occurred after Arnaldo and Angela
had established their relationship and thus were likely influenced by their
conversations. Arnaldo describes the principles that guided his redaction:
"I have done my best to try to assemble this remaining material into seven
steps or revelations. My guiding principle was to divide the subject matter
according to the state of divine grace I perceived Christ's faithful one to be
in, or according to what I perceived and learned of her spiritual progress; and
also according to what seemed to me most fitting and appropriate (*convenien-
tius et aptius*)."[28] The remaining seven steps are theologically the richest and

[22] Lachance provides a concise summary: "She '*looks* at the cross'; '*stands* at the foot of
it to find refuge'; '*sees*' the wounds of Christ 'while asleep and awake'; '*enters* into the sorrow
over Christ's passion suffered by the mother of Christ and St. John.'" *Complete Works*, 57–58.

[23] In the fourteenth step, Angela recounts the following: "Et tunc vocavit me et dixit
mihi quod ego ponerem os meum in plagam lateris sui, et videbatur mihi quod ego viderem
et biberum sanguinem eius fluentem recenter ex latere suo, et dabatur mihi intelligere quod
in isto mundaret me." *Il Libro*, 142–44 (*Complete Works*, 128).

[24] *Il Libro*, 152 (*Complete Works*, 131).

[25] God asked her, "Quid vis? Et ipsa respondit: Nolo aurum nec argentum, et si dares
mihi totum mundum, nolo aliud nisi te." *Il Libro*, 154.

[26] *Il Libro*, 154.

[27] "The step presented here as the twentieth is the first which I, the unworthy friar writing it, received and heard from the mouth of the faithful servant of Christ who related it to
me. . . . Having hardly begun this twentieth step, I abandon it for now and will return to it
after I have briefly related how, by the wonderful workings of Christ, I came to know of these
things and was compelled to write all about them." *Complete Works*, 132–33.

[28] *Il Libro*, 160 (*Complete Works*, 133).

contain Angela's increasingly sophisticated discourse on the profound revelations being given to her, but it is worth noting that Arnaldo's perception and sense of propriety guided their distinction. Briefly, these steps are as follows.

The first supplementary step (a continuation of the interrupted twentieth step) describes the indwelling of the Trinity that Angela was promised. It includes her vision of God as the "All Good," her definitive betrothal to Christ, and the resulting incandescence of her body. Supplementary steps two through five deepen her identity and union with Christ, both in his humanity and divinity. These steps include alternation of God's presence and absence, which causes Angela further suffering and increases her understanding of God's love, along with a series of eucharistic visions and her encounter with the lepers, in which she drank the water in which they were washed and swallowed a leper's scale, which tasted to her like the host.[29] The first five supplementary steps provide reassurance of God's love, knowledge of her own poverty and nothingness experienced through abjection, and knowledge of God's overwhelming goodness. But in the sixth step, Angela enters a "dark night" of illness, temptation, and spiritual suffering. This step coincides with the seventh.[30] It seems that Arnaldo here tried to distinguish for clarity's sake what was experienced almost simultaneously by Angela. The dark night lasted at its worst for two years, although it never entirely ended. In the seventh step, the suffering of divine abandonment was transformed or inverted into a great vision of divine darkness in the Pseudo-Dionysian tradition.[31] Together, these final two steps indicate complete abandonment by God and simultaneous union with the Godhead. Angela is both abjected and deified through her deep identification with the crucified Christ.

The content of the successive steps of Angela's spiritual journey can thus be extracted from her *Memorial*. The text itself, however, switches confusingly between a didactic form ("The first step is the awareness of one's sinfulness, in which the soul greatly fears being damned to hell"[32]) and a personal

---

[29] *Il Libro*, 200–334.

[30] "Sed duravit praedictus sextus passus parvo tempore, scilicet fere duobus annis, et cucurrit simul cum septimo passu qui incoepit ante sextum passum aliquantulum temporis, et qui sequitur omnibus mirabilior." *Il Libro*, 346.

[31] There is some question whether this interpretation is indeed Angela's or instead is a theological elaboration on her experience that was added in the second redaction; see Lachance, *Complete Works*, 65. The ambiguity stems from Angela's vocabulary, since in general she prefers the terms "abyss" and "uncreated" to refer to divine unknowability rather than Dionysian "darkness," at least in her *Instructions*.

[32] "Primus passus est cognitio peccati qua anima valde timet ne damnetur in inferno." *Il Libro*, 132 (*Complete Works*, 124).

narrative of different voices. For instance, in the second step, Arnaldo records Angela in the first person: "The very next morning, I went to the church of St. Francis,"[33] but after the fourth step, he interrupts: "I, brother scribe, declare that in all these steps I have not written about the remarkable penances which the faithful follower of Christ performed, for I learned about them only after I had written the aforesaid steps. She had only been telling me, at this point, what was necessary to distinguish one step from another."[34] For the first time, the reader becomes aware that a conversation is taking place behind the text as it is written. Almost apologetically, the scribe avers, "For my part, I did not want to write down one single word which was not exactly as she had said it. I even omitted many things which were simply impossible for me to write down properly."[35] The readers are not privy to the entire conversation. Although the scribe claims to be scrupulous in recording her words, he also screens what is written, for fear of misrepresenting what he has heard.[36]

The result is a narrative with multiple voices that collaborate in the production of the text and sometimes compete for control of its meaning. According to Paul Lachance, "There are three narrators: God speaks and reveals himself to Angela, and she in turn speaks to Arnaldo, who, as the prologue to the *Memorial* affirms, then narrates what he hears. At the end both claim that it is God who signed the book."[37] The result, however, is not so neatly distinguishable, and the divine origin and authorship of the book do not preclude the multiplicity of its voices. Indeed, on analogy with scripture (which Angela herself asserts by claiming God's signature),[38] we might say

[33] "Et mane statim ivi ad Sanctum Franciscum." *Il Libro*, 132 (*Complete Works*, 124).

[34] "Ego frater scriptor dico quod in omnibus passibus non scripsi paenitentiam eius mirabilem quam ipsa fidelis Christi faciebat et quam ego didici postquam scripseram passus praedictos, quia et ipsa non manifestavit mihi tunc nisi quantum oportebat eam dicere pro passibus distinguendis." *Il Libro*, 134 (*Complete Works*, 125).

[35] "Et ego nolebam unam dictionem plus scribere nisi sicut ipsa loquebatur, immo et plura dimittebam quae non poteram scribere." *Il Libro*, 134 (*Complete Works*, 125).

[36] For more on Angela and Arnaldo's relationship, see Mooney, "Authorial Role of Brother A." Lachance agrees that Arnaldo is more than a scribe: "Even if it is Angela's book, he is in many ways the artisan of its composition and, as such, a co-protagonist of her communications from God. Even if his intent is to report as faithfully as possible what she told him, he nonetheless is responsible for the internal organization of her account," *Complete Works*, 51.

[37] *Complete Works*, 47.

[38] On Angela's evangelical claims for her *Book*, see Bernard McGinn, "The Four Female Evangelists of the Thirteenth Century: The Invention of Authority," in *Deutsche Mystik im abendländischen Zusammenhang*, ed. Walter Haug and Wolfram Schneider-Lastin (Tübingen: Niemeyer, 2000), 175–94.

that divine authorship *requires* a plurality of voices. This heteroglossia also gives the text its immediacy and the feeling of orality.[39] Angela's *Book* is the product of a lived conversation and, before that conversation, a lived experience and revelation first narrated by Angela to her companion Masazuola and then to Arnaldo, who shares it with a wider audience. While the text presupposes and relates her experience, it is not a transcript of that experience but instead its rewriting through multiple voices.[40] The nature of the written text—its temporal distance from Angela's experience, its collaborative origins, its own apologetic and didactic urges—casts doubt on whether *any* transcript could accurately reproduce Angela's direct experience. Instead the *Memorial* is the transformation of experience into text, of somatic and spiritual and theological insight into speech, interpretation, and writing.

There remains the question of how the composition of the *Memorial* affected Angela's life. It was, after all, Arnaldo's questions that prompted Angela's narration and cowriting. Angela's book registers the interdependence of religious experience with the written word: as she was compelled to speak to Arnaldo for the sake of his writing, she turned to God for explanation of her visions.[41] Those visions were then translated back into narrative

---

[39] See Mikhail Bakhtin, *The Dialogic Imagination*, ed. Michael Holquist, trans. Caryl Emerson and Michael Holquist (Austin: University of Texas Press, 1981). For a reading of medieval women's texts using the literary theories of Bakhtin, see Laurie Finke, *Feminist Theory, Women's Writing: Reading Women Writing* (Ithaca, N.Y.: Cornell University Press, 1992).

[40] Most medieval women's mysticism is based on extraordinary "experience," which is then narrated or refined according to theological and literary genres and terms. That is not to say, however, that it is an unreflective or direct experience; their mystical experiences were available to them according to the religious categories of their day, and thus, in theoretical terms, highly constructed. Even more importantly, the mystic spent a great deal of time interpreting the nature and meaning of that experience (often in collaboration with a male confessor), and refining its expression according to the forms of a particular genre—in Angela's case, an *itinerarium* or spiritual journey that can serve as a didactic model for others. In other words, "experience" should not be divorced from interpretation and theology-making. Much contemporary feminist theory has struggled with the nature and status of "experience," as well, and especially its role in theoretical arguments and texts. For an incisive overview of the problem, see Joan W. Scott, "The Evidence of Experience," *Critical Inquiry* 17 (1991): 773–97.

[41] Lachance explains the interaction between mystic and scribe in gendered and institutional terms: "Arnaldo's faithful and demanding masculine presence thus served as a significant catalyst in Angela's development, calling on her to discriminate and focus inner meanings, as well as to articulate and name more clearly and precisely what she was experiencing. Moreover, as a representative of church tradition, Arnaldo performed the important function of certifying the authenticity and basic soundness of Angela's spiritual journey: a bridge between institution and praxis." *Complete Works*, 51.

form for the sake of the book. Arnaldo's questions thus impelled Angela to ever deeper consideration of her "divine secrets," which are recorded in the "supplementary steps" that occurred *after* he began writing.[42] His questions also seemed to provoke paramystical bodily symptoms as Angela received further graces. For instance, in the fifth supplementary step, she describes a superabundant joy that had bodily effects, confirmed by Angela's companion, who saw "the countenance of Christ's faithful one [become] white and radiant, then ruddy and joyful, and her eyes grew large and shone so brilliantly that she no longer seemed herself."[43] Arnaldo takes such graces as confirmation of the authenticity of Angela's revelations and the truth of what he is writing. His writing occasions the translation of Angela's experience into text and registers effects that are subject to further interpretation. This interdependence of life with text, of bodily symptoms with writing, is central to Hélène Cixous' literary theory as well.

Écriture féminine

Hélène Cixous' essay "Sorties," as the title indicates, both attacks and searches for exits from what she calls phallocentrism, the symbolic order of meaning and language that is governed by the Law of the Father.[44] Cixous identifies this Law, like Lacan and Freud before her, with the Name or "No!" of the father and the threat of castration that secures the symbolic system of language, culture, law, religion, and economy of exchange. This symbolic order is both phallocentric and logocentric, and its power derives from its abstraction and invisibility, represented by the absence of the Father.[45] It is God the Father who speaks the Logos but cannot be seen.[46] But while the

---

[42] Although it seems that Angela had already determined there would be thirty steps total. Evidence of Brother Arnaldo's influence on the text can be seen in his reduction of the ten remaining steps to seven. See Mooney, "Authorial Role of Brother A."

[43] "praedicta fidelis Christi effecta fuit alba, resplendens, laeta, rubicunda, et oculi erant facti grossi et in tantum resplendentes quod nullo modo videbatur esse ipsa." *Il Libro*, 320 (*Complete Works*, 190).

[44] Hélène Cixous, "Sorties," in Hélène Cixous and Catherine Clément, *La jeune née* (Paris: Union Générale d'Éditions, 1975). Hereafter, citations refer to the English translation: Hélène Cixous, "Sorties," in Hélène Cixous and Catherine Clément, *The Newly Born Woman*, trans. Betsy Wing (Minneapolis: University of Minnesota Press, 1986), 63–132.

[45] Sigmund Freud, *Totem and Taboo: Some Points of Agreement Between the Mental Lives of Savages and Neurotics*, trans. James Strachey (New York: Norton, 1950); Jacques Lacan, *Écrits: A Selection* (New York: Norton, 1977), esp. 67, 199, and 218.

[46] See Cixous' discussion of Freud's *Moses and Monotheism* in "Sorties," 100–103.

phallus promises plentitude and satisfaction, it is fantasy;[47] the Law both compels and forbids entry, but it is empty.[48] The patriarchal symbolic order or Law of the Father is powerful and omnipresent, but it is also both arbitrary and fictional.[49]

Cixous' essay examines the solidarity between logocentrism and phallocentrism and the way in which the figure of "woman" operates within them.[50] She notes how the law governs through the opposition of hierarchical pairs in which the devalued pole is associated with the feminine: "Shut out of his system's space, she is the repressed that ensures the system's functioning."[51] Because "she" provides the house or space for the (masculine) other, "She has not been able to live in her 'own' house, her very body . . . [Women's] bodies, which they haven't dared to enjoy, have been colonized."[52] Woman is exiled from her body and her sexuality by the law of the father, just as she is exiled from language by the phallogocentric symbolic order.[53] Cixous searches for the cracks in the system, the ruptures, gaps, or breaks that might allow the possibility of difference through the emergence of women's writing.

Cixous identifies and performs a practice of writing that she calls *écriture féminine*.[54] Writing as feminine, or "writing the body" as it is often referred to in Anglo-American literary theory, is a response to the paternal symbolic law that, according to Cixous, forbids women from writing and simultaneously

---

[47] Jacques Lacan, "The Meaning of the Phallus" (1958), in *Feminine Sexuality: Jacques Lacan and the école freudienne*, ed. Juliet Mitchell and Jacqueline Rose (London: Macmillan, 1982), 74–85.

[48] See Cixous' discussion of Kafka's "Before the Law" in "Sorties," 101–3.

[49] In the same section in which she discusses Kafka and Freud, Cixous refers to the fiction of paternity in Joyce's *Ulysses*; see "Sorties," 100–103.

[50] Cixous, "Sorties," 65.

[51] Cixous, "Sorties," 67. See one of the founding moments of Western metaphysics in the Pythagorean table of opposites in Aristotle, *Metaphysics* 986a (*The Basic Works of Aristotle*, ed. Richard McKeon [New York: Modern Library, 2001]).

[52] Cixous, "Sorties," 68.

[53] In answer to Freud's famous question, What does a woman want? Cixous writes, "It is precisely because there is so little room for her desire in society that, because of not knowing what to do with it, she ends up not knowing where to put it or if she even has it. This question conceals the most immediate and most urgent question: 'How do I pleasure?' What is it—feminine jouissance—where does it happen, how does it inscribe itself—on the level of her body or of her unconscious? And then, how does it write itself?" "Sorties," 82.

[54] Hélène Cixous, "Le rire de la Méduse," *L'Arc* 61 (1975): 39–54; English translation published as "The Laugh of the Medusa" in *New French Feminisms*, ed. Elaine Marks and Isabelle de Courtivron, trans. Keith Cohen and Paula Cohen (New York: Schocken Books, 1980), 245–64.

exiles women from their bodies.[55] Within the masculine symbolic order—
of language, law, property rights, and the economy of exchange—women's
bodies appear as sites of disruption. Women's bodies signify what cannot
otherwise be said through such phenomena as laughter, tears, milk, and,
classically, the contortions and symptoms of the hysteric. These bodily pro-
ductions operate at the borders of language—neither fully outside it nor
completely within it—and yet they carry meaning, they signify. In Cixous'
words, they *write* and can be read for what partially escapes, and therefore
threatens, the paternal symbolic order. Cixous draws feminist attention to
that which has been excluded and denied significance within phallocentric
language that privileges the proper and selfsame:[56] difference and otherness,
along with bodily phenomena and affects, which are coded as "feminine."
The repression of "the feminine" in the sense of alterity, difference, and corporeality is incomplete, and the repressed constantly threatens to return and
disrupt the law and language that excluded it. Consequently, the margins
and borders of what counts as "proper" language are fertile sites for feminist
intervention.

What Cixous means by *écriture féminine* has multiple dimensions and is
complicated by the fact that she says there can be no theory of it.[57] No theory
or logos could give an account or identify its essence; rather, *écriture féminine*
is enacted and can be identified, provisionally, by its effects. It has (at least)
the following features: interweaving of the personal with the historical and
literary;[58] deconstruction of binary opposition between speech and writing;[59]

---

[55] Cixous, "Le rire," 39–40 ("Laugh," 246).

[56] One of its philosophical rules is the law of identity, A=A.

[57] "Impossible de *définer* une pratique féminine de l'écriture, d'une impossibilité qui se
maintiendra car on ne pourra jamais *théoriser* cette pratique, l'enfermer, la coder, ce qui ne
signifie pas qu'elle n'existe pas." Cixous, "Le rire," 45 ("Laugh," 253).

[58] In "Sorties," for example, Cixous narrates her own story as a child in Algeria in
terms of the books she read and the historical events taking place. Cixous also writes in "Le
rire," 45: "En la femme se recoupent l'histoire de toutes les femmes, son histoire personnelle,
l'histoire nationale et internationale."

[59] Cixous describes women's voices, song, and gestures, their difficulty speaking, and
their hysterical resistances. Women already inscribe meaning with their bodies. "Sorties,"
92–94, esp. 93: "In feminine speech, as in writing, there never stops reverberating something
that, having once passed through us, having imperceptibly and deeply touched us, still has
the power to affect us—song, the first music of the voice of love, which every woman keeps
alive. The voice sings from a time before law, before the Symbolic took one's breath away and
reappropriated it into language under its authority of separation. The deepest, the oldest, the
loveliest Visitation. Within each woman the first, nameless love is singing."

stealing/flying (*voler*) from and through other texts;[60] and operating through an economy of giving without return to solid meaning.[61] These features differentiate *écriture féminine* from masculine or phallic writing. To be clear, these types of writing do not line up along biological bodies; just as women might adopt a masculine, phallic speaking or writing voice, Cixous identifies male writers such as Jean Genet and James Joyce who practice *écriture féminine*, who rejoice in the play of difference in written language. Masculine writing and feminine writing refer primarily to two different linguistic and literary economies—that of exchange and return versus that of the gift—rather than biologically essentialist modes of language.

What makes this style of writing "feminine" is not only its literal gender in French (the feminine noun *écriture*). It is also figuratively feminine in its practice as the expression of difference. Following Derrida, Cixous notes how writing operates through the play of difference (or *différance*): it both differs (signification being a function of difference between signifiers) and it defers final meaning.[62] Writing is productive of other writings, rewritings, and interpretations, so that every written text is, in a sense, unfinished. This notion of writing as productive, as the mark of difference, and as the repressed other of speech, presence, and representational systems of truth associates *writing* with the *feminine*, which is the repressed other of binary dualisms that operate to secure the law of phallogocentrism: activity/passivity, presence/absence, light/dark, self/other, male/female.[63] Writing as feminine, *écriture féminine*, subverts the law of the father from within the hierarchical pair of speech/writing. A practice of writing that highlights the differential features of writing and the multiplicity of senses it contains (such as that of Joyce, Genet, Marguerite Duras, Clarice Lispector, and Cixous herself) reveals the instability of the law of the father and of any attempt to divide the world into hierarchical pairs of opposites through force.

---

[60] Like Jean Genet, feminine writing thieves, stealing from other texts without acknowledging the property rights of paternal authority. This gesture allows the text to fly. Cixous, "Le rire," 49 ("Laugh," 258).

[61] Rather than an exchange/return to a foundation, to solid meaning or truth, *écriture féminine* operates through the economy of the gift. It is an adventure into the unknown, a giving without return. "Sorties," 87–88.

[62] See Jacques Derrida, *Of Grammatology*, trans. Gayatri Chakravorty Spivak (Baltimore: Johns Hopkins University Press, 1974), and idem, *Writing and Difference*, trans. Alan Bass (Chicago: University of Chicago Press, 1978).

[63] Cixous highlights these at the opening of "Sorties."

But writing is also "feminine" in that certain forms of writing—poetry, fiction—produce the "other" from within.[64] Writing is generative, gestational.[65] The desire to write is the desire to give birth to a multiplicity of forms, characters, and stories. These "others" inhabit the unconscious, the land of the repressed, the same place from which exiled women return.[66] Being repressed/oppressed themselves, Cixous claims, women have fewer boundaries separating them from this unconscious source of otherness. Writing as creation and birth appears as a feminine activity, even when performed by men. Cixous is particularly interested in reclaiming writing for women and finding a way for women to express their desires in language, and thereby to enter history and transform the symbolic order in the process.[67]

Cixous explicitly links this form of writing to women's bodies.[68] The rhetorical appeal to "write the body" has been frequently misunderstood by Anglo-American feminists and deserves some consideration.[69] It does not mean that women have direct access to their bodies outside of language. Nor does it simply mean that women ought to write *about* their bodies (though it does not preclude it). Cixous' imperative to "write the body" can be understood in several different ways: Since women have been exiled from writing as they have been exiled from their bodies, coming to writing is a return to

[64] "Today, writing is woman's. That is not a provocation, it means that woman admits there is an other. . . . It is much harder for man to let the other come through him. Writing is the passageway, the entrance, the exit, the dwelling place of the other in me—the other that I am and am not, that I don't know how to be, but that I feel passing, that makes me live—that tears me apart, disturbs me, changes me, who? une, un, des?—several, some unknown, which is indeed what gives me the desire to know and from all life soars." Cixous, "Sorties," 85–86.

[65] Cixous, "Le rire," 52: "toutes les pulsions sont nos bonnes forces, et parmi elles la pulsion de gestation,—toute comme l'envie d'écrire: une envie de se vivre dedans, une envie du ventre, de la langue, du sang." ("Laugh," 261).

[66] Cixous, "Le rire," 41: "Elles reviennent de loin: de toujours: du 'dehors', des landes où se maintiennent en vie les sorcières; d'en dessous, en deça de la 'culture'; *de leurs enfances*." ("Laugh," 247).

[67] "If woman has always functioned 'within' man's discourse, a signifier referring always to the opposing signifier that annihilates its particular energy, puts down or stifles its very different sounds, now it is time for her to displace this 'within,' explode it, overturn it, grab it, make it hers, take it in, take it into her women's mouth, bite its tongue with her women's teeth, make up her own tongue to get inside of it." Cixous, "Sorties," 95–96.

[68] E.g., Cixous, "Sorties," 94, among many other passages.

[69] See Ann Rosalind Jones, "Writing the Body: Towards an Understanding of *l'Écriture Féminine*," in *The New Feminist Criticism: Essays on Women, Literature and Theory*, ed. E. Showalter (New York: Pantheon, 1985), 361–77.

the body and its pleasures.[70] Writing is a practice of desire; in its unforeseen, expansive dimensions writing is a form of *jouissance*, a way of touching one's body through language and infusing that language with the body's drives.[71] Writing, like desire, is incomplete, an unfinished text, a giving without return. What is more, Cixous claims, women already write with their bodies: through laughter, gestures, song, milk, and blood, women inscribe meaning. Their bodies, like that of the hysteric, signify what cannot otherwise be said or heard in phallogocentric discourse.[72] Writing is an embodied practice. Writing is material: the text itself has a body and is written by a body. The imperative to "write the body" unveils the hidden and forgotten conditions of all language as embodied, and therefore sexed.

In the texts of Cixous, writing the body is a feminist practice that allows female flesh to become word—by disrupting paternal language and by signifying a feminine libidinal economy of difference that gives without return. By undertaking the practice of writing for themselves, women have the opportunity to write women's bodies back into history, into literature, in short, the symbolic. Writing the body is thus a way for women both to challenge the symbolic order that would exclude them and to shift the conditions of that order by changing its written culture. This aspect of *écriture féminine* falls under a utopian dimension in Cixous' writing, a space of the future that women have yet to create.[73]

When Cixous identifies and performs *écriture féminine* and encourages women to write their bodies, these are far from clear and distinct concepts. Cixous refuses to resolve the ambiguity of her claims, and much of the Anglo-American feminist discomfort with "writing the body" can be attributed to this lack of clarity, on the one hand, along with anxiety surrounding

---

[70] Cixous, "Le rire," 39–40 ("Laugh," 246).

[71] Cixous, "Sorties," 87–88.

[72] "In a way, *écriture féminine* never stops reverberating from the wrench that the acquisition of speech, speaking out loud, is for her—'acquisition' that is experienced more as tearing away, dizzying flight and flinging oneself, diving . . . Really she makes what she thinks materialize carnally, she conveys meaning with her body. She *inscribes* what she is saying because she does not deny unconscious drives the unmanageable part they play in speech." Cixous, "Sorties," 92.

[73] Cixous, "Sorties," 94. See also 97: "But somewhere else? There will be some elsewhere where the other will no longer be condemned to death. But has there ever been any elsewhere, is there any? While it is not yet 'here,' it is there by now—in this other place that disrupts social order, where desire makes fiction exist . . . But I move toward something that only exists in an elsewhere, and I search in the thought that writing has uncontrollable resources."

potential essentialism, on the other.[74] But the ambiguity of *écriture féminine* derives from the multiplicity of ways in which writing appears as feminine and embodied and in which women relate to, and rewrite, paternal language. Cixous turns to the female body not to claim an unmediated relationship with it, but to locate the specificity of female desires and a *jouissance* that signifies in writing by giving without return. By invoking women's desires and writing practices, by identifying poets who recognize and enjoy the differences within writing, and by highlighting the ways that women's bodies already signify at the borders of language, Cixous subverts the symbolic order and invites other women to follow her. *Écriture féminine* translates the body into language and makes female flesh into the written word.

Hysteria and Mysticism

The classic exemplar of writing the body and the frustration of speech is the hysteric, whose body signifies through its symptoms and physical contortions.[75] In Charcot's studies and Freud and Breuer's early work, these contortions (captured in photography) and symptoms (such as Anna O.'s cough and Dora's abdominal pains) were read and interpreted as psychological signs or conversion phenomena.[76] The hysteric "writes the body" in the sense that her body communicates what she is not capable of speaking. She cannot use words because what needs to be said cannot be heard within the symbolic order: repressed trauma, or repressed desire. Freud broke with the earlier medical model of hysteria as his view of its origin and treatment evolved; he hoped that psychoanalysis, rather than medical science, would cure the hysteric of her illness, since it stemmed from the unconscious repression of trauma or unacceptable desire rather than organic causes. The "talking cure" provided the setting, occasion, questions from the Other/analyst, and most importantly, the words to allow the hysteric to speak. If the hysteric could

---

[74] See Diana Fuss, *Essentially Speaking: Feminism, Nature & Difference* (New York: Routledge, 1989); and Naomi Schor and Elizabeth Weed, eds., *The Essential Difference* (Bloomington: Indiana University Press, 1994).

[75] "Women have not sublimated. Fortunately. . . . They have furiously inhabited these sumptuous bodies. Those wonderful hysterics, who subjected Freud to so many voluptuous moments too shameful to mention, bombarding his mosaic statue/law of Moses with their carnal, passionate body-words, haunting him with their inaudible thundering denunciations, were more than just naked beneath their seven veils of modesty—they were dazzling." Cixous, "Sorties," 95.

[76] See Georges Didi-Huberman, *Invention of Hysteria: Charcot and the Photographic Iconography of the Salpêtrière*, trans. Alisa Hartz (Cambridge, Mass.: MIT, 2003).

articulate her desire, could make conscious the unconscious, her body would no longer have to speak/write for her, and her symptoms would resolve.[77]

Feminists have questioned the early psychoanalytic focus on hysterical women's bodies and have critiqued the patriarchal and objectifying surveillance their cures occasioned. If the bodies of the hysterics were protesting their repression, perhaps hysteria is better seen as a form of rebellion, even if circumscribed, than an illness.[78] Dora, for instance, was well aware of her role in her family drama and rebelled against it; her ability to analyze her situation equals and confounds Freud's.[79] This view of the hysteric takes her as a revolutionary or protofeminist, anticipating "La Jeune Née" of the twentieth century described by Cixous and Catherine Clément. In the words of the Mouvement de libération des femmes (MLF), "nous sommes toutes des hystériques!"[80] The hysteric's ability to write her body through her protesting symptoms, in this view, foreshadows *écriture féminine* as described by Cixous. What the nineteenth- and early twentieth-century hysterics could not achieve in history or literature, circumscribed as they were by the Law of the Father—that is, the medico-psychoanalytic institution and practice—Cixous hopes that contemporary women might, by consciously writing the body, by translating flesh into word through *écriture féminine.*[81]

From the earliest neurological study of hysteria in the nineteenth century, comparisons to women mystics were made. Charcot, for example, noted the similarity between the bodily symptoms of hysteria and the paramystical

[77] For a memoir of psychoanalysis and hysteria, see Marie Cardinal, *Les Mots Pour Le Dire* (Paris: Grasset, 1975).

[78] See Catherine Clément's essay in Cixous and Clément, *The Newly Born Woman*, 3–57. For an overview of the feminist critical response to and even embrace of hysteria and hysterics, see Elaine Showalter, *Hystories: Hysterical Epidemics and Modern Media* (New York: Columbia University Press, 1997), 49–61.

[79] Sigmund Freud, *Dora: An Analysis of a Case of Hysteria* (New York: Collier Books, 1963).

[80] Leaving aside the question of whether hysteria is a viable *political* strategy, the slogan appropriates and subverts the common, and derogatory, appellation of feminists as hysterical. See Claire Duchen, *Feminism in France: From May '68 to Mitterand* (New York: Routledge, 1986).

[81] Amy Hollywood notes how Cixous aligns mystics (at least, Teresa of Avila) with hysterics (and both in opposition to patriarchal religion) through a transvaluation of values: "Cixous' argument leads to the conclusion that mystics, in that they are religious, are obsessive-compulsives, whereas in that they are hysterical, they are artists and revolutionaries." *Sensible Ecstasy*, 4; for the way in which hysteria was used to disparage women's writing, see also idem, *Sensible Ecstasy*, 242–43.

phenomena associated with rapture.[82] These comparisons have appeared in feminist works as well, from Simone de Beauvoir to Irigaray and Cixous. In both hysteria and paramystical phenomena, the body functions as a signifier—it conveys meaning, it "writes." Cristina Mazzoni, however, in her account of "Hysteria," points to an important difference between the mystic and the hysteric:

> In spite of this common function of the body as linguistic sign, one finds a crucial difference between the hysteric and the mystic in the articulation of the intersection between the body and its speech, or lack thereof. . . . For is the mystic's body language, then, a symptom, uttering and muttering a repressed trauma, like the hysteric's, or is it a miracle, the result of a porousness between the supernatural and the natural?[83]

In other words, because the frame of reference is different for mysticism (supernatural grace) and hysteria (illness), Mazzoni thinks the similarities between the two, while striking, are superficial. Following psychoanalyst Antoine Vergote, she argues for mysticism as a distinct form of discourse, despite its analogy to hysteria, on account of the mystic's unique claims of the ineffability of her experience of God and Christ's revelation as body in the incarnation and the Eucharist. Vergote distinguishes between the hysteric's "language through the body"—writing and speaking through conversion phenomena, symptoms of repressed trauma and desire—and the mystic's "language of the body," in which the mystic's desire for God "expresses itself through the metaphors of the body, and the body in turn becomes the metaphorical vessel that gives experience, including spiritual experience, a special resonance"[84] through her union with Christ. He contrasts the disgust the hysteric feels for her body with the joy of the mystic, who, "even in moments of abjection, revels in her corporeality as a means of coming into contact with God the bridegroom." In this way, "the mystic gives her body over to language"; she becomes the vehicle for Christ the Word, his flesh on earth, celebrated in the Eucharist and in her own rapture.

These are important distinctions. The mystic is not ill; she is blessed. Unlike the hysteric, she successfully negotiates her relationship to language through her encounter with the Word, making her own body into its vehicle. In a further step, she finds a way to translate her flesh into speech and even writing. But the two signification systems that Mazzoni and Vergote

---

[82] See Cristina Mazzoni, *Saint Hysteria: Neurosis, Mysticism, and Gender in European Culture* (Ithaca, N.Y.: Cornell University Press, 1996), 191.

[83] Mazzoni, *Saint Hysteria*, 191.

[84] Mazzoni, *Saint Hysteria*, 195–96.

oppose, symptom and miracle, are not mutually exclusive. The "porousness" of nature to grace can be experienced by mystics such as Angela precisely *as* trauma—as a disruption that exceeds her capacity to articulate or even experience it. This disruption results in an inability to speak coupled with bodily symptoms similar to the hysteric's. These symptoms are compounded by Angela's location within patriarchal religion along with her harsh ascetical practices.[85] It is only later in her spiritual journey that she finds a way to give "her body over to language" with the help of her confessor and the production of her book. This transition from traumatized and symptomatic flesh to spoken and written incarnate word begins with the incident that initiated the writing of her book.

Angela in Assisi

In 1291 Angela undertook a pilgrimage to Assisi. Her spiritual life had recently intensified (steps seventeen through nineteen) as she received a new quality of faith and focused on the passion of Christ and his mother: "What I wanted was to perform even greater penance. So I enclosed myself within the passion of Christ (*reclusi me in passione Christi*) and I was given hope that therein I might find deliverance."[86] We do not know why Angela became consumed with doing penance. Some scholars speculate that she had committed a sexual sin; her evident wealth and life of luxury may have also provoked feelings of guilt in a Franciscan context that valued poverty.[87] Whatever the reason, as her acts of penance led to a deeper experience of Christ, bodily symptoms signified her spiritual experience. She forgot to eat. She stood in prayer and never tired of genuflections. She screamed when hearing anyone speak of God and suffered from fevers when seeing depictions of the passion. Receiving a consolation, she fell to the ground and lost her power of speech. Her female companion thought she was "on the verge of death or already dead." Such somatic responses were only symptoms of her increased desire for Christ: "even if you should offer me the whole universe, I would not be satisfied. I want only you." The response to this prayer took her by surprise: "Hurry, for as soon as you have finished what you have set out to do the whole Trinity will come into you."[88] What she had "set out to do" was to undertake a pilgrimage to Assisi as a sign of her penance.

[85] For an account of how Angela's self-inflicted violence affected her mystical speech and writing, see Finke, *Feminist Theory, Women's Writing*, 75–107.

[86] *Il Libro*, 148 (*Complete Works*, 130).

[87] See Lachance's introduction, *Complete Works*, 16–17.

[88] *Il Libro*, 154 (*Complete Works*, 132).

Arnaldo interrupts his narration of Angela's journey at this crucial turning point in order to clarify how he "came to know of these things and
was compelled to write all about them," producing the book his reader now
holds.[89] Arnaldo's narrative aside marks the twentieth step and the road to
Assisi as a decisive moment in Angela's itinerary, as well as the episode that
brought Angela and Arnaldo together in their collaborative work.[90] Assisi is
properly where the story began, not in Angela's thirty steps on the way of
penance as told to her companion, and so Assisi is where Arnaldo, Angela,
and their reader pause in order to hear the background story of how the text
came to be. Assisi is also the place where Angela's bodily symptoms reached a
climax and then began to recede, as her speech was heard and written. Assisi
is so important, in fact, that the reader will learn of what happened there
twice, from two different perspectives.

First, from Arnaldo's perspective, Angela's behavior in Assisi was the
occasion of his writing: "The true reason why I wrote is as follows. One
day the aforementioned person, Christ's faithful one, came to the church of
St. Francis in Assisi, where I was residing in a friary. She screamed greatly
while she was sitting at the entrance to the portals of the church (*striderat
multum sedens in introitu ostii ecclesiae*)."[91] Arnaldo identified himself for the
first time in the text as her confessor, blood relative, and special counselor
and acknowledges that he was "greatly ashamed" (*multum verecundatus*) of
her behavior, especially in front of his Franciscan brothers who knew them
both. While her companions on the pilgrimage watched her behavior with
reverence, Arnaldo admits,

---

[89] *Il Libro*, 156 (*Complete Works*, 133).

[90] Brother Arnaldo represents it as a major turning point, in part, no doubt, because
that is where he entered her story. Mooney ("Authorial Role of Brother A.," 57) notes, "it
seems a strange coincidence that Angela's spiritual life should take such a dramatic swing
toward the sublime, begin again as it were, at just the moment when he happened to ask her
about it. My point, in short, is that the entire structure of the *Memorial* is built from the
perspective of Brother A. He inadvertently casts the day he intruded into her thoughts as a
central turning point in her experience and he correlates the beginning of their writing relationship with what he represents as the genesis of her most significant religious experience."
From the perspective of the production of her book, however, it is indeed crucial, precisely
because it is where he intervened and began writing.

[91] "Causa vero vel ratio quare incoepi scribere fuit ex parte mea ista, videlicet quia praedicta persona fidelis Christi quadam vice venerat Assisium ad Sanctum Franciscum, ubi ego
morabar conventualis, et striderat multum sedens in introitu ostii ecclesiae." *Il Libro*, 168
(*Complete Works*, 136).

[M]y pride and shame were so great that out of embarrassment and indignation I did not approach her; instead, I waited for her to finish screaming, and I kept myself at a distance. After she had ceased her screaming and shouting and had risen from the entrance and come over to me, I could hardly speak to her calmly. I told her that, henceforth, she should never again dare to come to Assisi, since this was the place where this evil had seized her.[92]

To Arnaldo, Angela's screams and shouts were too public, too ostentatious. Despite the reverence of her companions, Angela was out of order and out of place. Her shouting disrupted the peace and quiet of the church as her body blocked the door. He was embarrassed for her, and even more for himself. Was she possessed by an evil spirit? Arnaldo wanted to know.

"Wanting to know the cause of her shouts, I began to press her in every way that I could to tell me why she had screamed and shouted so much in Assisi."[93] After swearing her relative to secrecy, Angela began to tell of her spiritual journey, including the graces and visions of Christ she had received. Arnaldo tried his best to introduce doubt. "Amazed as I was and suspicious that it might come from some evil spirit, I made a strong effort to arouse her suspicions because I myself had so many. I advised her and compelled her to tell me everything." He began to take notes for himself, which he called a "memorial," to remember what she said and to show to another man. "I wished to write absolutely everything," he explains,

> so that I could consult with some wise and spiritual man who would have never heard of her. I told her that I wished to do this so that she could in no way be deceived by an evil spirit. I strove to inspire fear in her by showing her by examples how many persons had been deceived, and consequently how she could be similarly deceived. Because she did not yet have the degree of clarity and perfect certitude which she had later—as will be found in the writings which follow—she began to reveal the divine secrets to me and I wrote these down.[94]

---

[92] "tanta tamen fuit superbia et superba verecundia mea, quod prae verecundia non accessi usque ad eam, sed cum verecundia et indignatione expectavi eam vociferantem aliquantulum e longinquo ab ea. Et etiam postquam destitit ab illo stridoris clamore et surrexit de illo ostio et venit ad me, vix potui pacifice sibi loqui. Et dixi sibi quod nunquam de cetero iterum auderet venire Assisium, ex quo hoc malum accidebat ei." *Il Libro*, 168–70 (*Complete Works*, 136).

[93] "Et volens scire causam clamoris praedicti coepi cogere eam omni modo quo potui quod ipsa indicaret mihi quare sic et tantum striderat vel clamaverat quando venerat Assisium." *Il Libro*, 170 (*Complete Works*, 136–37).

[94] "ego volebam illud scribere omnino, ut possem consulere super illo aliquem sapientem et spiritualem virum qui nunquam eam cognosceret. Et hoc dicebam me velle facere ut ipsa nullo modo posset ab aliquo malo spiritu esse decepta. Et conabar incutere sibi timorem et dicere sibi exempla quomodo multae personae iam exstiterunt deceptae, unde et ipsa

And so begins their relationship, taken up time and again by mystics and
their confessors, witches and their inquisitors, hysterics and their doctors.
Arnaldo wants to know the cause of her screaming. And so he sets out to
write for other learned men. But instead of writing her condemnation, Angela
and Arnaldo together produce a book of mystical theology that affirms her
sanctity.

Immediately, however, communication is a problem: "In truth, I wrote
them [the divine secrets], but I had so little grasp of their meaning that I
thought of myself as a sieve or sifter which does not retain the precious and
refined flour but only the most coarse."[95] While Arnaldo claims to "add nothing of my own, not even a single word (*nec unam dictionem*)," his inability
to understand Angela's revelation affects his writing: "One day after I had
written as best I could what I had been able to grasp of her discourse, I read
to her what I had written in order to have her dictate more to me, and she
told me with amazement that she did not recognize it."[96] Angela calls his
words "dry and without any savor (*sicce et sine omni sapore*)," "very obscure
(*obscurissima*)," "inferior, and amounts to nothing (*deterius est et quod nihil*)"
in comparison to the precious feeling in her soul.[97] Arnaldo attributes his difficulty writing to his own inadequacy as a scribe and to fear of his brothers
who were suspicious of his relationship with Angela.[98]

After this lengthy aside explaining the origin of the book, Arnaldo
returns to the narrative and describes once again the screaming and shouting episode in Assisi. This time he writes from Angela's perspective and, to
the degree possible, in her own words. Angela had asked St. Francis to feel
Christ's presence, to observe his rule well, and for the grace of true poverty.
Her visions and consolations had increased, along with her somatic reactions—inedia, screaming, fever, aphasia—and she had been promised an

---

similiter poterat esse decepta. Et ipsa, quia non erat adhuc in gradu clarissimae et perfectissi-
mae certitudinis sicut postea fuit, sicut reperietur in ista scriptura quae sequitur, coepit mihi
scribenti manifestare secreta divina." *Il Libro*, 170 (*Complete Works*, 137).

[95] "De quibus in veritate ita parum capere poteram ad scribendum, quod ego cogitavi
et intellexi quod eram sicut cribrum vel setaccia quae subtilem et preciosam farinam non
retinet, sed retinet magis grossam." *Il Libro*, 170 (*Complete Works*, 137).

[96] "aliquando, dum ego scribebam recte sicut a suo ore capere poteram, relegenti sibi illa
quae scripseram ut ipsa alia diceret ad scribendum, dixit mihi admirando quod non recog-
noscebat illa." *Il Libro*, 172 (*Complete Works*, 137).

[97] *Il Libro*, 172 (*Complete Works*, 137–38).

[98] He was even forbidden to write and reprimanded by his superiors. "It is true," he
allows, "that they did not know what I was writing and how good it was (*nescientes tamen
quid ego scriberem et quae bona*)." *Il Libro*, 174 (*Complete Works*, 138).

indwelling of the Holy Trinity, although she was skeptical of its fulfillment. But on the road to Assisi, Angela received a revelation from the Holy Spirit, who comforted her and promised to accompany her as far as the church of St. Francis. The Spirit whispered to her all along the way: "My daughter, my dear and sweet daughter, my delight, my temple, my beloved daughter, love me, because you are very much loved by me; much more than you could love me."[99] With an indescribable feeling of joy and sweetness, the Holy Spirit repeated the promise to accompany Angela until the second time she entered the church of St. Francis, at which point this consolation would end.

> After he had withdrawn, I began to shout and to cry out without any shame: "Love still unknown, why do you leave me?" I could not nor did I scream out any other words than these: 'Love still unknown, why? why? why?" Furthermore, these screams were so choked up in my throat that the words were unintelligible . . . As I shouted I wanted to die. It was very painful for me not to die and to go on living. After this experience I felt my joints become dislocated.[100]

The arrival of the Holy Spirit was sweet and marked by his words of endearment. But his withdrawal was painful and provoked her protest. Angela's symptoms signified the end of her divine encounter as a traumatic experience—a desire for death, dislocation of limbs, incomprehension, and inability to speak. The words got caught in her throat and were unintelligible to those who merely saw a woman screaming and shouting on the floor by the doors to the church. Her utter lack of self-consciousness or shame (*sine aliqua verecundia*) during the incident contrasts strongly with Arnaldo's professed embarrassment at her behavior. This traumatic experience strikingly resembles the hysterical body, as Angela's symptoms signify her divine encounter. In this case, however, the symptom and miracle of Angela's tormented body are a response not to the divine presence, but to its absence.

The shouted words initially caught in Angela's throat were later elaborated and translated into written form with the assistance of Brother

---

[99] "Filia mea, dulcis mihi, filia mea, delectum meum, templum meum, filia, delectum meum, ama me, quia tu es multum amata a me, multum plus quam tu ames me." *Il Libro*, 180 (*Complete Works*, 139–40).

[100] "Et tunc post discessum coepi stridere alta voce vel vociferari, et sine aliqua verecundia stridebam et clamabam dicendo hoc verbum scilicet: Amor non cognitus, et quare scilicet me dimittis? Sed non poteram vel non dicebam plus nisi quod clamabam sine verecundia praedictum verbum scilicet: Amor non cognitus, et quare et quare et quare? Tamen praedictum verbum ita intercludebatur a voce quod non intelligebatur verbum . . . Et ego clamabam volens mori, et dolor magnus erat mihi quia non moriebar et remanebam; et tunc omnes compagines meae disiungebantur." *Il Libro*, 184 (*Complete Works*, 142).

Arnaldo. On the way home from Assisi, Angela began to speak about God to her companions. She received an experience of the cross and the love of God within her body and soul.[101] In the days that followed, Angela smelled extraordinary fragrances, her companion saw her body emanating a glowing star, and, after meditating on the flesh driven into the wood by the nails of the cross, Angela received a vision of the beauty of the body of Christ. Her own body stretched out on the ground in response. All of this was told to Arnaldo, who quickly wrote it down with the intent of showing it to those who could determine the authenticity and source of Angela's extraordinary experiences. While Arnaldo initially succeeded in making Angela doubt herself, the tables soon turned as she convinced him of the genuineness of her revelations and their divine source. Angela assuaged both their doubts with the reassurance she received: " 'God is present in all those things which you are writing and stands there with you.' My soul understood and felt that God indeed delighted over all that had been written."[102]

Angela began her spiritual journey before meeting Arnaldo. But Assisi was a turning point, and not simply because of the extraordinary consolation she received from the presence of the Trinity. In Assisi, Angela's experience was manifested physically, in inarticulate screams and shouts. Her words caught in her throat. It took Arnaldo's embarrassment, suspicions, and masculine authority as her relative and confessor to help her get those words out. Once her words were set to paper (and Angela told him he would need a lot of paper![103]), she quickly asserted control over what was written, accepting or rejecting Arnaldo's version of her speech. No longer screaming inarticulately, she claimed spiritual authority as she received further and richer divine secrets. She obtained God's approval of the book, and God occasionally even specified what to write.[104] At the end of the *Memorial*, God told Angela, " 'Everything which has been written is in conformity with my will and comes from me, that is, issues forth from me.' Then he added: 'I will put my seal to it.' " Charmingly, Angela did not understand what God meant, and so God "clarified these words by saying: 'I will sign

---

[101] *Il Libro*, 186 (*Complete Works*, 142).

[102] "Deus est praesens in omnibus istis quae scribitis et stat ibi vobiscum. Et comprehendebat anima quod Deus inde delectabatur, et anima istud sentiebat." *Il Libro*, 218 (*Complete Works*, 154).

[103] *Il Libro*, 166–68 (*Complete Works*, 136).

[104] During one session, Arnaldo wrote, "Then she added that today she had also been told: 'Have these words inserted at the end of what you say, namely, that thanks should be given to God for all the things which you have written.' " *Complete Works*, 156.

it.' "[105] Angela's shouted protest of God's departure in Assisi led to the production of a book in which she found God again—this time in what she and Arnaldo had written together, above God's own signature.

Angela's life repeated many of the themes of medieval women's piety identified by Bynum and others—focus on the humanity of Christ, and especially his passion; drinking from the wound in Christ's side; a strong eucharistic piety; abjection through the ingestion of a leper's scale; radical asceticism such as inedia; and so on—and Arnaldo admired her greatly for it. Her body mirrored the body of Christ repeatedly in prayer and in visions: she stood or lay down as required, stripped herself naked at the foot of the cross, and even entered into his tomb on Holy Saturday where he pressed her cheek against his. These bodily reactions intensified in the steps immediately prior to the incident in Assisi: when Angela was not screaming and shouting, she was struck with aphasia; she had a fever; she could not eat. They reached their apex when she choked on her own words and her screams made her appear possessed.

Arnaldo's *Memorial* could have taken the form of another hagiography, written by an admiring male confessor who reported (and constructed) the extraordinary phenomena surrounding a woman's body for his own didactic purposes. But something else happened in Assisi that brought Angela's *Book* much closer to the characteristics of the medieval women *writers* identified by Amy Hollywood. When Angela's screaming provoked Arnaldo's desire to know, she became the origin—and coauthor—of her book. Her body was no longer merely symptomatic of God's miraculous work on her. Through her conversations with Arnaldo, Angela asserted the authority to interpret her experience, and she increased in confidence and certainty until she became a spiritual mother to her Franciscan sons and daughters, as recounted in the second part of her *Book*, the *Instructions*. The transition from acting as a spectacular, if suspicious, female body on the margins of the church to exercising authority over the spoken and written word began in Assisi and continued with Arnaldo's collaboration. Through this collaboration, Angela's flesh was translated into written word.

From spectacular body to author, from ineffable mystical experience to book, from symptomatic flesh to written word—it is possible to account for this transition in Angela's life through the historical and literary evidence available to us through the production of her book. Her book, however, is heavily mediated by Arnaldo's influence and tells us little directly about her life before their collaboration. Consequently, this approach has no choice

[105] *Complete Works*, 217–18.

but to attribute primary agency to Arnaldo as the author of Angela's book; Angela herself appears only as one of the "saints" admired for her miraculous experience, rather than as a writer and producer of theology in her own right. Alternatively, psychoanalytic categories such as hysteria have been used to describe Angela's experience.[106] Certainly, her physical behavior frequently mimicked hysterical symptoms (such as bodily contortions, aphasia, and her inability to eat), which receded as she began to speak to her confessor. This approach places Arnaldo in the role of analyst who cures his patient by listening to her words. But psychoanalytic categories have been widely criticized as ahistorical and reductive when applied to the complexities of medieval religion. Although these theoretical categories, whether psychoanalytic or historical, can be helpful in highlighting different facets of Angela's experience, they do not exhaust the meaning of her extraordinary transformation. Neither, for instance, can easily account for her entry into a collaborative writing practice or consider her as a writing subject.

Angela's intense interest in the body of Christ is a clue to understanding the transformative journey her own life takes. Using a theological lens, Angela's transformation into a writer can be seen as a response to her experience of the incarnation of Christ. While the incarnation has traditionally been understood as both unique and hierarchical—in a top-down movement, the Word descends and becomes flesh for the sake of human salvation—Angela operates from a much more expansive interpretation of the incarnation, one that sheds new light on her entry into the written Christian tradition. Angela does not limit the incarnation to the historical body of Jesus. In her words as recorded in her *Book*, she encounters Christ's body in the world, in the host, and in the leper, as well as in her own body. Her transition from disruptive body to writer/theologian can best be understood through this broadened theological lens of the incarnation, at the intersection of word and flesh.

Angela's Incarnation

While at Mass one day, Angela heard a voice say to her, "My daughter, you are sweet to me." She describes what happened next when the divine voice added, "I want to show you something of my power":

> And immediately the eyes of my soul were opened, and in a vision I beheld the fullness of God in which I beheld and comprehended the whole of creation, that is, what is on this side and what is beyond the sea, the abyss, the sea itself, and everything else. And in everything that I saw, I could perceive nothing except the

---

[106] See Cristina Mazzoni's critique of this comparison in *Saint Hysteria: Neurosis, Mysticism, and Gender in European Culture* (Ithaca, N.Y.: Cornell University Press, 1996).

presence of the power of God, and in a manner totally indescribable. And my soul in an excess of wonder cried out: "This world is pregnant with God!"[107]

Angela's vision of creation as the incarnate presence of God recalls, or anticipates, Sallie McFague's metaphor of the body of God.[108] But rather than describe the world as Christ's body or as the cosmic Christ through the power of the Word, here Angela's wonder finds expression in the metaphor of pregnancy.[109] Here the body of God is female and maternal; like Hadewijch, Angela locates the incarnation in the body of Mary, extended sacramentally to the world. These metaphors—fullness, pregnancy—link the incarnation to creation and to the sacraments, and from them to Angela's own body, which also experiences the fullness of God.[110]

---

[107] "Et postea dixit: Ego volo tibi ostendere de potentia mea. Et statim fuerunt aperti oculi animae, et videbam unam plenitudinem Dei in qua comprehendebam totum mundum, scilicet ultra mare et citra mare et abyssum et mare et omnia. Et in omnibus praedictis non discernebam nisi tantum potentiam divinam, modo omnino inenarrabili. Et anima tunc admirando nimis, clamavit dicens: Est iste mundus praegnans de Deo!" *Il Libro*, 260–62 (*Complete Works*, 169–70).

[108] See introduction.

[109] Process theologians might call this "panentheism" to indicate that God is both immanent within and transcendent beyond the world because all is in God. At times, however, Angela's visions seem to pull her closer to pantheism proper, as in this metaphor; indeed, she often seems to struggle to leave the language of duality (God/world or Christ/soul) behind altogether.

[110] "You are full of God (*Tu es plena Deo*)." Angela's own body responded to this voice: "Et tunc revera sentiebam omnia membra corporis plena delectamento Dei; et desiderabam mori (I truly felt all the members of my body filled with the delights of God. And I wanted to die)." *Il Libro*, 200 (*Complete Works*, 148). Union with God for Angela is usually either an erotic assimilation to the God-man Christ or the union without distinction of "becoming nothing" in the darkness of God. See, e.g., *Complete Works*, 205: "When I am in that darkness I do not remember anything about anything human, or the God-man, or anything which has a form. Nevertheless, I see all and I see nothing. As what I have spoken of withdraws and stays with me, I see the God-Man. He draws my soul with great gentleness and he sometimes says to me: 'You are I and I am you.' . . . When I am in the God-man my soul is alive. And I am in the God-man much more than in the other vision of seeing God with darkness. The soul is alive in that vision concerning the God-man. The vision with darkness, however, draws me so much more that there is no comparison. On the other hand, I am in the God-man almost continually. It began in this continual fashion on a certain occasion when I was given the assurance that there was no intermediary between God and myself. Since that time there has not been a day or a night in which I did not continually experience this joy of the humanity of Christ." Angela's nondual awareness is the result of her contemplative practice.

Like other medieval mystics and saints, many of Angela's visions are occasioned by the elevation of the host or by her reception of the sacrament. In the host, she sees a beauty that "surpasses the splendor of the sun." Under intense questioning by Arnaldo, she insists, "This beauty which I see makes me conclude with the utmost certainty and without a shadow of a doubt that I am seeing God."[111] Sometimes the beauty takes a more specific bodily form, such as a pair of eyes or the Christ child. These visions, like the vision of creation as pregnant with God, affirm the extension of the incarnation beyond the body of Jesus. Christ is present in the world just as Christ's real presence is encountered in the Eucharist. And just as Angela experienced the "fullness" of God in her own body, she discovers herself within the ciborium with Christ, understanding "that Christ was at once in the ciborium and yet present everywhere, filling everything."[112]

Christ's presence extends to the most detested and marginalized bodies. Christ does not simply minister to these bodies, as in Jesus' ministry of healing; rather, Christ is paradigmatically present in those who are sick and suffering. Angela discovers Christ's presence, like St. Francis, in her encounter with the lepers. On Maundy Thursday, she says to her companion, "Let's go . . . to the hospital and perhaps we will be able to find Christ there among the poor, the suffering, and the afflicted." After her acts of charity, she follows the example of Jesus:

> And after we had distributed all that we had, we washed the feet of the women and the hands of the men, and especially those of one of the lepers which were festering and in an advanced stage of decomposition. Then we drank the very water with which we had washed him. And the drink was so sweet that, all the way home, we tasted its sweetness and it was as if we had received Holy Communion. As a small scale of the leper's sores was stuck in my throat, I tried to swallow it. My conscience would not let me spit it out, just as if I had received Holy Communion. I really did not want to spit it out but simply to detach it from my throat.[113]

Christ is present in the world and in the host, but he is present in a special way in the bodies of those who suffer; their washing water and scales become his body and blood. By ingesting these, Angela identifies with the leper and incorporates the body of Christ into her own. What appears as abjection, reveling in self-abasement, is transformed into divinization out of love. Following Christ, she inverts abjection into divinization through a radically inclusive understanding of Christ's incarnate presence.

[111] *Complete Works*, 146–47.
[112] *Complete Works*, 209, 215.
[113] *Complete Works*, 162–63.

The presence of God within the world, within the sacraments, and within the leper is the effect of the incarnation. In the incarnation, God unites us to himself, incorporating us within God just as God is incorporated within humanity.[114] Angela's final letter to her followers ("Angela's Testament") interprets the incarnation as the "highest mystery" of God—one of her "divine secrets"—and gives a taste of how she experienced the incarnation for herself:

> O incomprehensible love! There is indeed no greater love than the one by which *my God became flesh in order that he might make me God.* O heartfelt love poured out for me! You gave of yourself in order to make me when you assumed our form; You did not let go of anything in yourself in any way that would lessen you or your divinity, but the abyss of your conception makes me pour out these deep, heartfelt words: O incomprehensible one, made comprehensible! O uncreated one, made creature! O inconceivable one, made conceivable! O impalpable one, become palpable![115]

She continues this theme a little later: "O highest and transformed love! O vision divine! O ineffable one! When will you, Jesus Christ, make me understand that you were born for me? Oh, how glorious it is to truly understand— as I now see and understand—that you were born for me. This fills me with every conceivable delight."[116] For Angela, the incarnation has personal significance: God's birth results in her own divinization. God became flesh so that Angela might become God. What is more, God's conception and birth in the incarnation have a direct effect on her theological and pedagogical speech: "abyssus tuae conceptionis facit me dicere verba ista eviscerata."

---

[114] As she teaches in her *Instructions*, "God's desire is to unite us to himself, incorporate us in himself, and himself in us. Furthermore, he wishes that we carry him within ourselves as he himself carries us, consoling and strengthening us." God "vult unire nos sibi et incorporare se nobis et nos sibi. Et vult ut nos portemus ipsum ut ipse portet nos, confortando et fortificando nos." *Il Libro*, 666 (*Complete Works*, 294–95).

[115] Emphasis added. "O incomprehensibilis caritas! Supra istam non est maior caritas, quam quod Deus meus fiat caro ut me faciat Deum. O amor evisceratus! Dedisti te ut faceres me quando recepisti formam nostram; non defecisti in te ut aliquid minueretur a te nec a tua divinitate, sed abyssus tuae conceptionis facit me dicere verba ista eviscerata. O Incomprehensibilis, factus es comprehensibilis. O Increatus, tu es factus creatura. O Incogitabilis, tu es cogitabilis. O Impalpabilis, tu palpari potes." *Il Libro*, 714 (*Complete Works*, 308), translation modified. The editors of the critical edition of *Il Libro* date this letter to the middle of 1308; it appears to be authentic.

[116] "O amor summus et transformatus! O divina visio! O Ineffabilis! Quando tu, Jesu Christe, facis me intelligere quod mihi es natus? O quomodo est gloriosum istud intelligere in veritate, quod ego videam et intelligam quod tu es mihi natus. Plenum est omni delectamento." *Il Libro*, 716 (*Complete Works*, 309).

Angela pours out her own flesh as words in response to the mystery of God's word made flesh.

That the Word became flesh so that Angela's flesh might be translated into divine speech and writing can be seen at the beginning and the end of her narrative. When Brother Arnaldo first encountered Angela in Assisi, she was screaming incomprehensibly and making a scene. In their initial meetings, she repeatedly described the earliest steps of her spiritual journey in terms of bodily paramystical phenomena such as screaming, weeping, glowing, aphasia, fever, inedia, sweet fragrances, and visions, in part, no doubt, due to his line of questioning and his interests. Angela's screaming fit in Assisi led directly to Brother Arnaldo's desire to know, and then write, her experience, not least due to his suspicion of demonic influence on her body. As their discussions progress, however, Angela's extraordinary experiences result in greater insight into her divine revelations and eventually lead to her role as teacher and spiritual mother of her Franciscan disciples. Consequently, in her *Instructions*, Angela speaks with authority, and in her own voice, no longer filtered by Brother Arnaldo's amazed reactions.[117] Because her self-knowledge and theological interpretation are mediated through her book, as it is cowritten with her confessor, writing becomes the vehicle of her self-understanding. Whereas at the start of her journey Angela was "writing the body" through paramystical signs and symptoms, by the end of her life Angela has written her body into speech: her flesh poured out as word(s) in response to the mystery of Christ's incarnation.[118] Writing, as a record of Angela's divine words and in the production of her *Book*, assists the process of becoming divine.

"Writing Is God"

Writing can provide a pathway for women to enter a tradition in which authority is based on the written word. Angela gains spiritual authority by cowriting her book with Brother Arnaldo; her life is transformed through the self-awareness she gains as her understanding of the incarnation deepens. But women can have a troubled relationship with a written tradition that has been based, in part, on their exclusion from it. Until quite recently (and perhaps still), women have felt the need to justify their decision to write, often with considerable anxiety, or to write under a pseudonym, or to find a supportive man (which Arnaldo becomes) who is in a position to help them

[117] See Lachance's introduction in *Complete Works*, 81–84.
[118] See Petroff, *Body and Soul*, 214.

secure approval for their books. In her autobiographical essay "Coming to Writing," Hélène Cixous' describes her early desire to write, along with her perception that writing was forbidden to her:

> Wouldn't you first have needed the "right reasons" to write? The reasons, mysterious to me, that give you the "right" to write? But I didn't know them. I had only the "wrong" reason; it wasn't a reason, it was a passion, something shameful—and disturbing; one of those violent characteristics with which I was afflicted. I didn't "want" to write. How could I have "wanted" to? I hadn't strayed to the point of losing all measure of things. A mouse is not a prophet. I wouldn't have had the cheek to go claim my book from God on Mount Sinai, even if, as a mouse, I had found the energy to scamper up the mountain. No reasons at all. But there was madness. Writing was in the air around me. Always close, intoxicating, invisible, inaccessible. I undergo writing! It came to me abruptly. One day I was tracked down, besieged, taken. It captured me. I was seized. From where? I knew nothing about it. I've never known anything about it. From some bodily region. I don't know where. "Writing" seized me, gripped me, around the diaphragm, between the stomach and the chest, a blast dilated my lungs and I stopped breathing.[119]

In comparing herself to a mouse scampering up Mount Sinai, Cixous captures the anxiety surrounding writing for many. There is no reason to write for those who lack all authority. The desire to write is instead experienced as an irrational passion that seizes the body from within. Instead of the inspiration of the prophets, writing takes away her breath.

Cixous contrasts two modalities of writing in her essay: the male-identified tradition of Mount Sinai, the Torah, and the prophets, in which writing comes from on high as the sign of authority; and the passionate and embodied form of writing that seizes the mouselike from within. She perceives the first form of writing as the domain of the Father, forbidden to her as woman, as not-God, as a mouse; she both recognizes and resists its authority: "Writing is God. But it is not your God." But the corporeal passion that seizes her, which does not come from above,[120] also has dimensions of the divine: "Reading, I discovered that writing is endless. Everlasting. Eternal. Writing or God. God the writing. The writing God."[121] Although not a theologian, Cixous' essay points to a profound theological insight: if God is another name for writing, how we understand and practice writing

---

[119] Hélène Cixous, "Coming to Writing," in *"Coming to Writing" and Other Essays*, ed. Deborah Jenson, trans. Sarah Cornell et al. (Cambridge, Mass.: Harvard University Press, 1991), 9.

[120] The desire to write was "A joyful force. Not a god; it doesn't come from above. But from an inconceivable region, deep down inside my body." Cixous, "Coming to Writing," 10.

[121] Cixous, "Coming to Writing," 23.

is intimately related to how we picture and pray to God. In other words, our theological writing, in both form and content, should mirror our deepest theological beliefs. For feminist theologians of the incarnation, writing should take on an embodied form.[122]

Cixous encountered writing as at once forbidden and seductive, as a divine calling she could not refuse. But she soon discovered that she was equally exiled from a second tradition of writing because of her religion. Christian writing, she notes, is "like the Revelation of a cathedral," whose beauty is undeniable, but which also proclaims, "Admire me. I am the spirit of Christianity. Down on your knees, offspring of the bad race. Transient. I was erected for my followers. Out, little Jewess. Quick, before I baptize you."[123] In an incident that echoes Angela's pilgrimage to Assisi, Cixous was thrown out of a cathedral as a tourist for having bare skin. Whether it was her female flesh at issue, her Jewishness, or the simple fact of embodiment, she says she "felt naked for being Jewish, Jewish for being naked, naked for being a woman, Jewish for being flesh and joyful!" Her response turns shame into joy and boldly claims the right to a written tradition that attempted to exclude her: "So I'll take all your books. But the cathedrals I'll leave behind. Their stone is sad and male. The texts I ate, sucked, suckled, kissed. I am the innumerable child of their masses."[124]

Cixous identifies writing with God at first only negatively, as the realm of the Father, as the Torah given to prophets, priests, and rabbis, as the French Catholic cathedral whose architectural space identifies her as other, as intruder, as naked female flesh. But Cixous the mouse nevertheless finds a way to enter writing, to scurry up Mount Sinai, to suckle the texts of the Christian tradition by turning it on its head. If she is Jewish for being flesh and naked for being a woman then this physical underside of writing—the point of exclusion—becomes a point of entry.

> I don't "begin" by "writing": I don't write. Life becomes text starting out from my body. I am already text. History, love, violence, time, work, desire inscribe it in my body, I go where the "fundamental language" is spoken, the body language into which all the tongues of things, acts, and beings translate themselves, in my own breast, the whole of reality worked upon in my flesh, intercepted by my nerves, by my senses, by the labor of all my cells, projected, analyzed, recomposed into a book. Vision: my breast as the Tabernacle. Open. My lungs like the scrolls of the Torah.[125]

[122] These questions are examined more fully in chapter 5.

[123] Cixous, "Coming to Writing," 11.

[124] Cixous describes her attraction to Teresa of Avila in particular in "Sorties." Cixous, "Coming to Writing," 12.

[125] Cixous, "Coming to Writing," 52.

Writing cannot be forbidden if it is already present in her own body, if it begins there and seizes her as a passionate force from an unknown source within.[126] Before or beneath the writing of Mount Sinai, Cixous discovers an older language associated with the maternal body, the language of milk and honey, "The language that women speak when no one is there to correct them."[127] The language of the mother tongue, the land of milk and honey prior to the Law, is older than the paternal symbolic order. By writing, Cixous partakes of its nourishment and becomes a nourishing mother in turn: "So this is why, how, who, what, I write: milk. Strong nourishment. The gift without return. Writing, too, is milk. I nourish. And like all those who nourish, I am nourished."[128]

It would be a mistake to say that Cixous' theory of writing is theological, because no logos could contain it, and yet it is divine, an embodied spiritual practice of love. Like the mystics, she describes reading as writing (and writing as reading) as a spiritual exercise without end: "The flesh is writing, and writing is never read; it always remains to be read, studied, sought, invented. Reading: writing the ten thousand pages of every page, bringing them to light. Grow and multiply and the page will multiply. But that means *reading*: making love to the text. It's the same spiritual exercise."[129] Writing is an embodied spiritual practice of active passivity, a vocation and a technique, a refusal of mastery, and, most importantly, an act of love.[130] "Love opens up

[126] "And the source is given to me. It is not me. One cannot be one's own source. Source: always there. Always the vividness of the being who gives me the There." Cixous, "Coming to Writing," 43.

[127] "There is a language that I speak or that speaks (to) me in all tongues. A language at once unique and universal that resounds in each national tongue when a poet speaks it. In each tongue, there flows milk and honey. And this language I know, I don't need to enter it, it surges from me, it flows, it is the milk of love, the honey of my unconscious." Cixous, "Coming to Writing," 21.

[128] Cixous, "Coming to Writing," 49. See Lisa Walsh, "Writing (into) the Symbolic: The Maternal Metaphor in Hélène Cixous," in *Language and Liberation: Feminism, Philosophy, and Language*, ed. Christina Hendricks and Kelly Oliver (Albany: State University of New York Press, 1999), 347–65.

[129] Cixous, "Coming to Writing," 24. Cf. Cixous, "The Last Painting," in *Coming to Writing*, 104–31, 129: "When I have finished writing, when I am a hundred and ten, all I will have done will have been to attempt a portrait of God. Of the God. Of what escapes us and makes us wonder. Of what we do not know but feel. Of what makes us live. I mean our own divinity, awkward, twisting, throbbing, our own mystery."

[130] "All that I can say is that this 'coming' to language is a fusion, a flowing into fusion; if there is 'intervention' on my part, it's in a sort of 'position,' of activity—passive, as if I were inciting myself: 'Let yourself go, let the writing flow, let yourself steep; bathe, relax, become

the body without which Writing becomes atrophied. For Love, the words become loved and read flesh, multiplied into all the bodies and texts that love bears and awaits from love. Text: not a detour, but the flesh at work in a labor of love."[131] Cixous alludes to the prologue of John as the words become flesh: in the spiritual exercise of writing, love provides contiguity between the body and the text, between the word and the flesh, in multiple bodies and texts.

Hélène Cixous describes herself as *Juifemme*, and it is important to caution against a too-Christian reading of her embodied view of writing as incarnational in form. Christ is not the paradigm for her thinking, even if she alludes to the gospel of John, and it would do continuing violence to the distinctively Jewish aspects of her thought to find him there. But Christian theologians have much to learn from her theory and practice of writing the body, which gives insight into what embodied theological writing might look like. For the Christian theologian, that writing takes the incarnational shape of writing the body of Christ—an ongoing interpretation, reading, and writing of the incarnation "multiplied into all the bodies and texts that love bears and awaits from love." Cixous' writing touches upon a human mystery that the Christian doctrine of the incarnation also reveals: the mystery of word made flesh and flesh made word, the eternity and multiplicity of writing, the wonder of embodied writing and speech. This mystery is central to Angela's spiritual itinerary, and the incarnation provides the shape and direction of her theology just as it provides the path to her writing.

Writing the Body of Christ

Angela of Foligno and Hélène Cixous illuminate each other in mutually instructive ways on the central and shared questions of body and writing, writing and speech, authority and the divine. They each claim to speak or write from a position of humility (Cixous is only a "mouse" scurrying up the side of Mt. Sinai; Angela speaks under obedience to her confessor on the way of penance), but out of this humility they claim a remarkable authority: Cixous writes like a prophet and Angela claims nothing less than union with God. They each figure the complex relationship between writing and speech, as Angela's garbled speech becomes interpreted writing with the assistance

---

the river, let everything go, open up, unwind, open the floodgates, let yourself roll . . .' A practice of the greatest passivity. At once a vocation and a technique. This mode of passivity is our way—really an active way—of getting to know things by letting ourselves be known by them. You don't seek to master . . . But rather to transmit: to make things loved by making them known." Cixous, "Coming to Writing," 56–57.

[131] Cixous, "Coming to Writing," 42.

of Brother Arnaldo, and Cixous discovers writing in the way women already "write" with their bodies and gestures. Most importantly, the writings of each recognize the place of the body in coming to speech and writing: Angela, through her spiritual practices and quite physical imitation of Christ; and Cixous, in her description of the way the body, especially the female body, disrupts language and signifies at its borders, through signs such as hysterical contortions, laughter, and tears.

But there are important points of contrast as well, which equally illumine the notion of writing the body through their juxtaposition. For Cixous, for instance, hysteria provides an image of writing the body as the hysteric's inability to speak erupts in a constrained form of bodily writing. Set free from her circumscription, the hysteric might translate her bodily symptoms into a liberating and transformative writing that retains its contiguity with the body. In similar fashion, Cixous herself was seized by a bodily impulse to write that she translated into text, providing an entry point into the written tradition. Angela's inability to speak, however, is different from hysteria; it is not simply due to trauma or repression that she suffers from aphasia, garbled speech, or paramystical phenomena. Indeed, her extraordinary symptoms are read as signs of God's miraculous presence, not illness. Her initial difficulty speaking is due not only to her circumscription within patriarchal religion, along with the possible physical and psychic trauma she has undergone (due to the death of her family and her harsh ascetic practices). It also arises from the impossibility of finding adequate theological language for her ineffable experience of God.[132] The presence of the Holy Spirit on the road to Assisi renders Angela silent. It is only after his withdrawal that she begins to protest, in shouted and garbled words that are only later, and in ongoing conversation with her confessor, expanded into the self-explication that forms the basis of her *Memorial*. This piece of writing is the vehicle for Angela's self-understanding and transformation into authoritative spiritual mother. Writing becomes one of her spiritual practices in response to the incarnation; it preserves and transmits her theology of the incarnation; and it creates the body of a text to replicate the body of the beloved, Christ.[133]

[132] On Angela's self-conscious transgression of her own inability to speak, see Cristina Mazzoni, "On the (Un)Representability of Woman's Pleasure: Angela of Foligno and Jacques Lacan," in *Gender and Text in the Later Middle Ages*, ed. Jane Chance (Gainesville: University Press of Florida, 1996), esp. 250–51.

[133] This text would accompany, if not obviate, the forms of traumatic repetition through spiritual practices that Angela uses to induce bodily memories of Christ's suffering, which Amy Hollywood interprets, following Judith Butler and Freud, as a form of melancholic incorporation. *Sensible Ecstasy*, 260.

When Angela begins her spiritual journey, she "writes the body" through conventional spiritual practices that imitate Christ's suffering, but the body she is writing is not, strictly speaking, her own. With her own body she compensates for Christ's absence, making him present through imitation of his gestures, postures, and actions. *Imitatio* on the way of penance culminates on the way to Assisi, when she receives the grace of divine indwelling. Divine departure compels her into speech, the speech that occasions and eventually becomes Brother Arnaldo's writing. While Angela does not, as far as we can tell, physically write, at least in the beginning, she participates with Arnaldo in the construction of an artifact, going so far as to designate what size paper he should use, reviewing and approving (or not) his recording of her words, and obtaining God's signature on what, together, they have created. Angela begins writing the body of Christ by physically imitating him in his absence; her somatic "writing" is transformed through divine presence, and her silence into shouting, then speech, and then writing again, but this time of a different order—a writing that both records Angela's imitation of the body of Christ and writes it anew, incarnating it again in the text, just as Angela incarnates the Word in her own body, becoming divine in response to the incarnation. Like scripture, Angela's book both records and creates the community to whom it is addressed, beginning, as it does, with the community of Angela, Masazuola, and Arnaldo. In her teachings, Angela extended her understanding of the incarnation to this community, which remembers her in her absence, and to the entire Christian community, through the sacraments, the suffering of lepers, and beauty of creation, all of which, in her view, incarnate the divine.

Hadewijch's writings extend the incarnation to the body of Mary, the spiritual life of divinization, and to material dimension of poetic language, providing support for a view of theological writing as the spiritual practice of the incarnation. Angela, however, takes the incarnation personally. Her God became flesh in order to make her God. Because the word was made flesh, her flesh is poured out in words. The grace of insight that God dwells in her own body is coupled with the direct perception of God's presence elsewhere: in those who suffer, in the sacraments, in the beauty of creation. Writing emerges at a turning point in her life and, in the form of Brother Arnaldo's notes, provides the vehicle for her self-understanding. By shaping her spiritual life and establishing her authority, writing transmits her insights into the expansive graciousness of the incarnation—divine presence available to us in the multiple bodies and texts that love bears.

4

WRITING ANNIHILATION WITH
MARGUERITE PORETE

Near the end of Marguerite Porete's *Mirror of Simple Souls*,[1] the character Soul begins to sing. This song of love was found by the Soul; she calls it love's song, both in praise of and given by love.[2] The Soul fears that others may misunderstand her song because they are blinded by reason, but reason is surpassed by perfect love. Love sets the Soul free from imprisonment; love exalts, transforms, and unites her in being with divine love, and so she will love him, the lover finally named as the Holy Spirit. As the Soul nears the end of her song, she reflects:

> I have said that I shall love him.
> I lie, it is not I at all,
> But it is he alone who loves me:
> He is, and I am not . . .
> He is fullness,
> And from this I am full.
> This is the divine essence
> And love loyal.[3]

---

[1] All references are to the critical edition of Marguerite Porete, *Le mirouer des simples âmes / Speculum simplicium animarum*, ed. Romana Guarnieri and Paul Verdeyen; Corpus Christianorum Continuatio Mediaevalis 69 (Turnhout: Brepols, 1986), hereafter referred to as *Mirouer*, cited by chapter and page number. English translations are from *The Mirror of Simple Souls*, translated by Colledge et al., with modifications where noted.

[2] *Mirouer*, chap. 122, 342. "Amour m'a fait par noblece / Ces vers de chançon trouver." "Love caused me in her nobility to find the verses of this song." Translation modified.

[3] J'ay dit que je l'aymeray.

The Soul did not compose her song but merely found it.[4] She tells us she lies when she proclaims her love. And the "I" who sings, sings that she is not "I." Who is this singer? The content of the Soul's song belies the sound of her singing. The "I" is not "I": there is no songwriter, no lover, and no one to sing, simply a voice that paradoxically proclaims her own nonexistence. By the last lines of the verse, the "I" dissolves completely into the fullness of God.[5]

This final song in Porete's text encapsulates her doctrine of the soul's annihilation in love and the paradox it creates for writing and speech. Through annihilation of the will, the soul becomes nothing, but by becoming nothing, the soul returns to her origin in God, and so becomes everything. The annihilated soul does not compose songs, but love helps her find them. She no longer knows how to speak of God, for all telling, and even prayer, has been taken from her. Nor does she write books, and yet Porete produced a beautiful and complex work of mystical theology in her *Mirror*. Recognizable features of the self such as identity, authorial intent, and agency or will all dissipate in the annihilation of the soul. And yet through writing we hear a distinctive voice, singing the song of love.

———

Marguerite Porete was born in the middle of the thirteenth century and burned at the stake in Paris on June 1, 1310. Called a *pseudo-mulier* or "phony-woman" and a "beguine,"[6] but not associated with an institutional

---

Je mens, ce ne suis je mie.
C'est il seul qui ayme moy:
Il est, et je ne suis mie . . .
Il est plain,
Et de ce suis plaine
C'est le divin noyaulx
Et amour loyaulx. (*Mirouer*, ch. 122, 346; translation modified)

[4] "Finding" (*trouver*) songs was a common topos among the *trouvères*, meaning both "to find" and "to sing." Porete's writing is influenced by both *trouvère* lyrics and medieval French romance; see Barbara Newman, *From Virile Woman to WomanChrist: Studies in Medieval Religion and Literature* (Philadelphia: University of Pennsylvania Press, 1995), 137–67; and S. [Zan] Kocher, *Allegories of Love in Marguerite Porete's Mirror of Simple Souls* (Turnhout: Brepols, 2008), 60–69.

[5] Around 1300, the subject pronoun "je" was still grammatically optional (see Kocher, *Allegories of Love*, 186). Porete's choice of whether to write "je" in the context of union with God was surely deliberate.

[6] In light of the three possible denotations of "beguine" as "heretic," "devout Christian layperson," or "a member of a beguinage or beguine community," Kocher argues that inquisitors were using "beguine," circularly, in the first sense, and that Porete could be accurately described as a beguine in the second sense, but there is no documentary evidence for the third sense. Nor was Porete likely itinerant or mendicant, as she is sometimes described, since

beguinage, Porete was executed for writing and circulating a book judged as mystical heresy, the first documented case of such in the Christian West.[7] Porete was from the region of Hainault, and her book, *The Mirror of Simple Souls*, had been condemned and publicly burned in Valenciennes by the bishop of Cambrai sometime between 1296 and 1306. Porete, however, continued to copy, disseminate, and read aloud from her book. In 1308 she was arrested and sent to Paris, where she was tried by Guillaume Humbert, Dominican inquisitor and confessor to the king of France, Philip IV "the Fair." During the trial, she refused to cooperate with the inquisitors or even take the oath that would open the proceedings, her silence clearly indicating that she would not recant her teachings or even deign to respond to what her book calls "Holy Church the Little."[8] Instead, Guillaume Humbert extracted fifteen suspicious passages from her book, which he presented as propositions to a jury of twenty-one theologians assembled from the University of Paris. This jury unanimously declared the excerpts heretical; Porete was condemned as a relapsed heretic, handed over to the secular authorities, and executed by fire in the Place de Grève the next day. After her death, copies of her manuscript circulated anonymously; widely copied and translated, it was used in contemplative circles as a spiritual guidebook through the centuries.[9] It was only in 1946 that its author was identified and confirmed as the woman executed for heresy, Marguerite Porete.[10]

---

inquisitorial records document her possession of numerous books. See Kocher, *Allegories of Love*, 31, 37–38.

[7] See Bernard McGinn, *The Flowering of Mysticism: Men and Women in the New Mysticism (1200–1350)*, vol. 3 of *The Presence of God: A History of Western Christian Mysticism* (New York: Crossroad, 1998), 244. Her name was later linked to the so-called heresy of the Free Spirit after her death; see Robert E. Lerner, *The Heresy of the Free Spirit in the Later Middle Ages* (Los Angeles: University of California Press, 1972) and Herbert Grundmann, *Religious Movements in the Middle Ages: The Historical Links between Heresy, the Mendicant Orders, and the Women's Religious Movement in the Twelfth and Thirteenth Century, with the Historical Foundations of German Mysticism*, trans. Steven Rowan (Notre Dame, Ind.: University of Notre Dame Press, 1995).

[8] For details of Porete's encounters with ecclesiastical authority and subsequent trial, see Sean L. Field, *The Beguine, the Angel, and the Inquisitor: The Trials of Marguerite Porete and Guiard of Cressonessart* (Notre Dame, Ind.: Notre Dame University Press, 2012); and Paul Verdeyen, "Le Procès d'inquisition contre Marguerite Porete et Guiard de Cressonessart (1309–1310)," *Revue d'histoire ecclésiastique* 81 (1986): 47–94.

[9] On the manuscript tradition, see Kocher, *Allegories of Love*, 46–49. See also Ellen L. Babinsky's introduction to *Marguerite Porete: The Mirror of Simple Souls* (New York: Paulist Press, 1993); and Colledge, Marler, and Grant's introductory interpretive essay to Margaret Porette, *The Mirror of Simple Souls*.

[10] Romana Guarnieri, "Lo *Specchio delle anime semplici* e Margherita Poirette," *L'Osservatore Romano*, June 16, 1946, 3.

While readers are often tempted to look for the ways in which her book mirrors her life, Porete eschews talk of her own experience. Instead, the book is structured as an allegorical dialogue among the principal personified characters of Love, Soul, and Reason, all of whom are gendered female. With didactic intent, Porete has the three personified ladies discuss, debate, argue, and teach the soul's progress toward God through three deaths (to sin, nature, and spirit) and seven states of noble being that culminate in what Porete calls annihilation. Annihilation transforms the soul from being "lost" and "forlorn" into "freedom," "nobility," "simplicity," and "nakedness," in which the soul becomes one with God without distinction, a union of being through love. The character Soul is an abstraction and personification of all souls;[11] Lady Love speaks for God and instructs the Soul and the inscribed audiences of the text; and Reason appears as an antagonist, comically ignorant of the subtlety of Love's teaching and a model of how *not* to interpret the text through scholastic logic.[12] A wide variety of other characters such as Truth, Desire, and Graciousness arise and disappear without explanation. There is no setting, no dream-narrative that frames the allegory, no account of visionary experience, indeed, no bodies to these personified characters. The book begins with a parable of romantic love (derived from the *Roman d'Alexandre*) of a maiden for a king, which is immediately applied to divine love; it proceeds through dialogue and, in its midst, occasionally breaks into song. At the end of the book, the prose dissolves entirely into the songs of Truth, Holy Church, and the Holy Trinity, ending with the song of the Soul. The book is appended with a series of "considerations" or meditations on saints, divine attributes, and the soul's journey that are meant to assist those "whose state of being is forlorn, and who ask the way to the land of freedom"[13] (these were likely added by Porete after the first condemnation). The book is more obviously didactic in aim than the writings of Angela or even Hadewijch, in that it is meant to instruct the sad or forlorn in the path to freedom through annihilation in love, and Porete reaches for the widest possible audience in her efforts at instruction through literary techniques such as personification, allegory, and dialogue.

The contemporary French feminist philosopher Luce Irigaray provides a striking juxtaposition to Marguerite Porete. Rather than discovering resonance or likeness in their writings, however, this particular pairing

[11] See *Mirouer*, chap. 9.

[12] See Kocher, *Allegories of Love*, 6.

[13] "pour ceulx qui sont en l'estre des marriz, qui demandent la voye du pays de franchise." *Mirouer*, chap. 123, 348.

underscores difference, even dissonance. Luce Irigaray's philosophical and psychoanalytic writings examine women's status in the social and symbolic order, what she calls subjectivity. For Irigaray, not only is subjectivity constituted in language, but also it is primarily a matter of enunciation—that is, the ability to speak "I" to an other in a context of changing linguistic relationships.[14] The problem, according to Irigaray's reading of the history of philosophy and psychoanalysis, is that women have never been able to say "I" in a way that acknowledges their sexual difference. Taking up subjectivity in a patriarchal symbolic and political order requires identifying with the masculine generic, making oneself into a neutral, universal/masculine human subject, if not an object of masculine desire and exchange. Recognizing women's difference requires rethinking the relationship between sexed bodies and language, which, as Irigaray notes, is not simply a linguistic or psychoanalytic issue, but is equally a theological problem of word and flesh. The incarnation provides Irigaray a paradigm and a path for women to become divine.

Porete operates with a very different understanding of the incarnation, which the soul imitates not in flesh or word but through the annihilation of the will. Christ is the soul's exemplar in the movement of annihilation, which transforms the soul so that it becomes the place of love's incarnation in the world. The same annihilation that allows the soul to incarnate divine love, however, also appears to make ordinary, willful acts like writing a book seem tricky, if not impossible. Both Irigaray and Porete address the problem of writing in relation to the incarnation, but they do so in very different ways, with different interpretations of the incarnation and its implications for women.

In *The Mirror of Simple Souls*, we encounter a connection between writing and the incarnation that is distinctive from the writings of both Hadewijch and Angela. Hadewijch draws attention to the maternal origins of Christ's incarnation, the material aspects of language, and the effect of both of these on the spiritual life at the heart of her own writings, while Angela coproduces a book in response to the effect of the incarnation on her body and her speech. In contrast, Porete's writings are notable for their striking *lack* of attention to Christ's body or, for that matter, bodily phenomena in general. Scholars such as Amy Hollywood have noted the absence of bodies in the *Mirror*, in contrast to the excessive bodily phenomena displayed by other medieval women mystics.[15] Porete resists the popular women's

---

[14] This concern is especially evident in Irigaray's early work, such as *Parler n'est jamais neutre* (Paris: Minuit, 1985); see also Margaret Whitford, *Luce Irigaray: Philosophy in the Feminine* (New York: Routledge, 1991).

[15] See Amy Hollywood, "Suffering Transformed: Marguerite Porete, Meister Eckhart,

piety that embraced imitating Christ's bodily suffering as a path to sanctity.
Instead, she transfers the suffering of the body to the suffering, and eventual
annihilation, of the will, partly in order to free the body from the burden
of extreme asceticism, which she relegates to a lower stage of the spiritual
life.[16] But like her near contemporaries Hadewijch and Angela, Porete also
provides important resources for thinking about the incarnation inclusively
and for extending it theologically through spiritual practices. And like these
other medieval women writers, she helps us understand how writing can be
a way of practicing the incarnation, of writing the body of Christ, for Christ
remains central to Porete's teaching because he is the soul's mirror and exemplar. Like Christ, the soul sacrifices her will in a kenotic gesture. Through
the detachment and annihilation of the will, the soul is transformed into the
place of divine love. This transformed soul, which Porete represents as the
character Soul, sings (and writes) in her book from a place of detachment or,
as the *Mirror* puts it, "without a why." Juxtaposing Irigaray's feminist philosophy with Porete's mystical theology helps to underscore the uniqueness
of Porete's approach to both writing and the incarnation and to place these
diverse approaches, which both support an inclusive interpretation of the
incarnation, in relief. Here the differences are as illuminating as similarities.

Annihilation

The Mirror of Simple Souls teaches that souls, in this life, may return to
their primordial oneness with God through a process Porete calls *anéan-
tissement*, which translates as "being brought to nothing" or "annihilation."
In Porete's development of apophatic anthropology, the human will, a gift
of creation, is gradually stripped away to reveal the soul as "nothing" apart
from God, purely reflective of her divine origin, and willing only what God
wills.[17] Porete's teaching on the necessity of the soul's annihilation can strike
modern readers as difficult and even disturbing. It is especially poignant,
no doubt, because of the historical circumstances surrounding Porete's trial

and the Problem of Women's Spirituality," in *Meister Eckhart and the Beguine Mystics: Hadewijch of Brabant, Mechthild of Magdeburg, and Marguerite Porete*, ed. Bernard McGinn (New
York: Continuum, 1994), 87–113; and idem, *The Soul as Virgin Wife: Mechthild of Magdeburg, Marguerite Porete, and Meister Eckhart* (Notre Dame, Ind.: University of Notre Dame
Press, 1995).

[16] See *Mirouer*, chap. 9, 32.

[17] See Michael Sells, *Mystical Languages of Unsaying* (Chicago: University of Chicago
Press, 1994), chap. 5; see also Denys Turner, *The Darkness of God: Negativity in Christian
Mysticism* (Cambridge: Cambridge University Press, 1995), 139.

and execution, the burning of her book, and its continued circulation with her own name erased and forgotten. At first glance, these events appear to confirm the annihilation of Marguerite Porete.[18] Within the text, the "annihilation" of the feminine-gendered soul (following grammar and tradition, Porete personifies Soul as a lady) can be troubling from a feminist perspective, for some readers veering dangerously close to a stereotypical feminine masochism that affirms "He is, and I am not" as she sacrifices herself for a male God.[19] The coincidence between life and text makes it tempting to interpret Porete's execution as the inevitable conclusion to a self-destructive death wish, a will to self-annihilation through martyrdom. A careful examination of Porete's writings on annihilation, however, and its theological rootedness in both the doctrine of creation and in Christology can help to explain this subtle teaching and avoid misreading. It can further help us understand how a soul that is annihilated in the love of its creator can write a book. In the *Mirror*, annihilation is not destructive, but productive of writing and speech. Writing emerges from annihilation as the soul becomes the place in which God works and love is incarnate.

According to the *Mirror*, the annihilation of the soul takes place gradually through seven steps, stages, or states of being. Movement from one stage to the next occurs through divine grace, figured narratively and theologically in the text as Lady Love, the representative of God and guide of the soul.[20] This process consists of two movements that together annihilate and transform the soul. First, what we might call renunciation or detachment: the soul renounces or detaches from her practices, good works, affections, and desires, including ultimately her desire for God. This movement that Porete calls annihilation (and Eckhart will call detachment) strips the soul of its creaturely accretions as the soul is increasingly oriented toward God and

[18] See Michael G. Sargent, "The Annihilation of Marguerite Porete," *Viator* 28 (1997): 253–79.

[19] A. C. Spearing, "Marguerite Porete: Courtliness and Transcendence in *The Mirror of Simple Souls*," in *Envisaging Heaven in the Middle Ages*, ed. Carolyn Muessig and Ad Putter (New York: Routledge, 2009), 120–36. On the problematics of "annihilation" for feminist theology, see the roundtable discussion of Mary Potter Engel, Carol P. Christ, et al., "Mysticism and Feminist Spirituality," *Journal of Feminist Studies in Religion* 24, no. 2 (2008): 143–87.

[20] "Je suis Dieu, dit Amour, car Amour est Dieu, et Dieu est amour, et ceste Ame est Dieu par condicion d'amour." ("I am God, says Love, for Love is God, and God is Love, and this Soul is God through its condition of Love.") *Mirouer*, chap. 21, 82. Like many vernacular writers of the thirteenth century, Porete refuses a distinction between worldly love and divine love, or between eros and agape, in naming God "Lady Love." See Newman, *From Virile Woman*, 137–67.

transformed on the model of its exemplar, Christ. Second, transformation: in a process of divinization that Porete describes as *muance d'amour*, the transformation or transmutation of, in, by, and through love,[21] Lady Love enlarges the capacity of the soul to love God for God, "without herself"—that is, without what we might call her own ego getting in the way. Love is both the initiator or source of this transformation and its destination as Love transforms the soul into herself. Through annihilation of the will on the model of Christ, the soul is transformed and divinized in love.

In chapter 118, Porete gives her most complete account of the soul's journey to God through seven stages. In the first, the soul renounces sin, lives a virtuous life, and obeys God's commands. This is the life of the ordinary Christian. It is sufficient for salvation, but it is only the beginning of the process of annihilation through the detachment of the will. In the second stage, the soul renounces the desires of her body through the imitation of Christ. This is the life of the popular women's piety that surrounded Porete, in which the flesh was mortified through voluntary poverty, fasting, celibacy, vigils, and acts of charity. In the third stage, the soul realizes that she has grown too attached to these good works, which have only strengthened her will. She continues the process of detachment by renouncing the works that she loves so much and offering them to her beloved. By sacrificing the good works that once gave her pleasure, she further detaches from her desires and begins to annihilate her will—not just her inclination to sin but her will as created by God. When the soul gives up these works out of love of God, she is drawn by love into the fourth stage: joyous ecstasy. The soul becomes inebriated and swims in a sea of divine love. She thinks she has reached the summit of her journey: what could be better than ecstatic love? But union with God through mutual love is still a union of wills; the soul, in effect, loves herself loving as much as she loves God. Porete claims that at this stage the soul is "deceived" and must renounce even the joys of ecstasy.[22]

Renunciation and detachment from love catapult the soul from the pinnacle of ecstasy into an abyss of nothingness. This fall, the fifth stage, is

---

[21] *Muance* (or *mutatio* in the Latin translation) is Porete's favored term for divinization. See, e.g., *Mirouer*, chap. 117, 316: "Et puisque j'ay toute sa bonté," Soul claims, "donc suis je ce mesmes qu'il est, par muance d'amour. Car le plus fort mue en luy le plus foible. Ceste muance est moult delicieuse, ce scevent ceulx qui essayé l'ont." ("And since I have all his goodness, I am therefore what he is, through the transmutation of love. For the stronger changes the weaker into himself. This transmutation is all delight, as those who have experienced it know.") Cf. chaps. 39, 110, and 115.

[22] *Mirouer*, chap. 118, 324.

initiated by a dual recognition: the soul considers carefully "that God is he who is, of whom all things are, and that she is not, and that it is not from her that all things are."[23] God is all and she is nothing, in relation to God. The perception of her own nothingness is metaphysical; she recognizes her utter dependence on God, who created her out of nothing. But it is also moral: she perceives her sinfulness through the misuse of her will in a way contrary to God's will. She therefore gives up her will and returns it to God: "And so the Soul abandons this Will and the Will abandons this Soul, and then returns and surrenders and submits to God, there whence it was first derived, without keeping back anything of its own, in order to fulfill the perfect divine will which, unless such a gift is made, cannot be fulfilled in the Soul without the Soul's experiencing conflict or deprivation."[24] By renouncing her will, the soul annihilates that which separated her from God in creation. Her gift fulfills the divine will, erases all conflict and deprivation, perfects and frees her, and transforms her into divine love. She is "wholly at rest" and "in possession of her own state of free being."[25] Annihilation of the will is not violent or painful for the soul, but a gentle transformation into freedom, love, and equanimity.[26] The soul now rests in an abyss of nothingness, whence she sees that God is everything.

If the fifth stage describes annihilation from the soul's perspective, the sixth stage shifts to God's perspective.[27] Here the soul no longer sees at all:

> The Soul does not see herself at all, whatever the abyss of humility she has within herself, nor does she see God, whatever the exalted goodness he has. But God of his divine majesty sees himself in her, and by him this Soul is so illumined that she cannot see that anyone exists, except only God himself; and so she sees nothing

---

[23] "Le quint estat est que l'Ame regarde que Dieu est, qui est dont toute chose est, et elle n'est mie, si ne'est dont toute chose est." *Mirouer*, chap. 118, 324.

[24] "Et pource se despart l'Ame de ce vouloir, et le vouloir se despart de telle Ame, et adonc se remect et donne et rent a Dieu, la ou il fut premierement prins, sans rien propre de luy retenir, pour emplir la parfaicte voulenté divine, laquelle ne peut estre emplie en l'Ame sans tel don, que l'Ame n'ayt ou guerre ou deffaillance." *Mirouer*, chap. 118, 326.

[25] "et pource est elle toute en repos, et de franc estre mise en possession, qui la repouse par excellente noblesse de toutes choses." *Mirouer*, chap. 118, 330.

[26] Porete's doctrine of annihilation contrasts with those of John of the Cross and her near-contemporary Mechthild of Magdeburg, for both of whom annihilation is at times painful, even violent. See John of the Cross, *The Dark Night of the Soul*, trans. E. Allison Peers (New York: Doubleday, 1990); Mechthild of Magdeburg, *The Flowing Light of the Godhead*, trans. Frank Tobin (New York: Paulist Press, 1998).

[27] See Bernard McGinn's comparison of this passage to Meister Eckhart, who writes in German sermon 12, "the eye in which I see God is the same eye in which God sees me." *Flowering*, 259–60.

except herself, for whoever sees that which is sees nothing except God himself, who sees himself in this very Soul by his divine majesty. . . . But this Soul, thus pure and illumined, sees neither God nor herself, but God sees himself of himself in her, for her, without her, who—that is, God—shows to her that there is nothing except him.[28]

By annihilating everything that separated her from her divine origin, the soul is completely transformed into God through love.[29] There is nothing but God, and God is nothing but love. The previous five states take the soul by grace through a process of detachment and transformation, a kind of apophatic polishing in which everything that separates the soul from God is stripped away. The soul is confirmed in the fifth stage of detachment, from which she does not fall. But from time to time, the soul is caught up into the sixth stage, a momentary manifestation of life after death (stage seven), in a flash of glory by which she becomes free and "clarifiée" or illumined, purely reflective of the divine.[30] In these moments, she becomes the mirror of God: she no longer sees God nor herself, but God sees himself in her, without her. By becoming nothing in nondual union with God, she also becomes everything: "she cannot see that anyone exists, except only God himself; and so she sees nothing except herself."

The transition from one stage to the next is led by grace, figured in the narrative by Lady Love, but it is also driven by a certain restlessness or

---

[28] "Le siziesme estat est, que l'Ame ne se voit point, pour quelconque abysme d'umilité que elle ait en elle; ne Dieu, pour quelconque haultiesme bonté qu'il ait. Mais Dieu se voit en elle de sa majesté divine, qui clarifie de luy ceste Ame, si que elle ne voit que nul soit, fors Dieu mesmes, qui est, dont toute chose est; et ce qui est, c'est Dieu mesmes; et pource ne voit elle sinon elle mesmes; car qui voit ce qui est, il ne voit fors Dieu mesmes, qui se voit en ceste Ame mesmes, de sa majesté divine. Et adonc est l'Ame ou siziesme estat de toutes choses enfranchie et pure et clariffiee,—et non mie glorifiee; car le glorifiement est ou septiesme estat, que nous aurons en gloire, dont nul ne sçait parler. Mais ceste Ame, ainsi pure et clariffiee, ne voit ne Dieu ne elle, mais Dieu se voit de luy en elle, pour elle, sans elle; lequel (c'est assavoir Dieu) luy monstre, que il n'est fors que lui." *Mirouer*, chap. 118, 330.

[29] On Porete's doctrine of the virtual existence of the soul within the Trinity prior to creation, see Joanne Maguire Robinson, *Nobility and Annihilation in Marguerite Porete's Mirror of Simple Souls* (Albany: SUNY Press, 2001), 52–66. Meister Eckhart has a similar account of the "poverty of the will" as a return to the soul's precreated oneness with God; see especially "Sermon 52: Beati pauperes spiritu," in Meister Eckhart, *The Essential Sermons, Commentaries, Treatises, and Defense*, trans. Edmund Colledge and Bernard McGinn (Mahweh, N.J.: Paulist Press, 1981).

[30] See *Mirouer*, chap. 61, 176, 178: "et le siziesme est glorieux car l'ouverture du doulx mouvement de gloire, que le gentil Loingprés donne, n'est aultre chose que une apparicion, que Dieu veult que l'Ame ait de sa gloire mesmes, que elle aura sans fin . . . Laquelle demonstrance est si tost donnee, que celle mesmes, a qui ce est donné, n'a de son don, qui est donné,

dissatisfaction in the soul who only wants to love God more completely, and so the process is assisted by meditative spiritual exercises. These "considerations" (*regars*) are offered in the final chapters of the book for the benefit of the sad souls who wish to become free and noble through annihilation. Through dialectical considerations of God in relation to herself and the *demandes d'amour*, in which God asks the soul to sacrifice her love for God, the soul's "wits failed,"[31] her "will is martyred,"[32] and she is brought to nothing[33] in union with God:

> She is all his, never knowing how, and when she is one with him she is nothing. Then she has no more to do for God than God has to do for her. Why? Because he is, and she is not. When she has become nothing, she has kept nothing of herself, for this is enough for her, that he is and she is not. Then she is stripped naked of all things, for now she is without being, there where she had being before she might be. And so she has what she has from God, and she is that which God is, through the transmutation of love, there at the point where she was before she could flow forth from the goodness of God.[34]

Annihilation is a difficult teaching, and Porete's love of paradoxical language and pushing logic to extremes—beyond the rational discourse

---

nulle apparcevance." ("The sixth is glorious, for the opening of the sweet movement of glory, which the noble Far-Near gives, is nothing else than a manifestation which God wishes the Soul to have of her own glory which she will have forever . . . This manifestation is given so swiftly that the very one to whom it is given has no perception of the gift which is given to her.") These openings are called pledges given by the noble Far-Near (*Loingprés*). Porete describes the mysterious Far-Near as a manifestation of the Trinity, both immanent and transcendent, who conveys pledges of betrothal to the soul through flashes of glory.

[31] "et adonc me faillit le sens, et ne sceu que respondre, ne que vouloir, ne que escondire." *Mirouer*, chap. 131, 384.

[32] "et pource est mon vouloir martir, et mon amour martire: vous les avez a martire amenez." *Mirouer*, chap. 131, 388.

[33] "Adonc, je respondi tantoust que j'estoie pur nient." ("and so I answered at once that I was pure nothingness.") *Mirouer*, chap. 132, 390.

[34] There is a lacuna in the Middle French (Chantilly, Musée Condé ms. F xiv 26) manuscript on which Guarnieri bases her translation, from chapters 134–37. These missing passages are preserved in the Latin and Middle English copies and are included in Guarnieri and Verdeyen's edition. "Totum est sibi unum sine propter quid, et est nulla in tali uno. Tunc nichil habet plus facere de Deo quam Deus de ea. Quare? Quia Ipse est et ipsa non est. Ipsa nichil plus retinuit in nichilo sui ipsius, quia istud est sibi satis, scilicet quod Ipse est et ipsa non est. Tunc est omnibus rebus nuda, quia ipsa est sine esse, ubi ipsa erat, antequam esset. Et ideo habet a Deo id quod habet; et est id quod Deus est per mutationem amoris, in illo puncto in quo erat, antequam a Dei bonitate fluxisset." *Mirouer*, chap. 135, 396–97. This passage resonates with Beverly Lanzetta's description of the apophasis of woman, or the "dark night of the feminine," in *Radical Wisdom: A Feminist Mystical Theology* (Minneapolis: Fortress, 2005), 119–36.

represented by Reason—does not make it any more palatable. Rather than reading her as advocating a rejection of the goodness of the body, the will, or nature, or as self-destructive or masochistic, however, annihilation can be better understood in relation to two fundamental Christian doctrines: creation and Christ.

Christ and Creation

Following Thomas Aquinas, one might view the will as a created source of intellectual and affective motion that draws the human being back to her creator. Original sin corrupts the original justice of the subordination of the human will to God's will; as the will turns toward mutable goods rather than the Good for which it was created, it is characterized by what Thomas calls concupiscence or disordered craving.[35] The human desire for the good is diminished by sin but it is not destroyed. Oriented once again in the right direction, the will finds its completion in the presence of God. The will is then no longer exercised—in Porete's phrase, it "wills nothing"—because it comes to rest in the beatitude for which it was created. By willing nothing *other than God*, the soul exercises the will in the proper capacity for which it was created, and so returns her will to its source. The soul annihilates the difference between God and herself through a loving union of wills.

But Porete goes further than Thomas. The will is not only the source of the movement of love that draws her, a created being, back to God. It is also the marker of her ontological difference from God and thus her perceived estrangement from him. The problem with the will is not that it too often wills the wrong object in an inordinate manner, but the fact that it separates her from her beloved in creation. In Porete's uncompromising account, even her love for God merely strengthens her will, and thereby separates her further from the one she loves. To become truly one without any difference between the two, the soul must annihilate the will itself and recognize her own nothingness—but without rejecting the goodness of God's creation. What is required is what Meister Eckhart calls the virtue of "detachment" (*abegescheidenheit*) and what Simone Weil calls "decreation": a radical shift in perspective that reorients the soul back toward creation, properly viewed from the perspective of God's love.[36] In Porete's own terms, the annihilated

[35] Thomas Aquinas, *Summa Theologica* I–II q.1–3 and q.82.
[36] See Meister Eckhart, "On Detachment," in *The Essential Sermons, Commentaries, Treatises, and Defense*, trans. Edmund Colledge, O.S.A. and Bernard McGinn (Mahwah, N.J.: Paulist Press, 1981), 285–94. On Weil, see J. P. Little, "Simone Weil's Concept of Decreation," in *Simone Weil's Philosophy of Culture: Readings toward a Divine Humanity*,

soul acts effortlessly "without a why" and "without herself" getting in the way. Such reorientation to creation is made possible by the *muance d'amour*, the transformation into love that brings awareness of the soul's fundamental oneness with God.

Bernard McGinn notes how previous Christian mystical itineraries were mainly christological in that Christ provided both the path and the goal of union.[37] At first glance, Porete stands apart from this tradition: there are scant references to Christ in her book; he is not mentioned in the seven-stage itinerary; and her theology as a whole is much more theocentric than christocentric. The suffering Christ is not held up for meditation, as with Angela and Hadewijch; if anything, Porete rejects and subverts contemporary religious practices imitating the suffering of Christ's body through her emphasis on the will.[38] Nor does Porete use the traditional bridal imagery of Song of Songs to describe Christ as her bridegroom (instead, her beloved is the Holy Spirit or the entire Trinity).[39] And yet she discusses Christ in over twenty chapters of her book and she explicitly names him as her exemplar in annihilation. In chapter 109, she writes,

> The Son of God the Father is my mirror in this: for God the Father gave us his Son, to save us. In giving this to us he had no other concern than that alone of our salvation. And the Son redeemed us by dying, paying obedience to his Father. He had no other concern in doing this than only the will of God his Father. And the Son of God is our exemplar, and so we must follow him in this regard, for in all things we must will only the divine will; and thus we shall be the sons of God the Father, after the example of Jesus Christ his Son.[40]

---

ed. Richard H. Bell (Cambridge: Cambridge University Press, 1993), 25–51; and Simone Weil, *First and Last Notebooks*, trans. Richard Rees (New York: Oxford University Press, 1970), 120, 297. See also Anne Carson, *Decreation: Poetry, Essays, Opera* (New York: Vintage, 2005), who fruitfully reads Porete together with Weil and Sappho.

[37] McGinn, *Flowering*, 260.

[38] See Danielle Dubois, "Spiritual Practice and Learned Traditions in Marguerite Porete's *Mirouer des simples ames*" (Ph.D. diss., Johns Hopkins University, 2012).

[39] See *Mirouer* chaps. 68, 96, 115, and 122.

[40] "Le Filz de Dieu le Pere est mon mirouer de ce; car Dieu le Pere nous donna son Filz, en nous sauvant. Il n'eut nul aultre regart, en ce don donnant a nous, que le regart de nostre salut tant seulement. Et le Filz nous racheta en mourant, en l'obedience de son Pere faisant. Il n'eut aultre regart, en ce faisant, que la voulenté de Dieu son Pere tant seulement. Et le Filz de Dieu est exemple de nous, et pource le devons nous en ce regart ensuir, car nous devon vouloir en toutes choses tant seulement la divine voulenté; et ainsi serions nous filz de Dieu le Pere, a l'exemple de Jhesucrist son filz." *Mirouer*, chap. 109, 298. See also chap. 117.

Christ is the first manifestation and the model of annihilation: self-emptying (kenotic) descent into nothingness and sin as the expression of the goodness and love of God.[41] In this framework, Christ brings redemption not (only) by his ontological union with humanity or by his death on the cross, but by the obedience of his will to the Father. By relinquishing his own will, he becomes the exemplar of every creature, who, according to Porete, is likewise called to give up or annihilate the will that separates her from God. Christ's atonement does not substitute for the individual; instead, each soul can and must repeat Christ's gesture of annihilation for herself out of her love for God. By willing only the divine will with Christ as her mirror, the soul likewise becomes a son of God the Father.[42] The implications for Porete's understanding of the incarnation are rather startling.

[41] See Robin O'Sullivan, "Model, Mirror, and Memorial: Imitation of the Passion and the Annihilation of the Imagination in Angela da Foligno's *Liber* and Marguerite Porete's *Mirouer des simples âmes*" (Ph.D. diss., University of Chicago Divinity School, 2002); Ellen Babinsky, "Christological Transformation in *The Mirror of Souls*, by Marguerite Porete," *Theology Today* 60 (2003): 34–38; Bernard McGinn, "Suffering, Emptiness and Annihilation in Three Beguine Mystics," in *Homo Medietas: Aufsätze zu Religiosität, Literatur und Denkformen des Menschen vom Mittelalter bis in die Neuzeit*, ed. Claudia Brinker-von der Heyde and Niklaus Largier (Bern: Peter Lang, 1998), 155–74; McGinn, *Flowering*, 255–61; and Hollywood, "Suffering Transformed ," 108, who also finds a radical (but disembodied) incarnational theology in Porete, read together with Meister Eckhart: "Throughout these mystical movements, the role of the body, so central in thirteenth-century depictions of female sanctity, is consistently downplayed. Yet . . . Porete and Eckhart are radically incarnational in that the divine works in and through the soul who has become detached. Such souls embody Christ insofar as annihilation and the birth of the Son occur within them. This language is, of course, problematized by both Porete and Eckhart, for the detachment of such souls is so great that they have no 'place' within which God works, but rather the divine works in himself. Properly understood, however, these claims underline the radically incarnational tendencies of their thought, for it is insofar as God or the Trinity works in his/her own ground that divine action is manifest upon earth."

[42] See also chapter 128, in which Porete reiterates the model of the soul's annihilation in her consideration of the humanity of Jesus Christ: "no-one will ascend [to heaven] except him alone who descended from Heaven, that is the Son of God himself. That is to say that no-one can ascend there except only those who are sons of God by divine grace. And therefore Jesus Christ himself says that 'He is my brother, my sister and my mother who does the will of God my Father.'" ("C'est a entendre, que nul n'y peut monter, sinon seulement ceulx qui sont filz de Dieu par divine grace. Et pource dit Jhesucrist mesmes que cil est mon frere, ma seur, et ma mere, qui fait voulenté de Dieu mon pere.") *Mirouer*, chaps. 128, 370. Here Porete relies on her interpretation of several key New Testament passages, which she combines: "No one has ascended into heaven except the one who descended from heaven, the Son of Man" (John 3:13) and "For whoever does the will of my Father in heaven is my brother and sister and mother" (Matt 12:50). Porete proposes that the soul becomes the sister of

Instead of *imitating* Christ, the annihilated soul *becomes* Christ. As the place in which Love/God works, without herself and without a why, she becomes the son of "God the Father, after the example of Jesus Christ his Son." God is incarnate in every annihilated soul as Love transforms the soul into herself. This radical interpretation of the incarnation becomes much more explicit in the writings of Meister Eckhart, who claims that the soul should be united with the Father just as the Son is united with him and that the birth of the Son takes place within the ground of the soul, but it is equally present in Porete (indeed, he may have learned it from her book).[43] The question remains of the effect this form of the incarnation has on the body and its actions in the world.

Effects of Annihilation

The movement of annihilation through detachment and transformation in love takes Christ as its exemplar and makes the soul into the place of love's incarnation. But the soul's journey remains relatively abstract and seemingly disembodied. The absence of bodies and bodily phenomena in the *Mirror* stands in contrast to the excessive bodily phenomena displayed by other medieval women mystics. Unlike Angela of Foligno, Porete gives little indication of what happens to the body in her itinerary. Nor, like Hadewijch, does she employ sensory metaphors for the movements of the soul. The personified characters of the allegorical dialogue speak in a nebulous setting devoid of space and time as the action takes place within the soul. As the soul moves through the seven stages of annihilation, the created world fades from view. Ordinary Christian life is insufficient, and masses, sacraments, prayers, and good works are renounced, leaving the soul "naked" and "nothing." The body of Christ, central to medieval Christian piety, seems largely absent from the *Mirror*. The only materiality obviously present is that of the text itself.

But one implication of Porete's teaching on annihilation is a remarkably positive attitude toward the body. She rejects physical suffering in service to the virtues,[44] and she acknowledges the ordinary needs of the body,

---

Christ and Christ herself by giving up her will on the model of Christ. Only by "descending" through annihilation can the soul, like Christ, return to her precreated oneness with God.

[43] See Amy Hollywood, "Preaching as Social Practice in Meister Eckhart," in *Mysticism and Social Transformation*, ed. Janet Ruffing (Syracuse, N.Y.: Syracuse University Press, 2001), 83–84; and McGinn, ed., *Meister Eckhart and the Beguine Mystics*.

[44] See Hollywood, "Suffering Transformed," 87–113; and idem, *Soul as Virgin Wife*, 87–119.

encompassed in what she calls "Nature."[45] Once the soul has been transformed in love, she can, famously, "grant to Nature all that it requires, with no qualm of conscience." Extracted as a "proposition," this teaching worried Porete's inquisitors, but it is clear she is not endorsing antinomianism, which would be the result of a proud and selfish will. Rather, the annihilation of the will, the source of human sin,[46] results in a more immediate, more honest, and ultimately more loving relation to the human body and the created world. As Porete explains, "this Nature is so well ordered through having been transformed in the union with Love . . . that it never asks anything which is forbidden." Her acknowledgment of the legitimate demands of human "nature" (food, shelter, security?) and her rejection of excessive physical suffering indicate the benign, if underrecognized, presence of the body in the soul's progress. At times, Porete goes so far as to include the body in the transformation of the soul, healed of its physical weakness by the rays of the true Sun.[47] There is no Cartesian dualism here; rather, in many cases Porete uses the term "Soul" metonymically to refer to the whole person, as in, for example, "the Soul who had this book written." The will (not the body) is the principal obstacle to union with God, and so Porete primarily focuses on the soul as the site of the will.

Nor is Porete an otherworldly thinker. References by Love to the transformed soul dwelling in the "sweet land of complete peace"[48] indicate Porete's vision of heaven on earth in the equanimity of the soul. Rather than transcending the created world and leaving it behind, annihilation reorients the

---

[45] See *Mirouer*, chap. 9, 32: "Laquelle Ame ne desire ne ne desprise pouvreté ne tribulation, ne messe ne sermon, ne jeune ne oraison, et donne a Nature tout ce qu'il luy fault, sans remors de conscience; mais telle nature est si bien ordonnee par transformacion de unité d'Amour, a laquelle la voulenté de ceste Ame est conjoincte, que la nature ne demande chose qui soit deffendue." ("This Soul neither longs for nor despises poverty or tribulation, Mass or sermon, fasting or prayer; and gives to Nature all that it requires, with no qualm of conscience; but this Nature is so well ordered through having been transformed in the union with Love, to whom this Soul's will is joined, that it never asks anything which is forbidden.") Similar claims are repeated in chapters 13 and 17.

[46] McGinn notes Porete's redefinition of sin as any use of the will removed from God; see McGinn, "Suffering, Emptiness, and Annihilation," 171.

[47] To support this assertion, she makes explicit reference to the healing miracles of the gospels: "Et quant tel soleil est en l'ame, et tel raiz et telz resplendisseurs, le corps n'a plus foiblece, ne l'ame crainte; car le vrai Soleil de Justice ne sana ne garit oncques ame sans garir le corps, quant il faisoit ses miracles en terre." ("When such a sun is in the soul, and such rays and such resplendence, the body has no more weakness and the soul no more fear, for never did the true Sun of Justice heal or cure any soul without curing its body, when he performed his miracles on earth.") *Mirouer*, chap. 78, 220.

[48] *Mirouer*, chaps. 52 and 81.

soul back to this life, this world.[49] But annihilation does result in a remark-able spiritual freedom with respect to the world. Once the will is annihilated, the desires that would make God and others into objects of her own longing are gone. The soul is no longer enslaved to her worst impulses. She is now free and noble,[50] liberated not only from burdensome spiritual practices but also from her desires, including even her desire for God.[51]

In the process of annihilation, the soul realizes her own ontological and moral nothingness: she is utterly dependent on God for her being and for her goodness. Such recognition is an annihilation of the ego: she is no-thing, no-self, apart from God.[52] However, in Porete's account, annihilation is not an end in itself. Detachment from the will and transformation into love together reorient the soul back toward the created world. Because the soul has given up her own selfish desires, she can at last love creation as God loves it and love others as they are loved by God. Instead of acting out of her own inter-ests, "with herself," she can love more fully, "without herself."[53] The result is liberation—she is "free" and "naked"—through which the annihilated soul can, for the first time, directly engage the created world free of attachment.

The effect of annihilation is a renewed understanding and appreciation for the active life. Porete views the body, nature, and creation largely posi-tively. Because of this positive—but detached—orientation, free and anni-hilated souls do not rest in quietism (another worry of inquisitors). Instead, they turn back toward the world, engaging fully in the work of teaching and preaching.[54] As Porete puts it, "these souls could govern a country if it were

[49] See Spearing, "Marguerite Porete," 126.

[50] On Porete's use of the language of nobility and the allegory of social rank, see Kocher, *Allegories of Love*, 107–25.

[51] The *demandes d'amour* in chapter 131 describe a vertiginous freedom from desire, including the desire to make God into an object of desire.

[52] In this, Porete's "annihilation" and "without herself" are strikingly similar to Bud-dhist teaching of anatta/anatman, no soul or no self. But whereas the Buddhist teaching is rooted in the metaphysics of interbeing, including the causes and conditions that together form the self, Porete's Christian view of no-self or annihilation is grounded in an Augustin-ian doctrine of creation, in which everything that exists is utterly dependent upon God for its existence.

[53] See Emilie Zum Brunn, "Self, Not-Self, and the Ultimate in Marguerite Porete's 'Mirror of Annihilated Souls,'" in *God, the Self, and Nothingness: Reflections Eastern and Western*, ed. Robert E. Carter (New York: Paragon House, 1990), 83.

[54] What we know of Porete's life and her persistence in copying, disseminating, and reading aloud from her book, even after its condemnation by her bishop, supports this view of an active life of writing and teaching very much in the world and for a wide and diverse audience. See Kocher, *Allegories of Love*, 29–34 and 49–53.

needed, but it would be without themselves."[55] This view of the active life, infused by contemplative union with Love/God, fully engaged in the world but "without herself," has important implications for the writing of her book.

The Speculum of *La Mystérique*

Porete presents her book as a "mirror" of simple souls, a title that announces both its aim to reflect and instruct and that it will require the audience's active interpretation.[56] Nearly seven hundred years later, another woman living in France wrote a book and called it a mirror: the *Speculum of the Other Woman*.[57] Luce Irigaray's philosophical and psychoanalytic work reads the history of philosophy from Freud, in reverse chronological order, back to Plato. In the middle of the book is a collection of essays again called "Speculum," and at the heart of this section, a mirror within a mirror, Irigaray reflects (on) the writings of medieval mystics in a chapter called "La Mystérique." The chapter opens with quotations from Ruusbroec, Eckhart, and Angela of Foligno, and contains allusions to Mechthild of Magdeburg, Hadewijch, Teresa of Avila, and Catherine of Siena. "La Mystérique" is situated as the central chapter of the book, and it repeats the mirror imagery of the larger work.[58]

Irigaray opens the chapter with the claim that mysticism "is the only place in the history of the West in which woman speaks and acts so publicly."[59] Her claim is perhaps exaggerated, but not by much. As many scholars have shown, women were prominent contributors to the flowering of late medieval mysticism, as seen not only in the paramystical bodily phenomena and miracles recorded in vitae but especially in the number of books of theology and spirituality written by their own hands. In these texts, spoken and

---

[55] *Mirouer*, chap. 58; see also chap. 81; and Zum Brunn, "Self, Not-Self," 87.

[56] On the use of "mirror" in this title and its precedents, see Kocher, *Allegories of Love*, 8–10; McGinn, *Flowering*, 247; and Herbert Grabes, *The Mutable Glass: Mirror Imagery in Titles and Texts of the Middle Ages and English Renaissance* (Cambridge: Cambridge University Press, 1982).

[57] Luce Irigaray, *Speculum de l'autre femme* (Paris: Éditions de Minuit, 1974). Future references are to the English edition, *Speculum of the Other Woman*, trans. Gillian C. Gill (Ithaca, N.Y.: Cornell University Press, 1985).

[58] See Philippa Berry, "The Burning Glass: Paradoxes of Feminist Revelation in *Speculum*," in *Engaging with Luce Irigaray*, ed. Carolyn Burke, Naomi Schor, and Margaret Whitford (New York: Columbia University Press, 1994), 235. Irigaray herself claims to have read "many mystics," but Porete was not among them. Irigaray, in discussion with author, June 23, 2006.

[59] Irigaray, *Speculum*, 191.

written by women, Irigaray finds a mystical alternative to the "dry desolation of reason," a place where "subject" and "Other" mingle and embrace, where *jouissance* flourishes, and where language and subjectivity are interrogated, annihilated, and reconfigured.[60] "La mystérique" (in which one can also hear "l'âme hystérique," an allusion to the psychoanalytic conflation of hysteria with mysticism) is culturally coded as feminine: the soul is grammatically feminine; women were associated (by men) with both mysticism and hysteria; and, most importantly for Irigaray, mystical speech and writing present an alternative discourse to the predominantly male philosophical tradition of reason. Here Irigaray discovers and mimics the mystical speech and writing preeminently associated with women in the Middle Ages.

According to Irigaray, this outpouring of public speech was made possible by the mystic's identification with the body of Christ through the incarnation and crucifixion.[61] The wounded body of Christ provides a divine mirror of the female sex, whose morphology is otherwise unrepresentable in the categories of male-authored psychoanalysis and philosophy. When the mystic gazes upon the body of Christ, Irigaray claims that she equally sees and loves herself: "In this way, you see me and I see you, finally I see myself seeing you in this fathomless wound which is the source of our wondering comprehension and exhilaration. And to know myself I scarcely need a 'soul,' I have only to gaze upon the gaping space in your loving body."[62] When Irigaray discusses the divine mirroring between God or Christ and the feminine soul or woman mystic, her writing shifts to first person and the subject "I" appears.[63] According to her reading of the history of Western thought, at this particular moment in European history, symbolic identification between

---

[60] Irigaray, *Speculum*, 191–92.

[61] Thinking perhaps of Angela of Foligno, she writes, "one man, at least, has understood her so well that he died in the most awful suffering. That most female of men, the Son. And she never ceases to look upon his nakedness, open for all to see, upon the gashes in his virgin flesh, at the wounds from the nails that pierce his body as he hangs there, in his passion and abandonment. And she is overwhelmed with love of him/herself." Irigaray, *Speculum*, 199–200.

[62] Irigaray, *Speculum*, 200.

[63] Cf. Irigaray, *Speculum*, 197: "What if everything were already so intimately specularized that even in the depths of the abyss of the 'soul' a mirror awaited her reflection and her light. Thus I have become your image in this nothingness that I am, and you gaze upon mine in your absence of being . . . A living mirror, thus, am I (to) your resemblance as you are mine." Irigaray is also alluding to Lacan's discussion of the mirror stage and retrieving an alternative possibility of subjectivity, or the formation of the "I," through a mirror that could reflect feminine specificity. Irigaray suggests that a concave mirror might provide a better representation of the ego-ideal for women in sexual difference.

women and Christ opened a space for women's public speech and writing, or what she might describe as their subjectivity. When women identified themselves with Christ, seeing in his wounded, bleeding flesh that is broken and eaten a mirror of their own bodies that bleed and birth and feed, their flesh was transformed into word in mystical discourse, writing and speech.

Irigaray's multiple references to mirrors, descent, and the nothingness and nakedness of the soul point past the epigraphs opening her chapter to her predecessor, Marguerite Porete. Both *Speculum*s are attempts to write what escapes representation within ordinary discourse: for Irigaray, women's difference; for Porete, the soul's union with God.[64] For each writer, Christ figures as a mirror, model, and exemplar for the feminine-gendered soul and love provides the path to transformation—although, it must be noted, they are working with very different theologies of the incarnation (to which I return later). Reflections between the two mirrors are most striking in the form of writing each author uses to convey her teaching. Irigaray's method, informed by both poststructuralism and psychoanalysis, uses mimicry to engage with the texts she reads and to uncover hidden assumptions and operations of the feminine or the maternal in philosophical texts. "La Mystérique" is one of her few essays on the writings of women, and in it, mimicry takes the form of homage, celebrating a (circumscribed and relatively constrained) space for women's voices in the Western written tradition. Irigaray's writing style repeats the excesses and paradoxes of mystical discourse, both apophatic and Christocentric, to emphasize the emergence of women's voices in the Christian Middle Ages as they speak and write of their experience of God.[65] Porete, too, employs feminine imagery in the form of Ladies Love and Soul; she uses both same-sex and mixed-sex metaphors to describe the soul's love of God; and, although addressing a diverse and mixed audience (both inscribed in the text and real), she at times refers to her listeners and readers as "unknown ladies." These personifications are conventional in allegorical literature, but they must also be seen as a deliberate choice: in the *Mirror*, gender is fluid and permeable, but Porete chooses language and imagery to emphasize the inclusion of the feminine in relation

---

[64] See Ann-Marie Priest, "Woman as God, God as Woman: Mysticism, Negative Theology, and Luce Irigaray," *Journal of Religion* 83, no. 1 (2003): 1–23.

[65] But not only women's voices. Irigaray's references to Ruusbroec and Eckhart indicate that this form of discourse, a mystical *écriture féminine*, could be adopted by men as well, but from relatively securer positions of authority within identifiable religious communities. On the construction of mysticism in the Christian tradition and the influence of power and gender on who counts as a mystic, see Grace Jantzen, *Power, Gender and Christian Mysticism* (Cambridge: Cambridge University Press, 1995). Marguerite Porete provides an important test case for Jantzen's thesis.

to, and as, the divine.[66] Despite these commonalities, Porete's mystical writing diverges from Irigaray's, and other modern feminist projects, on the topic of women's subjectivity. Porete relentlessly "unsays" everything that might characterize either God or the soul, including, ultimately, gender, which, like other attributes of God or the soul, is nonessential.[67] Instead of establishing women's agency, identity, and subjectivity, Porete wants to annihilate it—a difficult feat to accomplish if the author is one of the annihilated souls of which she speaks.

Writing Annihilation

"This book," as the *Mirror* frequently and self-referentially describes itself, is preoccupied with the status of its own writing. At first glance, Porete's doctrine of annihilation appears to contradict her act of writing the book, forcing her to justify or explain the creation of the book by an annihilated soul who "no longer knows how to speak of God."[68] If we take the author of the text to be one of the simple souls of which she speaks, whose will has been annihilated in the love of her creator, then the book seems to contradict the author's claim to annihilation.[69] Writing appears to demand reason and agency—annihilate the will and the words of the annihilated soul fall silent. Stephanie Paulsell speaks for many readers of the *Mirror* when she remarks, "Obviously, such a soul cannot possibly be the author of this text or any other text."[70] But this reading assumes a form of writing—willful, agential,

---

[66] See Kocher, *Allegories of Love*, 98–101. The spiritual path of "Lady Soul" is, of course, available to both men and women—the femininity of the soul does not correspond to the sex of the body. But because the stages of grace take the soul beyond the works of the body, especially those ascetic practices that were increasingly viewed as marks of female sanctity in the late Middle Ages, Porete's more speculative or intellectual path can be seen as especially liberating for women whose primary relationship with God was often established through physical suffering in imitation of Christ.

[67] See Sells, *Mystical Languages of Unsaying*, chap. 7.

[68] *Mirouer*, chap. 7, 26.

[69] Some critics view her book as a kind of self-evident contradiction, so that the author cannot be identified as an annihilated soul. In 1968, Edmund Colledge, e.g., asserted, "The entire book is characterized by a stubborn, willful determination to persist in its opinions, by a spiritual arrogance, which could surely find no place in a truly 'simple soul.'" "Liberty of Spirit: 'The Mirror of Simple Souls,'" in *Theology of Renewal*, vol. 2, ed. L. K. Shook (Dorval, Quebec: Palm, 1968), 114. See also Amy Hollywood's description of readers approaching Porete and other mystics for the first time, "'Who Does She Think She Is?' Christian Women's Mysticism," *Theology Today* 60 (2003): 5–15.

[70] Stephanie Paulsell, "Dreaming the King, Writing God: Hope, Desire, and Fiction in Marguerite Porete's *Mirror of Simple Souls*," in *Literature, Religion, and East/West Comparison*, ed. Eric Ziolkowski (Newark, N.J.: University of Delaware Press, 2005), 67.

authoritative—that the *Mirror* itself resists. While Porete recognizes the
paradox of writing from an apparent position of annihilation, her writing
negotiates this problem in multiple ways: through didactic explanations of
the function of author and audience; through the literary form of the text
(allegorical dialogue); through claims to divine inspiration; and through her
teaching on the effects of annihilation.

In passages addressing the motivation for writing, the *Mirror* indicates the difficult position of its author. The "poor begging creature" who
authored the book wrote "what you hear; and it was her wish that her neighbors would find God in her, through her writings and her words."[71] Porete's
book attempts to guide her neighbors to the "light of truth" and set them
"free."[72] In writing for the benefit of her neighbors, Porete addresses a double
audience: those who are sad or "forlorn," who desire something better but
do not know the way to freedom, and those who are already free and annihilated. While the *Mirror* attempts to effect a transformation in the former,
it repeatedly apologizes to the latter for its long-windedness and baseness. It
hints that annihilation is necessary before one can completely understand
the book. Reason, for example, asks Soul to "tell us how many kinds of
death you had to die before you came to understand this book perfectly."[73]
But those who can already understand the book presumably would have no
need to read it. Soul explains the reason for the double audience: "so that
you [the forlorn] might be like this without delay, at least in will, if that is
still in you; and if you are already freed from all things, and are without
will and living a life beyond your understanding, so that you may at least
provide the glosses for this book!"[74] As the *Mirror* transforms the forlorn by
teaching them how to become free and annihilated, it also creates a community among the annihilated "unknown ladies" who see themselves in Porete's
book and help to interpret it for others.[75] At the same time, Soul frequently

---

[71] "ce que vous oez; et voult que ses proesmes trouvassent Dieu en elle, par escrips et par
paroles." *Mirouer*, chap. 96, 268.

[72] "ce livre monstrera a tous vraye lumiere de verité." *Mirouer*, chap. 13, 54.

[73] "dictes nous de quantes manieres de mort vous convint il mourir ains que vous
entendissez ce livre." *Mirouer*, chap. 54, 156.

[74] "affin que vous soiez ce mesmes, sans arrest, au moins en voulenté, se vous l'avez encore;
et se vous estes ja descombree de toutes choses, et se estes gens sans voulenté, en vie qui soit
dessus vostre entendement, affin que au moins vous diez les gloses de ce livre!" *Mirouer*, chap.
60, 176.

[75] *Mirouer*, chap. 119, 332. The reference to an inscribed audience of "unknown ladies"
does not restrict Porete's real audience to women, however. In this context, "ladies" may refer
to the gender and rank of the annihilated souls. Porete seems to have deliberately made her
book accessible to the widest possible audience both inside and outside the text, as Kocher

expresses ambivalence toward the material constraints of her speech: "the body is too gross to speak of what the spirit has grasped."[76] Porete seems to dream of an ideal speech that would be purely transparent and complains of the limitations of language to express the ineffable. She is a master, however, at writing apophatic theology—that is, at using the very limits of language to point beyond itself through negation, paradox, and contradiction, to "unsay" everything she says so that language never reaches a point in which meaning becomes stable and fixed. One way in which she achieves this effect is through the literary form of the book.

Like a mirror, the form of Porete's book reflects its content. Writing annihilation happens indirectly; the literary features enable the book both to mirror the soul's annihilation and to mask the author's own experience. In the prologue, the Writer and Love explain the didactic purpose of the book: to remind the soul of its beloved and to teach the soul how to attain perfect being in love through seven states.[77] This progression through seven states, three deaths (to sin, nature, and spirit), and three categories of souls (lost, forlorn, and annihilated), however, is anything but systematic. Porete has little interest in leading her readers in a step-by-step fashion; her preferred method of teaching disorients readers and frustrates their expectations at the same time as it solicits their desire to understand. The dialogical form engages her "forlorn" readers who are asking "the way to the land of freedom." As she writes, "by asking questions one can travel very far, and it is by asking questions that one comes to one's right way, and comes back to it when one has wandered from it."[78]

The dialogue takes place in the space of the soul, using attributes of God and the soul's faculties to stage a dramatic portrait of the soul's transformation.[79] The principal characters of Ladies Love, Soul, and Reason guide the

---

notes, "by writing in the vernacular, varying the lessons' level of difficulty, and using cycles of repetition and analogy. The fact that Porete wrote the book and read it aloud (in French) suggests that she believed or wished her broad audiences to be capable of subtle spiritual understanding, and thought that they could be encouraged to attain it by means of hearing spoken words as well as written ones." *Allegories of Love*, 53.

[76] "car le corps est trop gros pour parler des emprises de l'esperit." *Mirouer*, chap. 32, 108. Soul also complains of her "meschant corps" (wretched body) in chap. 38 and the burden of her weak body ("mon corps est en foiblesse") in chap. 77.

[77] "Ils sont sept estres de noble estre, desquieulx creature reçoit estre, se elle se dispose a tous estres, ains qu'elle viengne a parfait estre; et vous dirons comment, ains que ce livre fine." *Mirouer*, prologue, 14.

[78] "car par demandes vait l'en moult loing, et par demandes s'adresse l'en a sa voie, et radresse l'en, quant on en est yssu." *Mirouer*, chap. 123, 348.

[79] See Hollywood, *Soul as Virgin Wife*, 95.

reader through the gradual transformation of the soul in loving union with
God. Love is the voice of God and speaks with authority.[80] Soul learns from
Love, her divine instructress, and affirms her teaching. Reason is puzzled and
outraged and asks the questions that might be posed by a confused reader—
such as a cleric of what Porete calls "Holy Church the Little," trained in what
she views as an inferior way of thinking. Other characters arise, fracture or
multiply, and disappear without explanation. The momentum of the dialogue
is driven by Reason's questions, which object to the claims of Love (e.g., "this
book says astonishing things about the Soul!"[81]) until reason fails and the
soul is set free. The book unfolds in the form of a dialectical spiral, as Love
instructs the Soul and baffled Reason demands an explanation, all the while
circling around, or within, the soul's annihilation in the love of its creator.
The literary form of allegorical dialogue makes use of a multiplicity of voices
and characters that allow Porete to mask her own perspective and experience,
which, unlike many of her contemporaries, Porete never describes.[82] Porete's
substitution of allegory and dialogue for a first-person narrative fractures and
decenters anything that could be construed as a consistent authorial voice
into the multiple and often contradictory voices of the text. The multiplicity
of voices is demanded by the divine origin of the book.

Claiming a divine origin for her book is another strategy that helps
Porete negotiate the problem of writing annihilation.[83] Other medieval
women writers (Hadewijch and Angela, for instance) appeal, explicitly or
implicitly, to their visions to claim the authority to write theology. The status
of visionary was recognized by the medieval church; even women might be
graced with visions from God, which they could and should share with others through writing. Porete, however, takes a different approach, while also
claiming divine inspiration—and even evangelical status—for her book. In
the prologue, Porete tells a tale of a princess who fell in love with the reputa-
tion of Alexander and had an imagined likeness of him painted in order to
make him present. "Truly, says the Soul who had this book made," glosses
Soul, "I speak to you of matters similar to this." She, too, fell in love with

---

[80] "Je suis Dieu, dit Amour, car Amour est Dieu, et Dieu est amour." *Mirouer*, chap.
21, 82.

[81] "ce livre dit de ceste Ame grans admiracions." *Mirouer*, ch. 13, 54.

[82] On the multiple functions of allegory in the *Mirror* and its relation to authorship, see
Kocher, *Allegories of Love*, esp. 165–76.

[83] See Bernard McGinn, "The Four Female Evangelists of the Thirteenth Century: The
Invention of Authority," in *Deutsche Mystik im abendländischen Zusammenhang*, ed. Walter
Haug and Wolfram Schneider-Lastin (Tübingen: Niemeyer, 2000), 175–94.

a far-off "noble Alexander . . . and to remind me of him, he gave me this book."[84] This first self-referential description of the book calls it a gift from God. Shortly thereafter, Love tells the children of Holy Church for whom and why the book was made: "it is for you that I have made this book, so that you may hear of and so hold in greater worth the perfection of life and the state of peace, to which the creature can attain by the power of perfect charity, which gift is made to it by the whole Trinity; and you will hear this gift described in this book."[85] Love made the book so that the forlorn souls will understand annihilation "in its true sense; for this is how she is while she is in this state of being; and may God grant it to you to be always there, without ever departing. I say this for those persons for whom Love has caused this book to be made, and to those for whom I have written it."[86] In the style of the *trouvères*, Porete even refers to Soul having "found" the verses of her book, singing rather than writing it.[87] In positing the origin of her book outside herself, Porete attributes the authorship of her text to God, Love (God's manifestation), or the annihilated Soul who has been transformed in love: "This work is nothing. . . . But what is in me or comes through me, which is from divine knowledge, you yourself, Lady Love, have said it in me or through me out of your goodness, for my profit and that of others."[88] Just as the movement of the text increasingly identifies the soul with divine Love, so too, the author identifies her writing with the agency of Love—a love made possible through her annihilation and transformation.

The final way in which the *Mirror* negotiates the problem of writing is through Porete's teaching on annihilation itself. Properly understood, annihilation is not masochistic, self-destructive, or quietist. It is neither otherworldly nor anti-body. Rather, annihilation is the realization of the soul's

---

[84] "pour moy souvenir de lui il me donna ce livre qui represente en aucuns usages l'amour de lui mesmes." *Mirouer*, prologue, 12.

[85] "pour vous ay je fait ce livre, affin que vous oyez pour mieulx valoir la parfection de vie et l'estre de paix, ouquel creature peut venir par la vertu de parfaicte charité, a qui ce don est donné de toute la Trinité; lequel don vous orrez diviser en ce livre." *Mirouer*, chap. 2, 14.

[86] "Entendez sainement, car c'est tant comme elle est en cest estre: Dieu vous y done, sans en yssir, toudis estre. Je le di aux personnes pour qui Amour a fait faire ce livre, et a celles pour qui je l'ay escript." *Mirouer*, chap. 84, 238.

[87] For example, in the song with which this chapter began: "Amour m'a fait par noblece / Ces vers de chancon trouver." *Mirouer*, chap. 122, 342.

[88] "Nyent est de l'oeuvre, quant il convient que elle soit nyent; par quoy il convient, dit ceste Ame, que je soie certaine que ce que j'ay dit est moins que nyent. Mais ce qui est en moy ou par moy, qui est de divine cognoissance, vous mesmes, dame Amour, l'avez dit en moy et par moy de vostre bonté, pour mon prouffit et celluy des aultres." *Mirouer*, chap. 27, 120.

primordial oneness with God through creation. This realization causes a radical shift in perspective through which the soul gives up her will out of love of God. Once there is no will or what we might call ego in the way, the soul becomes the pure conduit and mirror of God's love. She exists "without herself," detached from her desires, free to engage others and the world around her, as Porete puts it, "without a why." Annihilation reorients the soul to engage the world more fully out of love.

The effect of annihilation is to free the soul to act, without herself and without a why, out of love of God and neighbor. In Porete's case, the active life includes the writing and dissemination of her book, offered out of love for her readers (or "listeners"). The writing of Porete's book becomes less puzzling in this regard. Love authors the book because the author's own ego has been abandoned. Divine love is incarnate in the transformed soul, whose writing emerges from the space of annihilation. This annihilation is not self-destructive, but freeing and empowering as it enables the active life of writing and teaching others, "without herself."[89] Porete's writing is both didactic and performative, and it intends to effect in her readers the annihilation of which she speaks, just as Soul is dramatically transformed by the words of Love:

> Ah, Love, says this Soul, the meaning of what has now been said has made me nothing, and the nothingness of this alone has placed me in an abyss, below what is immeasurably less than nothing. And the knowledge of my nothingness, says this Soul, has given me everything, and the nothingness of this everything, says this Soul, has deprived me of orison and prayer, and [I] do not pray at all.[90]

The form of writing that emerges from annihilating and transformative love aims for a similar effect on its readers:[91] disorientation, as we are thrown into

---

[89] Paulsell resolves the contradiction differently, by reading a split identity in the speaking Soul, who at some moments seems identified with the annihilated soul, at others identified with the author, who acknowledges she "remained a beggar and encumbered with herself" in the act of writing (chap. 96). Certainly, in the *Mirror*, words can mean two things (chap. 13), and so one aspect of the Soul does not rule out the other. While Paulsell's interpretation of a fluid or split identity resolves the different (and apparently contradictory) literary representations of the Soul, it requires a view of both writing and annihilation that is not always operative in the text. See Paulsell, "Dreaming the King."

[90] "Hee, Amour, dit ceste Ame, le sens de ce qui est dit m'a fait nulle, et le nient de ce seul m'a mis en abysme dessoubs moins que nient sans mesure. Et la cognoissance de mon nient, dit ceste Ame, m'a donné le tout, et le nient de ce tout, dit ceste Ame, m'a tollu oraison et priere, et ne prie nient." *Mirouer*, chap. 51, 150; translation modified.

[91] Hollywood sees a similar operation in Porete's writing process: "The process of writing the book transforms or transfigures the author in the same way that the Soul is transformed in the text, and the same transfiguration is meant to be brought about in the reader. This is the work that the author/the Soul/Porete has been called to perform. When the Soul

the paradoxical dialogue of the *Mirror*; detachment from our own willful desires and expectations for the text; transformation from being lost and forlorn into freedom through the work of Lady Love; and reorientation back to the world around us with a renewed sense of loving wonder.

When the soul is transformed and annihilated in love on the model of its exemplar Christ, she "no longer knows how to speak of God."[92] Instead, Love speaks in and through her. Porete's mystical writing is crafted to convey this apophatic paradox—both speaking and not speaking—in both content and form. Love (God) is the ultimate origin of the book, which is written "without a why," through allegory and dialogue. Annihilation makes the soul the place in which God acts in the world—the place of love's incarnation as the soul imitates Christ through self-emptying annihilation. Porete compares the soul to both wax and parchment, the surface on which writing (by the Holy Spirit) appears.[93] Annihilation clears the soul of all previous markings as it becomes a blank surface, like a mirror, that is open to the action of God, ready to receive an image, imprint, or inscription. Transformed in love, the soul becomes a purely reflective surface, the tain of the mirror that allows divine self-reflection. The soul becomes the mirror of God through annihilation, by mirroring her exemplar Christ, just as the written text becomes a mirror—a *Mirouer* or *Speculum*—of the soul's transformation.

In a very different way from Hadewijch and Angela, Porete also evokes an incarnational mode of writing that discloses God in the materiality of the written text. Her writing of the body of Christ is less *about* the body of Christ than a textual mirroring of the annihilated soul, the place of Love's incarnation, in self-emptying imitation of Christ. Writing transmits Porete's teaching, without a why, out of love for God and love for her neighbors, to show them the way to freedom, even at moments bursting into song: "I sing, says this Soul, now the melody and now the harmony, and all for those who are not yet free, so that they may hear something of freedom."[94] Writing

---

completes that work, she is united with Love and it is possible to speak of Love herself as the author. Although the soul who has learned to live 'without a why' might be unfit for or unable to carry out such a mission, Love is not. And it is precisely the simple soul who provides the space in which Love can operate in the world." *Soul as Virgin Wife*, 114–15. The transformation, however, happens before (and not just through) the writing; writing the book is an effect of transformation rather than its culmination.

[92] "ne sçait plus de Dieu parler." *Mirouer*, chap. 7, 26.

[93] See *Mirouer*, chap. 50, 148 and chap. 66, 188–90.

[94] "Je chante, dit ceste Ame, l'une heure a chant, l'aultre a deschant, et tout pour ceulx qui ne sont mie encore frans, affin qu'ilz oyent aucuns poins de franchise, et quelle chose il convient, ains que on parviengne a elle." *Mirouer*, chap. 80, 226.

mirrors the transformation of the soul just as the soul mirrors Christ: it is the manifestation of love, the place where divine instruction occurs, the vehicle of annihilation and transformation. Christ appears in the mirror of the soul and in the parchment of the text.

Sexual Difference, Incarnation, and *Parler-femme*

In 1987 Luce Irigaray published a review of *In Memory of Her*, Elisabeth Schüssler Fiorenza's classic work in feminist biblical hermeneutics and theology.[95] Irigaray praises the book for its insights into early Christian history, and for perspectives that "let in a breath of fresh air and a bit of spirit as well,"[96] but she disagrees with Schüssler Fiorenza's focus on the "discipleship of equals."[97] Instead of discovering women's historical equality with Jesus' male disciples, Irigaray wants to claim for women "an equal share in the divine."[98] It quickly becomes clear that Schüssler Fiorenza's book is the starting point for Irigaray's own theological reflections. For Irigaray, the most interesting thing about Jesus is not his radical social teachings and practices but the divinity of his body and the possibilities his incarnation offers for "a spiritualization and divinization of the flesh." Because Jesus was male, he "is the manifestation of only a part of this: he is God made man. But at least he's flesh and blood, living in the confines of a body and therefore sexuate."[99] Following Schüssler Fiorenza's discussion of the historical elimination of women from central roles as Christian witnesses to the Jesus movement, Irigaray suggests that the denial of Christ's sexual/sexuate incarnation "results from the exclusion of women from preaching the Gospels and from the priesthood."[100] Because "women, who were his witnesses as much as men, were eliminated from all evidence relating to him,"[101] Christ's divine body, his revolutionary attitudes toward marriage and women, his use of touch to heal and console,

---

[95] Luce Irigaray, "Egales à qui?" *Critique* 43, no. 480 (1987): 420–37. Translated as "Equal to Whom?" in *The Essential Difference*, ed. Naomi Schor and Elizabeth Weed, trans. Robert L. Mazzola (Bloomington: Indiana University Press, 1994), 63–81. Subsequent quotations are from the English translation. Irigaray's review is of the French translation of Elisabeth Schüssler Fiorenza, *In Memory of Her: A Feminist Theological Reconstruction of Christian Origins* (New York: Crossroad, 1983).

[96] Irigaray, "Equal," 64.

[97] Schüssler Fiorenza, *In Memory of Her*, 130–54.

[98] Irigaray, "Equal," 74.

[99] Irigaray, "Equal," 72; translation modified.

[100] Irigaray, "Equal," 74.

[101] Irigaray, "Equal," 70.

and his respect for the fruits of the earth in his memorial meal have been forgotten and denied. The Christian witness of Jesus might have been very different had his women followers written of their experience of his incarnation and been the ones to transmit the Eucharist in memory of him—and of her.

In this review, Irigaray links her own philosophical and linguistic interest in the question of women's subjectivity to the theological theme of incarnation. For Irigaray, sexual (or sexuate) difference refers to an ontological difference between the sexes that is prior to other human social differences (such as race, culture, and class).[102] Pheng Cheah and Elizabeth Grosz define it as "an originary nonanthropocentric form of negativity that issues from nature itself [which] undoes the binary opposition between nature and spirit because it is nothing other than the internal natural means by which nature becomes spiritualized,"[103] while Irigaray increasingly emphasizes the relational aspect of sexual difference: "A woman is born of a woman, of someone of her gender, whereas a man is born of someone of another gender than himself; a woman can engender in herself like her mother, whereas a man engenders outside of himself."[104] This evolutionary, ontological difference has been erased or forgotten in the history of Western thought as the male gender has been, until quite recently, considered the standard and norm for

---

[102] Irigaray's concept of sexual difference has been the topic of a lively debate surrounding essentialism and heterosexism within feminist theory. Early critics include Toril Moi, *Sexual/Textual Politics: Feminist Literary Theory* (London: Methuen, 1995), and Ann Rosalind Jones, "Writing the Body: Towards an Understanding of *l'Écriture féminine*," in *The New Feminist Criticism: Essays on Women, Literature and Theory*, ed. E. Showalter (New York: Pantheon, 1985), 361–77; and, more recently, Morny Joy, *Divine Love: Luce Irigaray, Women, Gender and Religion* (Manchester: Manchester University Press, 2006). Defenders include Elizabeth Grosz, *Sexual Subversions: Three French Feminists* (Sydney: Allen & Unwin, 1989); Margaret Whitford, *Luce Irigaray: Philosophy in the Feminine* (New York: Routledge, 1991); Tina Chanter, *Ethics of Eros: Irigaray's Rewriting of the Philosophers* (New York: Routledge, 1995); Naomi Schor, "This Essentialism Which Is Not One: Coming to Grips with Irigaray," in *Engaging with Luce Irigaray: Feminist Philosophy and Modern European Thought*, ed. Carolyn Burke, Naomi Schor, and Margaret Whitford (New York: Columbia University Press, 1994), 57–78; and Pheng Cheah and Elizabeth Grosz, "The Future of Sexual Difference: An Interview with Judith Butler and Drucilla Cornell," *Diacritics* 28, no. 1 (1998): 19–42. A nuanced appreciation of Irigaray coupled with a sophisticated critique of sexual difference as the "undeconstructed and fetishized ideality" within her thought can be found in Hollywood, *Sensible Ecstasy*, 187–273.

[103] Pheng Cheah and Elizabeth Grosz, "Of Being-Two: Introduction," *Diacritics* 28, no. 1 (1998): 8–9.

[104] Luce Irigaray, "Toward a Divine in the Feminine," in *Women and the Divine: Touching Transcendence*, ed. Gillian Howie and J'annine Jobling (New York: Palgrave Macmillan, 2008), 13–25, 14.

humanity. A more accurate philosophical anthropology would recognize that human beings are (at least)[105] two in kind; instead of assimilating differences to a single common or universal humanity that is, in fact, male, those relational differences might instead inform culture, politics, and religion. Irigaray's interest in sexual difference extends all the way to the divine, but rather than rejecting the Christian belief in the incarnation as upholding a male standard of both humanity and divinity (as some feminist theologians have done),[106] Irigaray embraces the concept of an embodied, sexed divinity.[107] For her, however, because Jesus was male, the incarnation of Christ remains partial and incomplete. Because there is no female incarnation of the divine, no Word of God made female flesh, women lack a divine model of their own being.[108] One way in which women might claim their own incarnation is through the development of their subject-position (or subjectivity) through self-affection, love of the other, moments of silence and practices of breathing, as well as through speech and writing. Irigaray's early interest in markers of sexual difference in linguistics and in the language or speech of women, what she calls *parler-femme* (speaking [as] woman), develops the incarnational manner in which female flesh becomes word.

In her early works *Speculum of the Other Woman* and *This Sex Which Is Not One*, Irigaray addresses the philosophical question of women's subjectivity through Freud's psychoanalytic description of women's bodies. She

[105] Although Irigaray does sometimes include "at least," she has not, to my knowledge, written on the full range of human sex-differentiation to include intersexed bodies or transgender identities, which challenge the neatness of her double ontology. Hollywood convincingly argues that Irigaray's sexual difference is an "ideal category that is incapable of encapsulating the complexity, ambiguity, and multiplicity of bodily experience. Human bodies may always be sexed, but, as both biological science and cultural theories of intersecting identities show, human bodies are not only nor simply sexed." There is no compelling reason, either politically or ontologically, for Irigaray to limit her philosophy of difference to the encounter between two sexes; there are, moreover, rich resources within Irigaray's own thought for expanding her understanding of both difference and the relation between bodies and language. See Hollywood, *Sensible Ecstasy*, 232–33.

[106] See, e.g., Mary Daly, *Beyond God the Father: Toward a Philosophy of Women's Liberation.* (Boston: Beacon, 1973) and Daphne Hampson, *Theology and Feminism* (Cambridge, Mass.: Blackwell, 1990).

[107] For the way in which Irigaray's thought intersects with the Christian notion of incarnation, see Anne-Claire Mulder, *Divine Flesh, Embodied Word: "Incarnation" as a Hermeneutical Key to a Feminist Theologian's Reading of Luce Irigaray's Work* (Amsterdam: Amsterdam University Press, 2006).

[108] See Irigaray's essay "Divine Women," in *Sexes and Genealogies*, trans. Gillian C. Gill (New York: Columbia University Press, 1993).

describes how female sexuality has always been represented as a castrated or inferior version of male sexuality according to what she calls phallocentric language or the logic of the same.[109] The phallocentric symbolic order of metaphysics, language, and logic cannot account for feminine erogenous multiplicity; the female body defies discrete forms, and therefore presents a challenge to the one form (the phallus) that would govern the symbolic. The female sex represents a disruptive excess because it is not *one*, but not nothing, either; it is multiple, different. Irigaray's poetic writing offers images of female morphology that emphasize multiplicity and fluidity.[110] Images of the two lips, caves, mucous, and thresholds are not ontologically truthful images of female anatomy but are instead attempts to challenge the representation of the feminine as an inferior version of "the one" or "the same" and thereby shift the conditions of that representation.[111] Such images of female morphology are intended as space-holders, to keep open the possibility of women's self-representation.[112] Irigaray's proposal of *parler-femme* as an embodied linguistic practice must be understood in this context.

Like Cixous' *écriture féminine*, Irigaray's *parler-femme* has multiple meanings, not limited to but including speaking the feminine, speaking of/ to women, speaking as woman-subject, and action/speech by/on behalf of women (*par les femmes*).[113] With *parler-femme*, Irigaray suggests an economy

---

[109] This argument is found in various forms in Luce Irigaray's early works: *Speculum de l'autre femme* (Paris: Éditions de Minuit, 1974), translated by Gillian C. Gill as *Speculum of the Other Woman* (Ithaca, N.Y.: Cornell University Press, 1985), and *Ce sexe qui n'en est pas un* (Paris: Éditions de Minuit, 1977), translated by Catherine Porter as *This Sex Which Is Not One* (Ithaca, N.Y.: Cornell University Press, 1985). Woman's sex is either "un sexe-clitoris qui ne soutient pas la comparaison avec l'organe phallique valeureux, ou un trou-enveloppe qui fait gaine et frottement autour du pénis dans le coït: un non-sexe, ou un sexe masculin retourné autour de lui-même pour s'auto-affecter. De la femme et de son plaisir, rien ne se dit dans une telle conception du rapport sexuel." *Ce Sexe*, 23. In other words, woman is not really "other" at all, but only ever represented as an inferior version of the "same." See also Whitford, *Luce Irigaray*, 101–18.

[110] See Grosz, *Sexual Subversions*, 115.

[111] See Grosz, *Sexual Subversions*, 116, and Whitford, *Luce Irigaray*, 35 and 62–70, who both argue that Irigaray is waging an intervention (in a psychoanalytic sense) at the level of the imaginary and the symbolic, rather than proposing a biological essentialism.

[112] Her writing offers feminine images to effect a shift in the imaginary of the reader, but these are "empty images" that are themselves fluid and provisional; they do not describe, much less prescribe, a feminine essence. See Elizabeth L. Berg, "The Third Woman," *Diacritics* 12 (1982): 11–20.

[113] In Irigaray's words: "Parler-femme, ce n'est pas parler de la femme. Il ne s'agit pas de produire un discours dont la femme serait l'objet, ou le sujet. Cela dit, *parlant-femme*, on peut tenter de ménager un lieu à l'"autre" comme féminin." ("Speaking (as) woman is not

of signification that is not based on the phallic exchange of metaphor (the substitution of signs), but on the *metonymy* of the two lips, in contiguous relation. The language of *parler-femme* arises from desire, and what makes it distinctively feminine is that it is isomorphic with a different morphology of the imaginary: a female body that is fluid, multiple, not one, unlike the unity and identity of the phallus. The speaking subject remains in contact with her body; her language does not operate through a substitutionary chain of signifiers but a contiguous speaking of desire in which language touches itself.[114] Although women's subjectivity and sexual difference are obscured by their conflation with men (legally, politically, culturally, religiously), Irigaray finds incipient evidence of *parler-femme* in the way women's bodies signify, in the way they speak what otherwise cannot be said through laughter, gestures, and hysterical symptoms.[115] Establishing the link between those bodily gestures and a language of the symbolic is the problem of enunciation,[116] creating the conditions for women to speak as women subjects, without denying or disavowing their bodies, their self-affection, their mothers, and their relationships with other women.[117]

Part of the difficulty of women becoming speaking subjects, according to Irigaray, is that language rests on a hidden and unacknowledged debt to its own material—and maternal—conditions. The woman-subject should be distinguished from her confusion with the mother, just as the debt (that each of us owes) to the maternal—and to material reality more broadly—must be acknowledged. In order for women to become subjects of enunciation, they

---

speaking of woman. It is not a matter of producing a discourse of which woman would be the object, or the subject. That said, by *speaking (as) woman*, one may attempt to provide a place for the 'other' as feminine.") *Ce Sexe*, 133 (*This Sex*, 135).

[114] See, e.g., Irigaray, *Ce Sexe*, 28.

[115] See Irigaray, *Ce sexe*, 132 (*This Sex*, 134). Irigaray also finds evidence of *parler-femme* in a certain practice of poetic writing that aims to shift the conditions of speech, to provide a place for the advent of the other, through a different syntax. See Irigaray's description of a feminine syntax without subject or object, entailing proximity, but not appropriation, in *Ce Sexe*, 132 (*This Sex*, 135). She also claims to have practiced this syntax in *Speculum*, "mais pas simplement," because it is not a matter of resting in that other, feminine syntax, but ultimately of establishing a relation or chiasmus between the two. Her descriptions of women's writing are reminiscent of Cixous' *écriture féminine*; the notion of a double syntax also recalls Cixous' invocation of sexed bisexuality in *La jeune née*.

[116] See Irigaray, *Ce Sexe*, 134–35 (*This Sex*, 137).

[117] See Whitford's interpretation of *parler-femme* as *langage* (rather than *langue*) in *Luce Irigaray*, 38–49. *Parler-femme* thus refers to the position of enunciation (and consequently the conditions of women's subjectivity).

need language as a "shelter" for what Irigaray calls their "becoming."[118] In her later work, Irigaray links this transformation of language with God, both as divine verb or Word and as a divine representation specifically in the image of women. Without a "God in the feminine," Irigaray worries that women are fixed in the role of, at best, the mother through whom God becomes man.[119] The unacknowledged debt to the maternal in phallocentric language parallels the unacknowledged debt to the maternal in the incarnation of Christ: in both cases the woman is sacrificed or paralyzed as mother. As that which supports the language and divinity of men, the mother, and the women who are conflated with her, is excluded from access to her own language, her own divine representation, and her own incarnation. Representing the divine in the image of women would, according to Irigaray, serve as the perfection of women's subjectivity, as the infinite horizon toward which women could become divine in an ongoing process of "transfiguration" of flesh and speech.[120]

Porete's *Mirror* gives one example of what Irigaray seeks: a divine representation in the feminine, Lady Love, who encourages and transforms the character Lady Soul, who speaks for both the human soul gendered feminine (Everywo/man) and the author of the book, a woman, writing at least in part for other women (unknown ladies). Surely the gender of the characters is not unrelated to the gender of the author; beguines such as Porete, Hadewijch, and Mechthild of Magdeburg all refer to God as "Lady Love," who is, Barbara Newman argues, effectively a goddess in this literary and imaginative form of theology written by women and men.[121] Feminine imagery for God could very well have supported these women as writers, who saw themselves reflected in Lady Soul and Lady Love, just as the annihilated soul reflects God.[122] As Irigaray suggests in "La Mystérique," and as many other scholars

---

[118] See Whitford, *Luce Irigaray*, 45–48.

[119] Irigaray, "Divine Women," 62.

[120] "If she is to become woman, if she is to accomplish her female subjectivity, woman needs a god who is a figure for the perfection of her subjectivity . . . the deformity associated with women . . . all this is symptomatic of the fact that women lack a female god who can open up the perspective in which their flesh can be transfigured." Irigaray, "Divine Women," 64.

[121] Barbara J. Newman, *God and the Goddesses: Vision, Poetry, and Belief in the Middle Ages* (Philadelphia: University of Pennsylvania Press, 2003).

[122] On the erotic way in which the female characters interact, see Amy Hollywood, "Queering the Beguines: Mechthild, Hadewijch, Porete," in *Queer Theology: Rethinking the Western Body*, ed. Gerard Loughlin (Malden, Mass.: Blackwell, 2007), 163–75. Bernard McGinn also notes that, unlike some of her contemporaries, "Marguerite Porete never apologizes for being a woman." *Flowering*, 247.

have noted, a distinctive theological voice emerges in women's mystical writings from this period in Christian history: their flesh was transformed into word in something like the *parler-femme* of the mystics, feminine speech in relation to God, their divine Beloved. Porete's theology, the distinctive literary form in which it was transmitted, and the courage to persist in speaking and writing in the face of censure were no doubt sustained by her understanding of Christ as exemplar and her relationship to divine Lady Love. But her message was not limited to women or merely for their religious benefit; she wrote for everyone in the vernacular and read aloud from her book in public. The flexibility and fluidity of gender in medieval literature ensured that the feminine soul was not a cipher for women only, and such imagery regularly appears in male writers from the same period.[123] Reading Irigaray and Porete in conversation brings certain similarities in structure and imagery to the fore, but it does not imply equivalence. Juxtaposing Irigaray's writings with Porete's instead sharpens their differences and dissonances, particularly with regard to the implications of annihilation and incarnation for women.

Incarnation and/or the Annihilation of Difference

Where Irigaray and Porete diverge sharply is in how they respectively interpret the effect of the incarnation on women. Does Christ's incarnation demand imitation in the form of annihilation, sacrificing the will and transforming the soul into the place of God's incarnate love? Or does it call for imitation in the form of additional bodily incarnations, embodying sexual and other differences? Like the mystical discourse evoked in "La Mystérique," which Irigaray associates with a *parler-femme* before its time, Porete's writing presents a challenge to the theological discourse of reason. She offers multiple images of feminine characters and the feminine divine. But these figures are simply allegorical representations, without specifically female bodies. Porete's own body never appears, unlike the female bodies in Angela or Hadewijch's texts. And although Christ is the exemplar of the soul's annihilation and transformation in love, explicit references to Christ's body, much less meditative descriptions like those common to her contemporaries, are rare in Porete's *Mirror*. Despite the gendered characters and both same-sex and mixed-sex metaphors, there is no trace of sexual difference in Porete's writing beyond the linguistic.[124]

---

[123] See Carolyn Walker Bynum, "Introduction: The Complexity of Symbols," in *Gender and Religion: On the Complexity of Symbols*, ed. Caroline W. Bynum, Stevan Harrell, and Paula Richman (Boston: Beacon, 1988).

[124] The fact that centuries of readers identified her "anonymous" work as written by a man would seem to support this interpretation. For the history of the circulation of the text

In their interpretations of the incarnation through divinization, Angela imitates Christ's suffering and abjection; Hadewijch imitates his mother and becomes his lover. But Porete imitates the annihilation of the will, which means she is simply uninterested in what happens to the body: nature may be well ordered by the virtues, and the soul acts without a why out of (God's) love for creation, but these effects seem disconnected from bodies.

For a reader like Irigaray, there is a deeper problem. Porete's powerful writing, her brief challenge to the symbolic order through her written text, was expressed at the cost of annihilation—both the soul's annihilation in God and Porete's physical and historical annihilation at the hands of church authorities.[125] From a feminist perspective, it is troubling that Lady Soul sings, "He is, and I am not." Instead of finding love within herself, she seeks it elsewhere, in God, and in order to become one in perfect love with Him, she annihilates all distinction between them, including her will, her being, and even her love. However challenging *The Mirror of Simple Souls* may be in its theology of love, in its portrayal of the soul's relation to a feminine divine, and in its literary form, on a certain feminist reading, the text ultimately succumbs to the same patriarchal forces that executed Porete, annihilating the feminine soul, annihilating another woman writer.

Establishing the conditions for women's subjectivity, to prevent something like "annihilation," is a key concern of Irigaray's philosophical project. Uncovering the masculine bias in philosophy and psychoanalysis was the first stage of her writing, clearing the ground for the recognition of difference.[126] The second stage attempted to open a space for female subjectivity, for a female speaking subject in language that does not erase sexual difference. This second, constructive stage invited accusations of essentialism and heterosexism, which Irigaray in part addresses through the notion of the "sensible transcendental," the conditions for women's subjectivity that do not foreclose what women might be or become.[127] Irigaray locates the sensible

---

and its attribution to Richard Rolle and John Ruusbroec, see the "Introductory Interpretive Essay" by Edmund Colledge, O.S.A., J. C. Marler, and Judith Grant, in their translation of *The Mirror of Simple Souls*, lxxx–lxxxi.

[125] And scholars, who were initially also preoccupied with the question of orthodoxy; see Sargent, "Annihilation of Marguerite Porete."

[126] See Luce Irigaray, "Je—Luce Irigaray," interview by Elizabeth Hirsh and Gary A. Olson, *Hypatia* 10, no. (1995): 93–114, esp. 96–97.

[127] In addition to the linguistic possibility of *parler-femme*, Irigaray identifies further conditions for women's subjectivity in her later works: sexed rights, a maternal genealogy, sociality among women, an ethical relationship with the other sex, and a divine in the image of women as the horizon for their "becoming"—in short, a radical shift in the linguistic,

transcendental within an ethical and political vision for the future that has the power to transform the present. In addition to its quasi-transcendental function as a condition for the possibility of women's subjectivity, there are at least two additional connotations: metaphysical and theological.

The "sensible transcendental" is a deliberate putting in touch of what has been divided in most metaphysical systems: sensible and intelligible, semblance and form, matter and spirit, body and soul, immanence and transcendence. Like other French poststructuralists, Irigaray diagnoses these dualisms as a kind of pathological splitting, in which one side is valued while the other is rejected—even as the devalued pole lends identity and coherence to the pole of value. These binaries, furthermore, are gendered, so that the maternal-feminine (matter, body, immanence, etc.) bears the weight of the devalued side, while the masculine is allied with the intelligible, spiritual, transcendent side and explicitly associated with God as disembodied and all-powerful Father. Reference to the "sensible transcendental" attempts to heal the split in the sexual division of metaphysical labor by bringing into relation what has previously been kept apart.[128]

But Irigaray also uses theological language when she calls the sensible transcendental "the dimension of the divine par excellence."[129] The sensible transcendental functions in her writings as a name for God, or the divine in us, with an eschatological dimension. God, or the gods, or the divine, is yet to come—in and through the sensible world. After quoting Heidegger's claim that "only a god will save us," she writes, "Is a god what we need, then? . . . A god carried on the breath of the cosmos, the song of the poets, the respiration of lovers." She continues:

> We still have to await the god, remain ready and open to prepare a way for his coming. And, with him, for ourselves, to prepare, not an implacable decline, but a new birth, a new era in history. . . . This creation would be our opportunity . . . by means of the opening of a sensible transcendental that comes into being through us, of which we would be the mediators and bridges. Not only in mourning for the dead God of Nietzsche, not waiting passively for the god to come, but by creating him among us, within us, as resurrection and transfiguration of blood, of flesh, through a language and an ethics that is ours.[130]

---

political, cultural, and religious symbolic. See especially the essays collected in Irigaray, *Sexes and Genealogies*, and Whitford, *Luce Irigaray*, 47.

[128] See Whitford, *Luce Irigaray*, 93; and Jantzen, *Becoming Divine*, 270–71.

[129] Luce Irigaray, *An Ethics of Sexual Difference*, trans. Carolyn Burke and Gillian C. Gill (Ithaca, N.Y.: Cornell University Press, 1993), 114.

[130] Irigaray, *Ethics*, 129; translation modified.

This second coming of the incarnation, in her view, is here and now, "in and through the body."[131] In its theological aspect, the sensible transcendental refers to something yet to come, but not from an inaccessible or unknown future. Rather, it is the realization of the divine in bodies and language, a transformation of the symbolic order that creates space for "becoming": both becoming fully human, ethical subjects and—what is inseparable from human subjectivity for her—becoming divine.[132] This process of divinization is rooted in Irigaray's understanding of the incarnation. Both sensible and transcendent, the incarnation of God in Jesus is the sensible transcendental that provides the condition for the possibility of all bodies, female and male, becoming divine.

Irigaray expands her notion of "becoming divine" most explicitly in her essay "Divine Women," which has had a mixed reception among feminist theorists and theologians.[133] The essay is frequently read as calling for a deliberate projection of a feminine divine or goddess to serve as an ideal model or horizon for women's subjectivity. Just as, according to Feuerbach, a male God has supported men's subjectivity in idealized and perfected form, so too do women need a divine mirror for their gender.[134] But within the essay, self-conscious projection is ancillary to an incarnational mode of divinity,[135] which appears in the "transfiguration" of female flesh and in the "incarnation" of women as divine. Irigaray claims that our destiny is "to generate the

---

[131] Irigaray, *Ethics*, 148.

[132] See Irigaray, "Divine Women," 61–64; as well as Irigaray, "Toward a Divine," 13–25. On the way in which the figure of Mary in particular embodies the incarnation and becoming divine in Irigaray's thought, see Phyllis H. Kaminski, "What the Daughter Knows: Rethinking Women's Religious Experience with and against Luce Irigaray," in *Encountering Transcendence: Contributions to a Theology of Christian Religious Experience*, ed. Lieven Boeve, Hans Geybels, and Stijn Van den Bossche (Leuven: Peeters, 2005), 57–82.

[133] For the critical feminist reaction, see Elizabeth Grosz, "Irigaray and the Divine," in *Transfigurations: Theology and the French Feminists*, ed. C. W. Maggie Kim, Susan M. St. Ville, and Susan M. Simonaitis (Minneapolis: Fortress, 1993), 199–214; Serene Jones, "Divining Women: Irigaray and Feminist Theologies," *Yale French Studies* 87 (1995): 42–67; Jenny Daggers, "Luce Irigaray and 'Divine Women': A Resource for Postmodern Feminist Theology?" *Feminist Theology* 14 (1997): 35–50; Judith L. Poxon, "Corporeality and Divinity: Irigaray and the Problem of the Ideal," in *Religion in French Feminist Thought: Critical Perspectives*, ed. Morny Joy, Kathleen O'Grady, and Judith Poxon (London: Routledge, 2003), 41–50; and Hollywood, *Sensible Ecstasy*, 211–35.

[134] Irigaray, "Divine Women," 61–69. See Ludwig Feuerbach, *The Essence of Christianity*, trans. George Eliot (1841; Amherst, N.Y.: Prometheus Books, 1989).

[135] For instance, Irigaray, "Divine Women," 71: "Does respect for God made flesh not imply that we should incarnate God within us and in our sex: daughter-woman-mother?"

human, the divine, within us and among us."[136] The divine is both external ideal and sensible transcendental that provides a bridge for growth. "Love of God," she writes, "shows the way."

> It is the incentive for a more perfect becoming. It marks the horizon between the more past and the more future, the more passive and the more active—permanent and always in tension. God forces us to do nothing except become. The only task, the only obligation laid upon us is: to become divine men and women, to become perfectly, to refuse to allow parts of ourselves to shrivel and die that have the potential for growth and fulfillment.[137]

As in "La Mystérique," here, too, there are echoes of Porete. Porete describes divinization as a process of transformation through the love of God. Love is both guide and mirror of Lady Soul, a path or bridge to becoming divine, as she transforms the soul into herself. But the bodily dimension of this transformation, which is where Irigaray locates sexual difference, matters little to Porete. The superficial textual echoes rest on deeper differences.

Porete and Irigaray understand the incarnation, and its implications for women, in fundamentally different ways. They both take Christ's incarnation as the exemplar of human possibility. But Irigaray explicitly emphasizes the bodily dimension of the incarnation. Since sexual difference is ontological for her, the incarnation of God in Jesus is partial and incomplete. It points to the necessary junction of word and flesh, but incarnation of the divine must be repeated by each man and each woman who becomes divine. Divinization happens through practices of prayer and breathing, perception, listening, love of self and love of other, speech and silence, and even writing.[138] These practices are always embodied, and they are shaped by sexual (and other) differences.[139] For Irigaray, the incarnation is sexed, which

---

[136] Irigaray, "Divine Women," 60. See also Phyllis H. Kaminski, "Mysticism Embodied Differently: Luce Irigaray and the Subject of Incarnate Love," *Religious Studies and Theology* 17, no. 2 (1998): 59–79.

[137] Irigaray, "Divine Women," 68–69.

[138] See Luce Irigaray, "Ethical Gestures toward the Other," *Poligrafi* 57, no. 15 (2010): 3–23.

[139] See in particular Luce Irigaray, *I Love to You: Sketch of a Possible Felicity in History*, trans. Alison Martin (New York: Routledge, 1996) and *To Be Two*, trans. Monique M. Rhodes and Marco F. Cocito-Monoc (New York: Routledge, 2001). Irigaray's insistent focus on sexual difference as the fundamental ontological difference, for which she has been heavily critiqued, seemingly prevents her from considering the role of love in same-sex relationships or between races. Although her philosophical interest is more ontological and less interpersonal, this blind spot is a serious weakness in her later thought. Extending the notion of "difference," as Ellen Armour has called for, could apply the basic Irigarayan schema in

means multiple bodies incarnate the divine in different ways. Love provides a space for the recognition of difference, where each can say "I" to the other in the dialogical process of becoming divine.[140] Women speak and write out of their difference as their flesh becomes divine word.

According to Porete, in contrast, annihilation makes the soul the place of love's incarnation. The soul is not separate from her body, nor is she reduced to it. She does not leave the created world through annihilation; if anything, she is more fully present to others in the world, acting out of love for her neighbors "without a why." But Porete is uninterested in bodily sexual difference. Her persistent apophaticism undercuts all attributes of both God and the soul, including gender. Every soul has the potential to become Christ through annihilation and transformation in love. By fully incarnating love, by being transformed into divine love, the soul receives a new identity, what Christians since Paul have called an identity "in Christ." The voice that emerges from this incarnation has a fluid gender identity—she is transgendered or beyond gender entirely there where the soul is one with God. Love provides a space for the elimination, or better, the transcendence of difference there where the soul says "I" in identification with Love.[141] The (feminine) annihilated soul speaks and writes out of that place beyond place, beyond identity, beyond difference.

---

new directions of race and sexual orientation. See Ellen T. Armour, *Deconstruction, Feminist Theology, and the Problem of Difference: Subverting the Race/Gender Divide* (Chicago: University of Chicago Press, 1999).

[140] See Irigaray, *I Love to You*, 139.

[141] See *Mirouer*, chap. 87, 246. What seems a "strange language" to Reason and leads to Reason's death is the soul's utter identification with love: "Ce n'est mie merveilles, car dedans pou de temps elle ne sera mie; mais je suis, dit ceste Ame, et suis et seray toujours sans faillir, car Amour n'a commencement ne fin ne comprennement, et je ne suis, fors que Amour." ("But it is not strange, for soon she [Reason] will be no more, but I am, says this Soul, and I am and I shall be always without fail, for Love has no beginning or end or bounds, and I am nothing but Love.") See also the Soul's self-identification in chapter 70 when Reason asks, who are you? "Je suis, dit ceste Ame, de la grace Dieu ce que je suis. Donc suis je tant seulement et nulle aultre chose, ce que Dieu est en moy; et Dieu est aussi ce mesmes qu'il est en moy; car nient est nient. Ains est, ce qui est; donc ne suis je, se je suis, sinon ce que Dieu est; et nul n'est fors Dieu; et pource ne trouve je fors Dieu, quelque part que je m'enbate; car il n'est fort que luy, a verité dire." ("I am, says this Soul, by the grace of God that which I am. So I am that alone and nothing else which God is in me; and God is also that same which he is in me; for nothing is nothing. But what is, is. And so I am not, if I am, except that which God is; and there is no-one except God, and therefore I find no-one except God, wherever I enter, for, to say truly, there is no-one but him.") *Mirouer*, chap. 70, 196 (Cf. 1 Cor 15:10).

Reading these two thinkers together underscores different ways of under-standing how God is embodied in humanity and the place of our human differences in the incarnation of Christ. If our many human differences are transcended from the perspective of annihilation, we become the place of Christ's incarnation in the soul through love, and relate to the world as God does—without a why, without the limitation of our identities, positions, and perspectives. If our differences are retained as specific instantiations of the incarnation, we might be separated from one another by those differences. Both Irigaray and Porete look to Christ for an inclusive incarnation that is not limited to Jesus but is radically and hospitably extended to humanity. But they each work out of different ontological assumptions: Irigaray argues for a double ontology or being-two, while Porete is a Christian nondual-ist. For Irigaray, difference, or at least sexual difference, is fundamental to human ontology; it cannot be erased, and the desire for annihilation of dif-ference, including the difference between God and humanity, is illusory at best. In contrast, Porete argues that human ontology is ultimately rooted in God, with whom we are one prior to our creation, but from whom we differ in the fact of our being created. While that ultimate oneness is fun-damental to human nature—it is the image of God in us that can be cov-ered over or forgotten, but never erased—our human differences are equally real, both to our experience and to the goodness and diversity of creation.[142] Porete acknowledges many social differences in her characters and imagery as well as in her inscribed audience: female, male, and transgender; same-sex

---

[142] Discussing the influence of Dionysius the Areopagite on Porete and others, Denys Turner offers a helpful explanation of this principle: "To deny that God is 'different' from creatures by way of *created* distinction does not entail that God is identical with creatures by way of created identity. For God, as Meister Eckhart says, differs *maximally* from creatures in that whereas every creature is 'different' from every other in some respect, God is differ-ent from creatures only in this: that God is 'one', but not one among many, and is identified precisely by the fact that God is the one and only being who is 'indistinct,' an *unum indistinc-tum*. Which is no more than to say, as Dionysius says, that God is 'beyond every assertion,' or, as he also says, 'God is not some kind of being.' It follows from this that statements of the soul's 'oneness' with God, such as those of Marguerite, Meister Eckhart, and Ruusbroec can be maximally emphatic—not merely rhetorically hyperbolic—without imperilling the created soul's created identity." Denys Turner, "Dionysius and Some Late Medieval Mystical Theologians of Northern Europe," in *Re-thinking Dionysius the Areopagite*, ed. Sarah Coakley and Charles M. Stang (Oxford: Wiley Blackwell, 2009), 121–35, 133. Emphasis in original.

and mixed-sex love relationships; differences of rank and class (such as serfs and nobility); differences of religious affiliation (actives and contemplatives, beguines, Austin Friars, Dominicans, Friars Minor, Carmelites); differences of literacy and understanding.[143] These real human differences can be lovingly acknowledged and embraced as such, even in the annihilation that transforms the soul.[144] Rather than destroying human nature and eliminating all difference, annihilation recovers exactly what we are meant to be: the incarnation of God's love for others on earth.

Both Irigaray and Porete present examples of writing as a practice of the incarnation, however differently conceived—writing as (sexually) different flesh made word, or writing as the practice of love without a why. Writing gives women an entry point into the Christian tradition, and a subject-position within the tradition of Western thought more broadly. In relation to Christ, writing allows female flesh to become word; it is a way of practicing the incarnation. But writing need not exhaust revelation or limit divine transcendence. A certain form of theological writing that is associated with mysticism in particular points beyond itself through its own negation. How the mystical writing of medieval women can be at once incarnational and apophatic is examined in the final chapter.

---

[143] See Kocher, *Allegories of Love*, 49–55.

[144] Although Porete herself does not explicitly say so, the positive valuation of nature that results would affirm human differences as real but relatively unimportant expressions of nature that pour out from God in creation but are each ultimately rooted in oneness with him. This Christian Neoplatonic picture of the God-world relationship is developed further by Meister Eckhart.

5

Transcendence Incarnate

Apophatic Discourse

Hadewijch of Antwerp, Angela of Foligno, and Marguerite Porete each write theology with keen awareness of the limitations of their own language in the face of God's transcendence. Because their mystical writings fall in the rich tradition of apophatic or negative theology, it is worth concluding by examining the effect this way of speaking might have on our understanding of the incarnation. In its Christian form, apophatic theology is rooted in the writings of the sixth-century Pseudo-Dionysius the Areopagite,[1] who practiced a way of writing that emphasizes the limitations of human beings to know what God is in God's nature or essence. Both God and the human experience of God are ineffable, beyond the capacity of words to bear meaning.[2] Because God exceeds the human capacity to know, grasp, or speak, "we do not know what kind of being God is."[3] God is not a being like other beings and therefore cannot be described through the same categories used for creation. Language functions differently when it comes to God. Theology itself becomes a "strategy and practice of unknowing," issuing in a distinctive form of theological discourse: "speech about God which is the failure of

---

[1] Pseudo-Dionysius, *The Complete Works*, trans. Colm Luibhéid and Paul Rorem (New York: Paulist Press, 1987); see also the excellent essays in *Re-thinking Dionysius the Areopagite*, ed. Sarah Coakley and Charles M. Stang (Oxford: Wiley Blackwell, 2009).

[2] Denys Turner, *The Darkness of God: Negativity in Christian Mysticism* (Cambridge, UK: Cambridge University Press, 1995), 19.

[3] Thomas Aquinas, *Summa Theologica*, I, q.12, a.13, ad 1.

speech."[4] Language fails. Words lie. But it is in and through written language that these self-subverting claims are made, using techniques of contradiction, paradox, and excessive speech to say, and unsay, and say again what cannot be said.

The Dionysian apophatic tradition influenced the theology of the late medieval period from Thomas Aquinas to the women mystics. As Denys Turner puts it, in the late Middle Ages, Dionysius "is less what you speak about than he is the air you breathe when you speak."[5] Apophatic writings use both affirmation (cataphasis) and negation (apophasis), and the further negation of negation, to indicate the mystery and transcendence of God. Each affirmation of God taken from scripture and creation must be "unsaid" or negated in turn.[6] While it is true, for instance, following Pseudo-Dionysius, to say that God is like a rock or a lion, or is Love or Being, it is in some sense truer to say that God is not a rock or a lion, nor our human conceptions of love, and certainly not a being like other beings; truer still to leave both affirmation and negation behind (negating the opposition between affirmation and negation) and to unite "to the completely unknown by an inactivity of all knowledge . . . [to know] beyond the mind by knowing nothing."[7] This mystical union of the unknown with the unknown by means of unknowing takes place, according to Pseudo-Dionysius, beyond language in the "brilliant darkness" of a "hidden silence."[8] But something like it is conveyed in writing through a distinctive form of discourse characterized by the "self-subverting utterance,"[9] paradox, the coincidence of opposites, and the collapse of spatiotemporal and subject-object distinctions. In other words, apophasis proceeds not only through negative statements (saying what God is not), but also through the performance of negation that doubles back upon

[4] Turner, *Darkness of God*, 19–20. See also Michael Sells, *Mystical Languages of Unsaying* (Chicago: University of Chicago Press, 1994), 2–4 and 9–10.

[5] Denys Turner, "Dionysius and Some Late Medieval Mystical Theologians of Northern Europe," in *Re-thinking Dionysius the Areopagite*, ed. Sarah Coakley and Charles M. Stang (Oxford: Wiley Blackwell, 2009), 121.

[6] See Turner, *Darkness of God*, 252; and Sells, *Mystical Languages*, 2: "The formal denial that the transcendent can be named must in some sense be valid, otherwise ineffability would not become an issue. Insofar as it is valid, however, the formal statement of ineffability turns back upon itself, and undoes itself. To say 'X is beyond names,' if true, entails that it cannot then be called by the name 'X.' In turn, the statement 'it cannot then be called X' becomes suspect, since the 'it,' as a pronoun, substitutes for a name, but the transcendent is beyond all names. As I attempt to state the aporia of transcendence, I am caught in a linguistic regress."

[7] Pseudo-Dionysius, *Mystical Theology*, in *The Complete Works*, 137.

[8] Pseudo-Dionysius, *Mystical Theology*, 135.

[9] Turner, *Darkness of God*, 21.

itself in an unending motion, as in Meister Eckhart's prayer: "let us pray to God that we may be free of God."[10] God's reality is never perfectly reflected in human knowledge or language; this is the basic point of apophatic theology. But writing can point to what transcends it through a form of discourse that strains beyond its capacity to the point of breaking into fractured, paradoxical, disordered utterances.[11]

Apophatic discourse, then, in its strictest delineation, is "collapsed, disordered language,"[12] a way of speaking about what cannot be said by unsaying. Acts of subterfuge, contradiction, paradox, and self-subversion proliferate in this form of writing that *performs* what it asserts.[13] Michael Sells makes an important distinction between apophatic theory and apophatic discourse. While apophatic theory affirms ineffability and the transcendence of God (a feature of all theology), it can do so without necessarily "turning back upon the naming used in its own affirmation of ineffability."[14] Apophatic discourse, in contrast, performs its own self-subversion. While Hadewijch, Angela, and Porete each affirm "apophatic theory" in the form of the mystery and transcendence of God, each also engages in particular linguistic strategies of "unsaying"—that is, what Sells calls "apophatic discourse," as when Porete uses the little word "without" to convey

---

[10] Meister Eckhart, "Sermon 52: *Beati pauperes spiritu*," in *The Essential Sermons, Commentaries, Treatises, and Defense*, trans. Edmund Colledge and Bernard McGinn (Mahweh, N.J.: Paulist Press, 1981), 200.

[11] Apophaticism exceeds the lineage of Dionysius and appears outside of theology, in philosophy, literature, and the arts. See, for instance, Harold Coward and Toby Foshay, eds., with Jacques Derrida, *Derrida and Negative Theology* (Albany, N.Y.: State University of New York Press, 1992); John D. Caputo, *The Prayers and Tears of Jacques Derrida: Religion without Religion* (Bloomington: Indiana University Press, 1997); Arthur Bradley, *Negative Theology and Modern French Philosophy* (London: Routledge, 2004); Sanford Budick and Wolfgang Iser, eds., *Languages of the Unsayable: The Play of Negativity in Literature and Literary Theory* (Stanford: Stanford University Press, 1987); and William Franke, ed., *On What Cannot Be Said: Apophatic Discourses in Philosophy, Religion, Literature, and the Arts* (Notre Dame, Ind.: University of Notre Dame Press, 2007), who credibly argues for the presence of the apophatic in literature and the arts (and of course in non-Western religious discourse as well), and even as the basis of all language, the genre of genres: what cannot be said functions as a limit and condition for what can be said, in every genre across disciplines.

[12] "For the negation of the negation is not a *third* utterance . . . it is rather the collapse of our affirmation and denials into disorder, which we can only express, *a fortiori*, in bits of collapsed, disordered language . . . And that is what the 'self-subverting' utterance is, a bit of disordered language." Turner, *Darkness of God*, 22. Emphasis in original.

[13] See Sells, *Mystical Languages*, 3.

[14] Sells reserves "the term *apophasis* for those writings in which unnameability is not only asserted but performed" (*Mystical Languages*, 3).

her apophatic anthropology: "I am a soul created by him without me . . . and yet I cannot be in him, unless he of himself without me puts me there, as he of himself made me without me."[15]

Negation is not the only feature of apophatic discourse. These writers also make use of a different kind of apophasis, what Turner calls an "excess of affirmations."[16] This way of writing, which he identifies with Bonaventure and Julian of Norwich, reaches toward apophasis and "bursts its own bounds in a kind of self-negating prolixity" through sheer cataphatic multiplicity, for instance, in the repetition and excesses of Hadewijch's description of union with Christ:

> Where the abyss of his wisdom is, he will teach you what he is, and with what wondrous sweetness the loved one and the Beloved dwell one in the other, and how they penetrate each other in such a way that neither of the two distinguishes himself from the other. But they abide in one another in fruition, mouth in mouth, heart in heart, body in body, and soul in soul, while one sweet divine nature flows through them both, and they are both one thing through each other, but at the same time remain two different selves—yes, and remain so forever.[17]

This prolixity can also be seen in the multiplication of characters who speak in Porete's dialogue, in the multiplicity of genres in which Hadewijch writes, and in the way Angela's discourse exceeds Brother Arnaldo's ability to contain and organize it. For these and other "mystical" authors, as Grace Jantzen notes, claims of "ineffability" are not in fact ways of keeping *silent* about their experience (as modern philosophy of religion has often assumed); rather, ineffability is "a way of indicating the transcendence of God . . . that . . . must also be understood, for them, as inexhaustible fecundity, the very opposite of frustrated speechlessness."[18] In the best theological writing, the apophatic moment is not separate from the cataphatic, nor are they sequential

---

[15] Porete, *Mirouer*, chap. 111, 302: "Or suis je . . . ame creee de luy sans moy . . . et si ne puis estre en luy, se il ne m'y mect sans moy de luy, ainsi comme il me fist sans moy de lui mesmes."

[16] Turner, *Darkness of God*, 257.

[17] "Daer de diepheit siere vroetheit es, daer sal hi v leren wat hi es, Ende hoe wonderleke soeteleke dat een lief in dat ander woent, Ende soe dore dat ander woent, Dat haerre en gheen hem seluen en onderkent. Mer si ghebruken onderlinghe ende elc anderen Mont in mont, ende herte in herte, Ende lichame in lichame, Ende ziele in ziele, Ende ene soete godlike nature doer hen beiden vloyende, Ende si beide een dore hen seluen, Ende al eens beide bliuen, Ja ende bliuende." Hadewijch, *Letters*, 9.4–14 (CW, 66).

[18] Grace Jantzen, *Power, Gender, and Christian Mysticism* (Cambridge: Cambridge University Press, 1995), 284.

theological gestures: both function simultaneously as "we both say and unsay in the same theological word."[19]

Apophatic theology and discourse in this broader sense, inclusive of cataphasis that functions apophatically, characterizes much of the theology of the Middle Ages; indeed, it is a feature of all theological discourse insofar as it is properly theological.[20] Apophaticism has also been a powerful strand in contemporary feminist theologies. Beginning with Mary Daly, many Roman Catholic feminist theologians in particular have turned to the apophatic tradition as an effective tool to challenge patriarchal language and images for God as Father, King, Lord, etc. They have exposed these names and images as idols that function to support an unjust social and religious order that oppresses women. Because all names of God are relative and limited ways of speaking and writing, the apophatic tradition also supports supplementing or replacing traditional language with new names and images of God drawn from the Bible (e.g., Wisdom), tradition, and women's experience. Elizabeth Johnson, for instance, draws on the Dionysian tradition as it passes through Thomas Aquinas to argue that all speech about God is analogical and metaphorical, and that no one image or name is therefore sufficient. Rather, a multiplicity of names and images for God, both male and female, personal and abstract, and intelligible and sensible, can and must be used to point to the One who transcends them all.[21] This use of the tradition to critique itself from within is also the method of Protestant theologians such as Sallie McFague, Laurel Schneider, and Wendy Farley, among others, as well as Jewish theologian Judith Plaskow, all of whom write with a clear sense of the limits of theological language. Such limits provide opportunities for critique as well as possibilities for theological construction. Divine unknowability relativizes the authority of patriarchal religious language and traditions and loosens our ideas of God, opening space for new models, names, and images of the divine drawn from the wide diversity of human experience.

But the apophatic feminist argument has come under critique from two different directions. From one side, traditionalists argue against feminist theology by appealing to positive revelation in Jesus Christ and in scripture. On the basis of divine self-revelation, they accuse feminist theologians of

---

[19] Denys Turner, "The Darkness of God and the Light of Christ: Negative Theology and Eucharistic Presence," *Modern Theology* 15, no. 2 (1999): 143–58, 147.

[20] See Turner, "Darkness of God," 146.

[21] See Elizabeth A. Johnson, *She Who Is: The Mystery of God in Feminist Theological Discourse* (New York: Crossroad, 1997) and *Quest for the Living God: Mapping Frontiers in the Theology of God* (New York: Continuum, 2007).

idolatry, heresy, and goddess-worship for their critique of exclusively masculine language and substitution of feminine names for God.[22] This common response to apophaticism is not limited to antifeminists. As Turner points out, the (predictable) theological response to apophatic claims is to refer to revelation in Christ and in scripture: "For surely, it is said, Christ is the *visibility* of the Godhead, the source of all theological affirmativeness; so that, as it were, whatever license may or must be given to the apophatic in the meantime, in the end is the Word as it was in the beginning, therefore in the end there is speech, not silence."[23] God has spoken through Christ, his Word. What was hidden has been revealed and can be positively known and proclaimed. "No one has ever seen God," it is conceded, but "it is God the only Son, who is close to the Father's heart, who has made him known" (John 1:18 NRSV). Therefore God *is* Father and Christ *is* Son—because God has revealed as much.[24] In their critique of feminist apophatic theology, traditionalists invoke what should be the good news of the incarnation—Jesus the Christ, the Word of God made flesh—in order to argue against inclusive and multivalent language for God. Similar arguments based on revelation of God's Word—the maleness of the twelve disciples, the inability of women's bodies to image Christ—are used against the ordination of women.[25] In both

---

[22] The reaction to the 1993 Re-imagining Conference, in which God was named and worshipped as Sophia, provides a powerful but not isolated example of the backlash against feminist theological language. See Peter Steinfels, "Cries of Heresy after Feminists Meet," *New York Times*, May 14, 1994, http://www.nytimes.com/1994/05/14/us/cries-of-heresy -after-feminists-meet.html?src=pm, accessed July 15, 2012. See also Laurel Schneider, *Re-imagining the Divine: Confronting the Backlash against Feminist Theology* (Cleveland, Ohio: Pilgrim Press, 1998).

[23] Turner, "Darkness of God," 143–44.

[24] This may sound like a caricature, but not by much. See, for example, the reaction to Brian Wren's neo-Dionysian hymn "Bring Many Names" by Mark Tooley, affiliated with the watchdog group the Institute on Religion and Democracy, who says the hymn is "dangerous," because "when it refers to God as 'Mother,' it denies the authority of the bible, which uses the word 'Father' when speaking of God." He calls such changes in liturgical language "idolatry" and appeals to revelation: "Christians and Jews believe that God bends down and speaks to fallen humanity by revealing himself, primarily through the scriptures. And for reasons known entirely only to him, he does reveal himself exclusively in masculine terminology." See "Controversial Hymns Challenge US Methodists' View of God," Voice of America, July 2, 2002, http://www.voanews.com/content/a-13-a-2002-07-02-48-controversial -66290592/541141.html, accessed July 15, 2012.

[25] For instance, in the Vatican's response to feminist theology: "Letter to the Bishops of the Catholic Church on the Collaboration of Men and Women in the Church and in the World," Congregation for the Doctrine of the Faith, May 31, 2004. See also Tina Beattie, "Feminism, Vatican-Style," *The Tablet* (August 7, 2004), http://www.thetablet.co.uk/article/2190, accessed May 15, 2012.

arguments, overriding confidence in positively revealed theological language overpowers the apophatic impulse.

But from another direction, post-Christian, Goddess, and process feminist theologians also argue against the value of the apophatic tradition for feminist ends. Carol Christ, for instance, argues that apophaticism is rooted in a metaphysical dualism that makes God radically other, dominant and distant, over and against human beings and the world.[26] This God-world dualism, like other metaphysical dualisms, places God, perfection, and immutability on one side, and humanity, sin, and change on the other. Because the female body represents, to the Christian imaginary, change, sin, danger, and death, any theology that emphasizes God's transcendence supports a metaphysical system that disparages female bodies.[27] In particular, she worries about forms of apophatic mysticism that encourage annihilation or surrender of the self in the face of a transcendent deity who is wholly other to humanity. "The notion that the self must be annihilated or surrender or sacrifice itself in the presence of the divinity," she writes, "is firmly rooted in dualistic traditions in which God is defined as utterly transcendent." These traditions, in her view, cannot support "feminist theologies and thealogies that wish to affirm the female body, other bodies, natality, the earth body, and the world body. Because they are rooted in dualistic traditions, notions of divine unknowability and mystery and of radical divine otherness are not the appropriate beginning points for feminist theologies and thealogies."[28] In their appeals to mystical, apophatic strands within Christian tradition, feminist theologians reinforce dualistic assumptions of God's distance and otherness from the world. In Carol Christ's view, they are guilty of reinscribing, even unwittingly, the view of God as a dominant, distant judge, one who demands the annihilation of the human soul to achieve union with Him. For her, the problem

[26] See Carol P. Christ, "Embodied, Embedded Mysticism: Affirming the Self and Others in a Radically Interdependent World," *Journal of Feminist Studies in Religion* 24, no. 2 (2008): 159–67.

[27] For an alternative account of duality and the way difference is structured in medieval mystical theology, see Michelle Voss Roberts, *Dualities: A Theology of Difference* (Louisville, Ky.: Westminster John Knox, 2010).

[28] Christ, "Embodied, Embedded," 164. Christ argues that process metaphysics, which describes a panentheistic God-world relation and compassionate divine participation in a changing world, is more appropriate to feminist theological and thealogical construction; see her *She Who Changes: Re-imagining the Divine in the World* (New York: Palgrave Macmillan, 2004). But see also Beverly Lanzetta's counterargument, which addresses feminist criticism of annihilation language by arguing in favor of the resulting liberation of the self through annihilation, particularly in the form of the *via feminina*. See Beverly J. Lanzetta, *Radical Wisdom: A Feminist Mystical Theology* (Minneapolis: Fortress, 2005), 95–98.

with apophaticism is not so much the limits it places on human theological language, much less positive revelation, but the fact that in asserting God's ultimate transcendence and unknowability, apophatic theology works to the detriment of female bodies and the earth.

Carol Christ is right to focus on the effect on women's bodies (and the bodies of others) as the measure by which we judge the adequacy of a theological and metaphysical system. Chris Boesel and Catherine Keller describe the problem of apophaticism in a similar way, as seeming to indicate "too great a distance, too radical a separation, between divine and creaturely reality; too absolute a sense of divine transcendence in relation to the finite realm of creaturely embodiment. This transcendence smacks of indifference (and so, ethically, of quietism) in the face of needs, desires, and unjust sufferings of an embodied life."[29] But instead of rejecting apophatic theology in favor of sole focus on creaturely embodiment, they introduce the paradoxical notion of "apophatic bodies." Boesel and Keller suggest that it may be possible to "speak (and unspeak) of God without necessarily ceasing to speak of the body." In other words, it may be possible to find a theological language that is faithful and accountable both to the transcendence and infinity of God, on the one hand, and to the finitude, the needs, the desires, and the sufferings of the human body, on the other.[30] These theologians are cautiously optimistic that the apophatic tradition provides a powerful supplement to contemporary concerns for the well-being of bodies,[31] and they hint at a radically widened incarnationalism that appears in the juxtaposition of negation with embodiment.[32]

For Christians, God is revealed through the incarnation as radically embodied and inclusive love, overflowing compassion, justice, and equality, as practiced in the life and ministry of Jesus and extended to the bodies of those who incarnate the divine through him. Many feminist theologians

---

[29] Chris Boesel and Catherine Keller, *Apophatic Bodies: Negative Theology, Incarnation, and Relationality* (New York: Fordham University Press, 2010), 3.

[30] Boesel and Keller, *Apophatic Bodies*, 3.

[31] Boesel and Keller, *Apophatic Bodies*, 4. They write, "The coupling of apophasis and bodies, then, forges a heightened, ethically nuanced tension of obligation split between linguistic gestures toward a transcendent divinity on one hand, and flesh-and-blood commitments to the embodied life of creatures on the other," 7.

[32] They note that there is "one way that negative theology folds into—and has always in a certain sense folded into—a relational affirmation of bodies. Does a radically widened incarnationalism begin to appear in the void of the radical negation? If so, our presenting enigma of apophatic bodies would signify more than a simple oxymoron," but this possibility receives little attention in their collection. Boesel and Keller, *Apophatic Bodies*, 5.

have found in the incarnation affirmation of the human body, of nonhuman bodies and the world, and, in the life of Jesus, an ethics of justice, compassion and solidarity in suffering, and healing and liberation. For Christian theologians, what is revealed in the incarnation is not a distant, transcendent, radically divine Other who demands human surrender, but a God who surrenders him/herself out of love, and intimately embraces suffering humanity. The divine otherness is "kataphatically revealed as the God of love, in whom Christians profess their faith."[33] This understanding of incarnation, which stands in paradoxical tension with notions of divine otherness and transcendence, has sustained the speech and writings of women. Critics of apophatic theology overlook the role of the incarnation in an apophatic understanding of divine transcendence. The incarnation does not eliminate the transcendence and mystery of God, revealing once and for all what has been hidden as if apophatic caution were no longer needed.[34] But it does overturn concepts of divine otherness that set God over and against the world in a rigid dualism that has pernicious effects on bodies nonhuman and human, especially those that are poor and female. In Laurel Schneider's words, "The coming to flesh of divinity completely disrupts the smooth otherness of the divine, its separateness from the changeable stuff of earth, its abhorrence of rot, its innocence of death, and its ignorance of life or desire."[35] In the theological writings of Hadewijch, Angela, and Porete, the incarnation preserves apophatic mystery in the midst of revelation, the incarnation of Christ both reveals and conceals, and Christ appears in our own "apophatic bodies."

The incarnation authorizes women's mystical speech and writing through the creative interplay of word and flesh: God's Word became flesh so that their flesh might become word, extending the incarnation through practices of mystical speech and writing. But that revelation does not end all mystery; indeed, what is revealed by the "word" is a form of speech that is frequently self-negating, paradoxical, and opaque in the writings of the mystics. The incarnation claims that Christ is flesh of our flesh, but also divine,

[33] Lieven Boeve, "Christus Postmodernus: An Attempt at Apophatic Christology," in *The Myriad Christ: Plurality and the Quest for Unity in Contemporary Christology*, ed. T. Merrigan and J. Haers (Leuven: Leuven University Press, 2000), 591.

[34] See Paul S. Fiddes, "The Quest for a Place Which Is 'Not-a-Place': The Hiddenness of God and the Presence of God," in *Silence and the Word: Negative Theology and Incarnation*, ed. Oliver Davies and Denys Turner (Cambridge: Cambridge University Press, 2008), 35–60.

[35] Laurel Schneider, "Promiscuous Incarnation," in *The Embrace of Eros: Bodies, Desires, and Sexuality in Christianity*, ed. Margaret D. Kamitsuka (Minneapolis: Fortress, 2010), 232.

and, as God enfleshed, transcendent, ungraspable mystery. This transcendent mystery can be seen in the resurrected Christ, whose mystical body is encountered in the church and the materiality of its sacraments. It also can be found in the flesh of the incarnation, in the bodies of those who incarnate the apophatic Christ through their spiritual and ethical practices, and in encounters with the bodies of those on the margins in whom the face of Christ appears incognito. The transcendent mystery of God is both hidden and revealed, both written and unsaid, in our bodies and our words through the apophatic Christ.

Apophatic Writing/Writing the Incarnation

Writing within the apophatic Christian tradition, Hadewijch, Angela, and Porete were each acutely aware of boundaries of theological language and the risks of misrepresenting God. And yet each was compelled to speak and write of and for Christ in words, at turns startling and striking, that seemed to them both necessary and impossible. The transcendent mystery of God informs their writings, which strain to express what cannot be said through language that both affirms and denies in the same utterance. Compelled to speak and write of God, they each brush up against the limits of language. What results is not silence, but rather a fecundity of speech that is rooted in the incarnation and the love it reveals. The previous chapters have focused on the ways in which Hadewijch, Angela, and Porete write the incarnation. Here it is worth considering the ways in which they each write apophasis, to see how the transcendent mystery of God informs their understanding of Christ in both the content and form of their writing.

When Hadewijch writes lessons of divine love to her beguines, she immediately points to what cannot be said. Describing love is no easier than writing of God, for God is Love: "For with nothing the mind says can one put into words the theme of Love, which I desire and want for you. I say no more; here we are obliged to speak with our soul. Our theme is boundless; for this theme—Love—which we take, is God himself by Nature."[36] With reference to the apophatic claims of Isaiah, she writes that "earth cannot understand heavenly wisdom. Words enough and Dutch enough can be found for all things on earth, but I do not know any Dutch or any words that answer

---

[36] "Want met ghenen sinnen en machmen te worde brenghen die materie van Minnen, Daer ic v in meyne ende wille; Jc en segghe niet el; daer toe behoeftmen metter sielen te sprekene. Onse materie es te wijt; want wi nemen Minne die god selue bi naturen es." *Letters,* 19.27–32 (CW, 89).

my purpose."[37] Language applies more readily to earthly matters, but when it comes to love, Hadewijch struggles to express this boundless theme. Even in the midst of her prolific writing, she claims "I say no more," and refers to the speech of the soul because "no Dutch can be found for *all I have said to you.*"

Speaking even as she claims not to, Hadewijch's famous descriptions of mystical union make similar references to ineffability: "O *deus*! What a marvel takes place then—when such great dissimilarity attains evenness and becomes wholly one without elevation! Oh, I dare write no more here about this; I must always keep silence about the best, because of my sad lot, and besides no one can truly reproach himself because he knows nothing about God."[38] Respect for the mystery of God and concern for her audience lead to claims of silence—in the midst of writing. In other passages, words tumble over themselves in an excessive, ecstatic breathlessness in which God and the soul blend together: "But when God and the blessed soul are united he, together with the blessed soul, will be exalted from the earth in all beauty. For when the soul has nothing else but God, and when it retains no will but lives exclusively according to his will alone; and when the soul is brought to nought and with God's will wills all that he wills, and is engulfed in him, and is brought to nought—then he is exalted above the earth, and then he draws all things to him; and so the soul becomes with him all that he himself is."[39] Hadewijch both gestures toward the apophatic limits of language and then refuses them: instead of obligating silence, the boundless theme of love demands an equally boundless form of writing that bubbles over in profusion. Her apophatic discourse takes the form of an "excess of affirmations" that blend God and the soul at the level of syntax in a way that violates the law of noncontradiction: they are both one and two, both distinct and indistinct, forever. Speaking of God and the soul in the union of love demands this peculiar form of writing.

[37] "Want hemelsche redene en mach ertrike niet verstaen; want van allen dien dat in ertrike es, mach men redene ende dietsch ghenoech venden; Mer hier toe en weet ic gheen dietsch noch ghene redene." *Letters*, 17.114–22 (CW, 84).

[38] "Ay deus, wat wonder ghesciet dan daer, Daer groet onghelijc effene ende al een wert sonder verheffen. Ay ic en dar hier af nummer scriuen; ic moet emmer vanden besten meest swighen dore mijn ongheual, Ende om dat wel na nieman en ghemest ane hem seluen dat hi van gode niet en weet." *Letters*, 22.72–78 (CW, 96).

[39] "Mer alse god ende die salighe ziele een sijn, Soe es hi metter zalegher zielen alre scoenst volhoghet vander erden; Want alse haer el niet en es dan god, Ende si ghenen wille en behoudet Dan dat si sijns enechs willen leuet, Ende de ziele te nieute wart, Ende met sinen wille wilt al dat hi wilt, ende in hem verswolghen es ende te nieute worden, soe es hi volhoghet vander erden Ende soe trect hi alle dinc te hem; Ende soe wertse met hem al dat selue dat hi es." *Letters*, 19.52–61 (CW 90).

Angela of Foligno makes similar gestures toward the limits of language. She tells her confessor, "I know with the utmost certainty that the more one feels God, the less is one able to say anything about him, for the very fact of feeling something of this infinite and unutterable Good renders one incapable of speaking about it."[40] Angela seems to prefer silence—she repeatedly claims, "my secrets are mine"[41]—and experiences her own speech, at the behest of her confessor, as a kind of blasphemy: "Everything I say now about it seems to say nothing or to be badly said. . . . It seems that whatever I say about it is blasphemy. And when you asked me if this [divine darkness] drew me more than everything I had ever experienced, what I answered seemed to me to be blasphemy."[42] At the height of her mystical itinerary, when her words seem to blaspheme and fail, Angela nevertheless describes God with an affirmation that has the force of negation. She calls God the "All Good," who resides in a chamber in her soul (similar to Teresa's interior castle)[43] and gives her an inner equanimity and a revelation of God's goodness—the All Good beyond any particular truth.[44] Of this goodness, Angela claims, "I speak about it so badly because I cannot find words to express it—I nonetheless affirm that in this manifestation of God I discover the complete truth."[45] Despite the impediments of speech, Angela boldly names and affirms God's goodness.

Angela does not oppose apophatic and cataphatic theology; they coincide in her book. As Angela names God the All Good, she hedges that affirmation with cautions of speaking "badly" and apparent "blasphemy." The term

---

[40] "cognovi certissime quod illi qui magis sentiunt de Deo, minus possunt loqui de eo; quia eo ipso quod sentiunt de illo infinito et indicibili, de eo minus loqui possunt." *Il Libro*, 322 (*Complete Works*, 191). She even challenges her confessor to preach this message: "you would then say to the people with total self-assurance: 'Go with God, because about God I can say nothing.' " (*Complete Works*, 192).

[41] "Secretum meum mihi." *Il Libro*, 496 (*Complete Works*, 248).

[42] "et quidquid dico videtur mihi nihil dicere vel male dicere. Et postea dixit: Videtur mihi blasphemare. Et quando quaesivisti si trahit plus quam hactenus, [quod ita respondi] videtur mihi quod sit blasphemare." *Il Libro*, 360 (*Complete Works*, 205).

[43] Indeed, Teresa very likely borrowed the image from Angela. See Gillian Ahlgren, "Teresa of Avila and Angela of Foligno: Ecstatic Sisters," *Magistra: A Journal of Women's Spirituality in History* 10, no. 1 (2004): 88–116.

[44] Lanzetta elaborates on this correlation of Teresa of Avila with earlier mystics such as Angela and connects the incarnation with the *via negativa*, crucially reinterpreted as the "dark night of the feminine," in *Radical Wisdom*, 132.

[45] "Et in illo manifestare Dei, quamvis ego blasphemem dicendo et male dicendo illud quia non possum illud loqui, dico tamen quod in illo manifestare Dei est tota veritas." *Il Libro*, 388 (*Complete Works*, 214).

"Good" is modified as "infinite and unutterable," both spoken and unspoken by negation, and it is goodness ("All") unlike any human goodness. Likewise, when Angela's confessor asks about her vision of the darkness of God, Angela describes this darkness in dialectical tension with the incarnation of Christ, her vision of the "God-man":

> When I am in that darkness I do not remember anything about anything human, or the God-man, or anything which has a form. Nevertheless, I see all and I see nothing. As what I have spoken of withdraws and stays with me, I see the God-Man. He draws my soul with great gentleness and he sometimes says to me: 'You are I and I am you.' I see, then, those eyes and that face so gracious and attractive as he leans to embrace me. In short, what proceeds from those eyes and that face is what I said that I saw in that previous darkness which comes from within, and which delights me so that I can say nothing about it. When I am in the God-man my soul is alive. And I am in the God-man much more than in the other vision of seeing God with darkness. . . . The vision with darkness, however, draws me so much more that there is no comparison. On the other hand, I am in the God-man almost continually.[46]

As Paul Lachance notes, these two visions—of darkness and of the God-man—should not be seen as sequential, or even, for that matter, as separate moments.[47] They coincide as an approach to God through both the incarnation of Christ, with whom Angela experiences herself in continual union, and the transcendent darkness of God, the "unknown nothingness" beyond visions, beyond speech.[48]

While Angela worries that her words "blaspheme," Marguerite Porete claims that words speak "lies" more than the truth with respect to God, the soul, and annihilation. Near the end of the *Mirror*, the "Soul who caused this book to be written" laments the results of her efforts and concludes that "My heart is drawn up so high and plunged down so deep that I cannot reach it; for everything which one can say or write of God, or, what is more than saying, that one can think of him is far more lying than it is speaking the truth."[49] Like Thomas' analogies, Porete thinks truth can be spoken, but always within a context of greater dissimilarity that, for her, resembles lying. But where words weaken and fall short in lies, love speaks truth: "For the

---

[46] *Il Libro*, 362 (*Complete Works*, 205).

[47] See Lachance's introduction, *Complete Works*, 69–77.

[48] "O nihil incognitum!" *Il Libro*, 734 (*Complete Works*, 316).

[49] *Mirouer*, chap. 119, 334: "Mon cueur est tiré si hault et avalé si bas, que je n'y puis actaindre; car tout ce que l'en peut de Dieu dire ne escrire, ne que l'en en peut penser, qui plus est que n'est dire, est assez mieulx mentir que ce n'est vray dire." The internal rhymes of this sentence give a musical effect to its "unsaying." See also *Mirouer*, chap. 132, 390.

best that anyone could say to me about him is nothing, compared with what he is in himself. And so I needed to hear no more said of him, except to be told that my beloved cannot be comprehended. . . . And so my love would never reach an end of loving, for it always will have new love from him who is all love, immense though he be."[50] God's incomprehensibility is matched by infinite love both from and for God, for the nature of that incomprehensible mystery is love.[51] Divine hiddenness is not arbitrary or capricious but infinitely loving, and it is in the nature of love to give of itself. From love issues speech and writing—the Soul's song and Porete's book. The words of love (and of Love, the character) are not always easy to understand, however, and require interpretation, even translation between Reason's language and the language of Love.[52]

With great skill, Porete writes the limits and lies of language. She further introduces frequent repetition of short phrases that signal apophatic moments within the text: "the more,"[53] which points to that which exceeds language; the pairing of "all and nothing" to describe the paradox of the soul's annihilation and transformation in love; and "without" to unsay what has been asserted at the level of syntax. Porete also delights in the rhetorical figure of the chiasmus, such as "This is the uncreated goodness which loves the goodness she has created."[54] Here love anchors the crossing of goodness both created and uncreated. Indeed, the chiasmus functions for her as a way of holding in tension many of the dialectical pairs that structure the themes of the book, such as "is" and "is not" and the divine name "FarNear,"[55] who perfectly encapsulates, and personifies, what Nicholas of Cusa calls the coincidence of opposites in Porete's description:

> The far distance of this goodness is much nearer, for the soul sees more clearly that
> Far-Near in herself, who constantly makes her to want in union to be his, with no

[50] *Mirouer*, chap. 31, 104: "Car le mieulx que on m'en pourroit dire est nient, au regard de ce qui est de luy. Et plus ne me failloit oïr dire de luy, sinon que on me deist que mon amy est incomprehensible . . . par quoy mon amour ne trouvast terme en amour, pour avoir tousjours nouvelle amour de celluy qui est tout amour, tant grant qu'il soit."

[51] On this point, see Wendy Farley, *Gathering Those Driven Away: A Theology of Incarnation* (Louisville, Ky.: Westminster John Knox, 2011), esp. chs. 3 and 5.

[52] See, for instance, *Mirouer*, chap. 71, 198.

[53] See, e.g., *Mirouer*, chap. 52, 152.

[54] "C'est la Bonté increee qui ayme la bonté qu'elle a creee." *Mirouer*, chap. 111, 302; translation modified.

[55] On "Loingprés," the personified coincidence of immanence and transcendence, see Bernard McGinn, *The Flowering of Mysticism: Men and Women in the New Mysticism (1200–1350)*, vol. 3 of *The Presence of God: A History of Western Christian Mysticism* (New York: Crossroad, 1998), 256.

hindrance from anything else which may happen. She is all his, never knowing how, and when she is one with him she is nothing. Then she has no more to do for God than God has to do for her. Why? Because he is, and she is not. When she has become nothing, she has kept nothing of herself, for this is enough for her, that he is and she is not. Then she is stripped naked of all things, for now she is without being, there where she had being before she might be. And so she has what she has from God, and she is that which God is, through the transmutation of love, there at that point where she was before she could flow forth from the goodness of God.[56]

Porete's apophatic theology—of both God and the soul—indicates language's limits but no more keeps silent than Angela or Hadewijch in the face of those limits. Love anchors the goodness of creation and the writing that emerges from it to reveal the goodness of love. Writing theology may be folly, like lighting up the sun with a lantern or a torch, as Porete is keenly aware, but she also knows that those lies and blasphemies are the language of love.[57] They are the song of the soul.

All three writers can be considered superb apophatic theologians. They each have a clear sense of the limits of their own words to represent God, and they turn those words back upon themselves in a performative unsaying that points the reader or listener to what cannot be said, whether through an excess of affirmations and superlatives or through negation. They achieve this effect in both the content and form of their writings. These theologians combine and invent new genres into a mystical way of writing marked by creativity and multiplicity. As Jantzen notes, "a proper grasp of divine ineffability is an invitation to experiment with language, to stretch it to its limits so that its very articulacy may lead beyond itself to the silence of God."[58] This experimentation can be seen in the multiple genres in which Hadewijch writes, as if one genre is just not enough to say what cannot be said; in the way both she and Porete make creative use of secular vernacular literature and invent a new genre, "la mystique courtoise,"[59] to write Christian theology; in the way multiple authors (Angela, Arnaldo, God) coauthor Angela's narrative and combine spiritual itinerary with visions, theological reflection, and, in the *Instructions*, epistles and testimony; and in the way Porete's *Mirror* requires a vast array of *dramatis personae* through which to speak. With reference to Eckhart's "omninameable unnameable," Jantzen concludes that ineffability

---

[56] *Mirouer*, chap. 135, 396.

[57] See *Mirouer*, chap. 97.

[58] Jantzen, *Power*, 284.

[59] Barbara Newman, *From Virile Woman to WomanChrist: Studies in Medieval Religion and Literature* (Philadelphia: University of Pennsylvania Press, 1995), 137–67.

invites mystical writers "to stretch and pull language beyond all boundaries. 'To look for a way of speaking' does not result in finding no such way but in finding 'all of them', an embarrassment of riches, none of them ultimate, all of them penultimately provocative."[60]

This literary richness is rooted in a sophisticated medieval theology of language. God's transcendence exceeds linguistic expression but words do not fall silent. Revelation is the other side of the ineffable coin. Words themselves are the vehicle of divine self-revelation and the path to God, through both affirmation and negation, even if language does not quite reach all the way to God.[61] The confidence that words can reveal the divine is grounded in scripture and, particularly, in the incarnation of the Word, but not without remainder. The incarnation, the Word made flesh, gives confidence in language to say, imperfectly, through analogy and metaphor, but it does not lessen the need for unsaying.[62] Ineffability and revelation go hand in hand, at every moment. "As God is made available to humankind through the Word incarnate and through the words of scripture," Jantzen concludes with respect to the mystics, "so humans ascend to God through the words which reveal and conceal the divine mystery."[63] When we look to the theological writings of Hadewijch, Angela, and Porete, we can see just how clearly their writings are justified and supported by a theology of language grounded in the incarnation. But the incarnation is not limited to one revelation, given once and for all as the final Word. Just as a multiplicity of words, images, and genres are needed to name that which is unnameable and omninameable, so too, a multiplicity of bodies incarnate these words. A multiplicity of words and flesh both reveal and conceal divine transcendence in the incarnation.

In the midst of these apophatic writings, Christ is ever present not as a positive revelation of what has been concealed, eliminating all hiddenness, but as the one who reveals transcendence in both word and flesh—in writing. When Hadewijch approaches the incarnation through the figure of Mary, and in so doing taps into the semiotic undercurrent of language that gives revolutionary force to her poetry; when Angela encounters the Word, both suffering and beautiful, in her flesh and responds with her own words; when Porete writes the annihilated soul as the place of God's love on the model of Christ—each writes the incarnation as that which reveals and conceals, says

---

[60] Jantzen, *Power*, 286. See Meister Eckhart, "Commentary on Exodus," in *Meister Eckhart: Teacher and Preacher*, ed. Bernard McGinn (Mahwah, N.J.: Paulist Press, 1986), 54.

[61] See Jantzen, *Power*, 284; and Boeve, "Christus Postmodernus," 580.

[62] See Jantzen, *Power*, 289.

[63] Jantzen, *Power*, 284.

and unsays, through a multiplicity of bodies and words. None of these is the definitive revelation of the Word, no more than the historical body of Jesus is the final earthly encounter with the Christ. What we find are glimpses of God's love through Christ in multiple forms of flesh and word, both hidden and revealed.

The Apophatic Christ

Christ can be approached theologically in many ways: as the earthly Jesus of history known partially through the texts of scripture; as the Christs of faith and culture, appearing with different faces for different communities; and as the risen Christ, who is met in the Eucharist, in practices of prayer, in the bodies of the afflicted, and in the compassion of the just.[64] As divine word and wisdom and as fully human flesh, Christ appears apophatically in every form, always receding from our grasp. Human language gives way as we try to describe Christ just as it reaches its limits with respect to God.[65] What is revealed in Christ, as Turner makes clear, is "not only the visibility of the Godhead, but also the invisibility: if Christ is the way, Christ is, in short, our access to the *un*knowability of God, not so as ultimately to know it, but so as to be brought into participation with the *Deus absconditus* precisely as *unknown*."[66] For this reason, the prologue to the gospel of John claims both that Christ has made God known, and that God remains unseen (1:18). Instead of the word breaking silence, positively revealing what was hidden, the incarnation of the Word invites us into relationship and participation with the unknown God.[67]

One way of approaching the apophatic Christ is by thinking through the relationship, and the distinction, between the Word or Logos and the word—our human words. The Word remains unknown, transcendent, even as it is revealed in particular words, which provide the way to the Word. In his postmodern interpretation of the Chalcedonian definition, Lieven Boeve argues that "In his own person, Jesus Christ signifies . . . the relation between Word (Logos) and word. . . . The Logos incarnated in the word, becomes signified

[64] See Sallie McFague, *The Body of God: An Ecological Theology* (Minneapolis: Fortress, 1993), 195.

[65] Sarah Coakley argues for an apophatic reading of the Chalcedonian "definition" (*horos*) in "What Does Chalcedon Solve and What Does It Not?," 159–63. See also Elizabeth Johnson, who suggests that even the maleness of Jesus the Christ must be understood apophatically in *She Who Is*, 163.

[66] Turner, "Darkness of God," 145. Emphasis in original.

[67] See Fiddes, "Quest for a Place," 60.

in the word, but does not identify itself with the word. The word 'evokes,' thereby determining the indeterminable Logos, and precisely in this determining distinguishes itself from the Logos. The word never becomes Logos, but is the way to the Logos."[68] This relationship-in-distinction between Word and word is described by the Chalcedonian definition as the union between the divine and human natures of Christ. Through the incarnation, Christians encounter God (the Word) but only in and through Christ's humanity (the word), which, it should be noted, is marked by its own unknowability. Boeve continues: "Jesus Christ is considered by believers to be the definitive signification (revelation) of God—'Whoever sees me, sees the Father' (cf. John 14:9)—but it implies at the same time that his person, life and words, being signification of God, can only be known as the word about the Logos, while standing in a relationship to the Logos. In other words: God's superfluous love has been revealed in a particular life story that does not exhaust this love, but nevertheless signifies it in a definitive way."[69] This relationship between word and Word, both revealed and yet hidden, requires continuing interpretation in new contexts. For this interpretation, Christ *is* the hermeneutics, the signification, and revelation of God, but insofar as he is God, can be approached only hermeneutically, without knowing *what* God is.[70] Incarnation is one way of describing "this tensile relation between the particular, context-determined word and the indeterminate Word (Logos)."[71]

To encounter the transcendence of God through Christ, in particular, contextual words, is to recognize the need for continual interpretation of the incarnation in ever new contexts. Medieval women mystical writers interpreted the incarnation in a way that supported their own writing, indeed, their own becoming divine, and I have argued that these writings can support a feminist inclusive interpretation of the incarnation today, for the apophatic Christ is encountered not only in words, which demand interpretation, but in bodies as well. Just as in words, Christ appears in bodies in an apophatic manner. That is, Christ both is and is not incarnate in the flesh of human bodies, truly so but not simply or without remainder.[72] There is a both/and-ness about the logic of the apophatic Christ, who is absent, insofar as he is

---

[68] Boeve, "Christus Postmodernus," 589.

[69] Boeve, "Christus Postmodernus," 589.

[70] See Thomas Aquinas: "In this life what God is is unknown to us [even] by the revelation of grace; and so [by grace] we are joined to him as to something unknown." *Summa Theologica* I, q.12.13, ad. 1.

[71] Boeve, "Christus Postmodernus," 591.

[72] See Turner, "Darkness of God," 152.

risen, but nevertheless present in the bodies of his followers. In this way, the apophatic Christ transforms his followers into himself, who increasingly become divine as they meet him in sacrament, practice, and prayer.

The Christian apophatic tradition makes frequent use of vertical imagery (ladders, ascent, etc.), but these are metaphors: to refer to the "transcendence and 'otherness' of God from the world," as Paul Fiddes notes, "is not about absence, but about a mode of presence in which God cannot be confused with the world."[73] The transcendence of God is encountered in the world through embodiment, paradigmatically revealed within the body of Christ. Because of the incarnation, apophatic theology is not inevitably hierarchical or dualistic; those categories are put into question. Instead, transcendence is found within immanence, within human differences, and within the created world. Still speaking metaphorically, this encounter with transcendence is more "horizontal" than vertical, to use Luce Irigaray's language. Sallie McFague notes that "The transcendence of God is in its primary and most important sense the invisible face of God, that aspect or dimension that we never see, never know. . . . it is the mystery, the absoluteness, that relativizes all our notions and models of God."[74] While she claims that "We know God—we have some intimation of the invisible face of God—through divine incarnation in nature and in the paradigmatic Jesus of Nazareth,"[75] these forms of incarnation point to transcendent mystery rather than obscure it. In her model of the body of God, each form of the incarnation "radicalizes divine immanence and transcendence," or, to put it somewhat differently, each speaks both cataphatically and apophatically. To radicalize transcendence in this way is to extend what we mean by "incarnation" to other bodies: "This," McFague concludes, "is experiencing the world as God's body, the ordinariness of all bodies contained within and empowered by the divine."[76]

Transcendence can be found within the intrahuman sphere in our human differences, and this aspect of difference, especially insofar as it registers through language, is a feature of the French feminist theorists who inform this project. Irigaray, for instance, uses the term "horizontal transcendence" to indicate the alterity or otherness of the other person (particularly, for her, the other of sexual difference). Difference indicates the negative within (not above) human relationships and the transcendence of each one to the other. To recognize the transcendence of the other is to say,

[73] Fiddes, "Quest for a Place," 45.

[74] McFague, *Body of God*, 192.

[75] McFague, *Body of God*, 194.

[76] McFague, *Body of God*, 194.

"you will never be me nor mine": the other is not identical to me nor reducible to an object of my possession. Each one is transcendent to the other and irreducibly different—this difference is the negative that limits the pretensions of the self.[77] By relocating transcendence between human beings rather than in the heights above, Irigaray interprets the message of the incarnation: God made human reveals divine transcendence within flesh: "Flesh, the flesh of each one is not substitutable for the other. It is—prior to any God—transcendence here and now. While God can help to arrange space, space-time, he never takes 'the place of.' He lets difference be achieved, even invites it to happen."[78] Closely related to the concept of horizontal transcendence is Irigaray's "sensible transcendental," the discovery of divine transcendence within embodied difference and the possibility of the divinization of the flesh.[79]

With the juxtaposition of apophatic phrases such as "immanental transcendence or transcendent immanence"[80] and "horizontal transcendence" or "sensible transcendental," McFague and Irigaray identify interpretive possibilities within the incarnation of Christ. Christ does not offer a positive revelation that overturns the hiddenness of God, the invisible now made visible; rather, Christ retains all the transcendent mystery of divinity and brings that transcendence into the world, indeed, reveals it already within human flesh. Transcendence and immanence are not two opposing attributes of divinity any more than apophasis and cataphasis are two separate or sequential ways of speaking theologically. Instead, they coincide in the apophatic Christ, whose incarnation reveals transcendence within human embodiment and relationality. This apophatic Christ is met in apophatic bodies and apophatic words.

The Incarnation of the Word in Apophatic Bodies

The incarnation reveals the transcendent mystery within each of us. Thinking about Christology in apophatic terms supports an inclusive understanding of the incarnation through an equally apophatic anthropology. Human beings are, in Gregory of Nyssa's phrase, "an incomprehensible image of the

[77] Irigaray here writes out of the Hegelian tradition of recognition of the other through limitation, difference, or the negative. See Luce Irigaray, *I Love to You: Sketch of a Possible Felicity in History*, trans. Alison Martin (New York: Routledge, 1996), 13.

[78] Irigaray, *An Ethics of Sexual Difference*, trans. Carolyn Burke and Gillian C. Gill (Ithaca, N.Y.: Cornell University Press, 1993), 167.

[79] See chapter 4. See also Amy Hollywood, *Sensible Ecstasy: Mysticism, Sexual Difference, and the Demands of History* (Chicago: University of Chicago Press, 2002), 199–210.

[80] McFague, *Body of God*, 194.

incomprehensible"[81] no less incomprehensible through the renewal of their image in Christ. The appearance of the Word in the flesh only deepens the mystery of both God and humanity, and human beings are no less incomprehensible in their bodies than in other ways of identifying the *imago dei*. As Boesel and Keller note, "material embodiment may entail a strange and mysterious infinitude all its own," no less than the infinitude of God that is registered through apophasis.[82] Flesh in itself remains unknowable.[83] Kristeva's theory of the semiotic makes this clear: the drives and rhythms of the (maternal) body remain external to language (and therefore knowledge), even as the semiotic provides the material support that shapes and influences what we can know and speak. When theologians speak and write apophatically with respect to God and Christ, it is also necessary to turn that language back upon ourselves, to unsay objectifying speech about human bodies and desires in the same manner in which we resist objectifying speech about Christ or God. Objectifying speech about God and human beings, bad theology or bad anthropology, can have equally disastrous effects on vulnerable bodies.

Old and new theological sources—such as the medieval women mystics and the French feminist theorists and their interpreters—can help to resist objectifying speech and to write apophatic theology, Christology, and anthropology with loving attention to bodies. Krista E. Hughes, for instance, discovers in Cixous support for an apophatic theology of bodies—in a way that resonates both with the incarnation and with the erotic writings of the women mystics—in passages in which Cixous' written effort to describe her lover flounders at the limits of language. It is not the height of infinite transcendence that unsettles her words; rather, it is the lovely and immediate transcendence of the embodied other, whose difference eludes the grasp of language in a fully sensible moment. By finding apophasis within the human erotic relationship—and in difference rather than union—Cixous provides a postmodern supplement to traditional forms of apophatic theology. Hughes concludes that Cixous "models an apophasis of sensible

[81] See Kathryn Tanner, "In the Image of the Invisible," in *Apophatic Bodies*, 118, who argues that "an apophatic anthropology is the consequence of an apophatic theology. If humans are the image of God, they are, as Gregory of Nyssa affirmed, an incomprehensible image of the incomprehensible."

[82] Boesel and Keller, *Apophatic Bodies*, 10–11.

[83] Pheng Cheah notes that "with respect to the flesh of embodiment, one can say that one arrives but one never arrives at a true end because the embodiment of finite beings is a process that has no end. In flesh, one is always arriving." Pheng Cheah and Elizabeth Grosz, "The Future of Sexual Difference: An Interview with Judith Butler and Drucilla Cornell," *Diacritics* 28, no. 1 (1998): 33.

intimacy that theologians might read as analogous to divine-human love and
also supports the feminist theological affirmation that humans encounter the
divine within embodied relations. God . . . both inspires and emerges from
the multiple bodies of the cosmos and their interrelations."[84] Cixous' way of
writing a sensible apophasis, like Irigaray's horizontal transcendence and sensible transcendental, discovers the divine transcendence within the human
intersubjective realm, in bodies and in words. Bodies can be seen as "living
manifestations of the divine" in so far as we can perceive their difference as
transcendence—a transcendence that protects the vulnerability of the other
and a difference that makes relationship possible.[85] This apophatic anthropology found in Cixous, among others, recognizes human bodies as potential
instances of incarnation, as the divine enfleshed.

Human bodies are neither mute flesh nor static material. They are not
prelinguistic, waiting for the Word to give them meaning, but they already
signify within and beyond language.[86] Flesh carries meaning with it, as
Kristeva's theory of the semiotic shows, and yet something about flesh nevertheless resists our too-easy comprehension and pushes back against our
theological categories. Human flesh appears in the form of "volatile bodies,"[87] dynamic and marked by multiple differences; as "speaking bodies"[88]
articulating pleasure and pain, suffering and finitude; as "apophatic bodies," that is, as "those infinite incarnations that continually conceal and disclose the divine that moves among and within us."[89] The mysterious flesh of
Christ's incarnation seems to require multiple bodies in which to both hide
and appear. It signifies in the multiplicity of our human differences. It is in
and through these "sensible bodies that surround us, that make up our very
lives, preceding and exceeding language and ever mediating whatever we can
know of the divine or the infinite or the transcendent"[90] that we meet Christ,
that we incarnate divine transcendence.

But God is not a body and our bodies are not God. The apophatic
logic to the way in which human bodies incarnate divine transcendence is a

[84] Krista E. Hughes, "Intimate Mysteries: The Apophatics of Sensible Love," in *Apophatic Bodies*, 352.

[85] Hughes, "Intimate Mysteries," 357.

[86] See Judith Butler, *Bodies That Matter: On the Discursive Limits of "Sex"* (New York:
Routledge, 1993).

[87] See Elizabeth Grosz, *Volatile Bodies: Toward a Corporeal Feminism* (Bloomington:
Indiana University Press, 1994).

[88] See Hollywood, *Sensible Ecstasy*, 21.

[89] Hughes, "Intimate Mysteries," 363.

[90] Hughes, "Intimate Mysteries," 363.

logic of "yes and no," of "both/and," of affirmation and negation, presence and absence. The ancient danger of idolatry haunts efforts to perceive the divine transcendence in human bodies and human differences. We are icons of Christ, not idols; we are not divine ourselves but we live into divinity, as we participate in Christ through grace, sacrament, and practice. The medieval women mystics understood the way in which human beings participate in God (through creation and incarnation, but under the sign of negation), but it was not always clear to their readers, who sometimes mistakenly saw autotheism.[91] (This is one risk of apophatic discourse: because it functions dialectically, it is always subject to misreading.) We are not God but we can, with Hadewijch, Angela, and Porete, become divine through participation. In other words, the incarnation, even radically inclusive, remains rooted in Christ. Human beings, human bodies and human words, participate in the Word made flesh, but they are not God. The logic of apophasis is always at work: revelation is true, but partial, analogous, more dissimilar than similar, truer in negation than affirmation. Farley calls this the "ambiguity of incarnation;"[92] history and bodies are open to divine presence and power, but also to distortions of power, to trauma, forgetfulness, suffering, woundedness, and evil. Christ is incarnate, truly, in human flesh in a manner analogous to his presence in the sacrament and scripture and theological language, but Christ's body is wounded, suffering in solidarity unto death with wounded humanity. Even as we recognize the apophatic logic with which Christ is present and absent in bodies, we can also recognize the nature of that presence/absence: divinization is not divorced from tragedy, from suffering, and from the hurt and pain and loss attending human finitude.[93] As Angela and Hadewijch clearly recognized, it is precisely in Christ's wounds that we see ourselves and in our woundedness that we find God.

The incarnation of the Word means that multiplicity is ever a feature of our encounter with Christ in the flesh. Origen recognized the "fullness"

---

[91] See Robert E. Lerner, *The Heresy of the Free Spirit in the Later Middle Ages* (Los Angeles: University of California Press, 1972).

[92] Wendy Farley, *Tragic Vision and Divine Compassion: A Contemporary Theodicy* (Louisville, Ky.: Westminster John Knox, 1990), 114.

[93] On this point, in addition to Farley, see Hollywood, *Sensible Ecstasy*, along with recent feminist theologies of trauma, suffering, and the cross: Shelly Rambo, *Spirit and Trauma: A Theology of Remaining* (Louisville, Ky.: Westminster John Knox, 2010); Serene Jones, *Trauma and Grace: Theology in a Ruptured World* (Louisville, Ky.: Westminster John Knox, 2009); Kent L. Brintnall, *Ecce Homo: The Male-Body-in-Pain as Redemptive Figure* (Chicago: University of Chicago Press, 2012); and Wonhee Anne Joh, *Heart of the Cross: A Postcolonial Christology* (Louisville, Ky.: Westminster John Knox, 2006).

of Christ as multiplicity with respect to the many aspects, titles, and transcendent perfections of God that he reveals, writing, "in so far as Christ is
the Wisdom of God, he is a multiplicity," and "Jesus is many in accordance
with the *epinoiai* [aspects]."[94] But this multiplicity need not be gathered back
into divine unity; instead Christ is truly encountered as multiple. Schneider asserts that "If the Christian doctrine of incarnation insists upon God
actually becoming flesh (as it does), then it obliterates both the radical and
abstract otherness of God and the absolute oneness of God upon which it
also insists."[95] The radical otherness of God, vertical transcendence, is over-
turned as transcendence appears in human flesh, which is always, irreducibly,
multiple, not one. Divine transcendence is met in a multiplicity of bodies—
speaking bodies, volatile bodies, apophatic bodies—that incarnate Christ in
and through their embodied differences. These varied instances of flesh—
male and female, gay and lesbian and queer bodies, diverse races and abili-
ties—these bodies become word; they speak and write; they incarnate Christ
through their practices and when Christ appears incognito in them. Wonhee
Anne Joh interprets the mystical annihilation of the self in this way, as letting a "multiplicity of selves into my being in the world. . . . The annihilation
of self then is a call to practice a kind of way of being in the world whose
arch is being toward the other. To use Gayatri Spivak's term, such a way of
being in the world, bent and directed toward the other, is a kind of love."[96] As
Marguerite Porete shows, to empty the self in annihilation is to become the
place in which God works, the incarnation of God's love for the sake of one's
neighbor. Christ is incarnate in multiple bodies, our own and others' and in
our transcendent differences that evoke an ethics of love. Attuning ourselves
to the embodied divine, living into its presence and absence, requires spiritual practices that support divine becoming.

Practicing the Incarnation

Incarnating the divine in multiple ways, in and through our many differences, is not a matter of being, a form of idolatry. Rather, the apophatic logic
of the incarnation as it extends to other bodies is a question of becoming—
that is, a process of increasing perception, awareness, and attention to the
divine within the world and within the other. As Jantzen writes, following

---

[94] Origen, *On the Book of Joshua*, Homily 7.7; quoted in Fiddes, "Quest for a Place," 58.

[95] Schneider, "Promiscuous Incarnation," 241.

[96] Wonhee Anne Joh, "Authoring a Multiplicity of Selves and No-Self," *Journal of Feminist Studies in Religion* 24, no. 2 (2008): 171.

Irigaray, becoming divine has the "aim of increasing sensitivity to the face of the Other: the Other of this world" through "compassion and empathy, given and received, and . . . the work of justice imaginatively exercised."[97] Ethical and spiritual practices help to bend us in the direction of the other and engage in the work of compassion, justice, and hospitality.[98] These are the criteria for incarnation, for God appearing in human flesh, for it is in the body of the other that Christ is met, "the incognito appearance of Christ wherever we see human compassion for the outcast and the vulnerable."[99] Christ is present in bodies in need and in the care extended to those bodies. McFague concludes that "God is present when and where the oppressed are liberated, the sick are healed, the outcast are invited in . . . so also every creaturely body in need is Christ's body, if we can see it as such."[100] The parables of the Good Samaritan (Luke 10) and the Son of Man (Matt 25) specify how Christ is incarnate in the world. Through practices we meet Christ in the other; through practices we live into the reality of the incarnation; through practices we become divine. Hadewijch's elegant exhortation makes this clear: "The greatest radiance anyone can have on earth is truth in works of justice performed in imitation of the Son, and to practice the truth with regard to all that exists, for the glory of the noble Love that God is."[101]

A wide variety of spiritual and ethical practices develop incarnate identity in Christ. Participation in the sacraments incorporates the body of Christ into our own. Contemplative prayer develops our capacity for attention to God and to others. Theodramas invite individuals to merge their identities with the figures of the Gospels.[102] All practices are embodied, but certain practices of singing, dancing, pilgrimage, and hesychasm directly engage the body and harness the breath for spiritual ends. Human beings are remarkably plastic, as Kathryn Tanner notes. In many ways, we are our practices; that is, our practices make us what we are as they become habits and even virtues. When we engage in spiritual and ethical practices that attune us

[97] Grace Jantzen, *Becoming Divine: Towards a Feminist Philosophy of Religion* (Bloomington: Indiana University Press, 1999), 265.

[98] See Joh, "Authoring a Multiplicity," 172.

[99] McFague, *Body of God*, 195.

[100] McFague, *Body of God*, 195.

[101] "Die alre meeste claerheit die men hebben mach in ertrike Dat es ghewaricheit in ieghenwordeghen werken van gherechticheden, Ende van allen wesenen waerheit te pleghene omme claerheit der edelre minnen die god es." *Letters*, 1.8–12 (CW 47).

[102] See Nancy Pineda-Madrid, "On Mysticism, Latinas/os, and the Journey: A Reflection in Conversation with Mary Engel," *Journal of Feminist Studies in Religion* 24, no. 2 (2008): 178–83.

to God and our neighbor, "At the end of the day it is our bodies that are to be remade into Christ's body."[103] In other words, our practices assist us in becoming divine, in both recognizing and extending the incarnation into the world through our own bodies.

These practices orient us toward God and neighbor and attune us to the transcendence of the other, "the unfathomable mystery, the unutterable in the human flesh."[104] Practical encounters with the other are not solutions to the "problem" of divine transcendence; instead, spiritual and ethical practices deepen our attention to divine mystery, as the vertical transcendence of God is recognized in the horizontal transcendence of the human other. The horizon of encounter with the other is always in the future, never quite grasped or achieved, even in our most intimate, sensible encounters with the body of the other. As Irigaray notes, if our most intimate encounters and relationships with others are to be ethical, they must recognize our differences—the difference that signals the transcendent mystery of the other, that preserves the otherness of the other. In these future-oriented, embodied, ethical, spiritual, practical encounters with divine mystery in the face, the flesh, and the words of the other, we catch glimpses of the incarnation. It is worth remembering here that the "definition" of Christ's incarnation, as described by the council of Chalcedon, calls itself a horizon (*horos*), never achieved, ever fleeting, always deferred in transcendent mystery. If our practices are to function as ethical, as spiritual, they must deepen our awareness of the transcendence of the other, before whom we pause in wonder.[105]

Among these many practices, appropriate to different communities and individuals, writing emerges as a paradigmatic practice of the incarnation, particularly in the way it takes shape in the hands of certain medieval women. Because writing engages both word and flesh, it assists the process of women's flesh becoming word in response to Christ the Word-made-flesh. Writing, by its nature, is directed toward the other, the audience, reader, or listener to whom one writes. For medieval religious and beguine women, writing was a natural extension of the other practices in which they were engaged: prayer, asceticism, charity, participation in the liturgy and in the sacraments, mutual

[103] Tanner, "In the Image of the Invisible," 126. See also Tanner's discussion of practices in *Theories of Culture: A New Agenda for Theology* (Minneapolis: Fortress, 1997), 120–55.

[104] Ivone Gebara, *Longing for Running Water*, 185.

[105] See Luce Irigaray, "Wonder: A Reading of Descartes, *The Passions of the Soul*," in *An Ethics of Sexual Difference*, trans. Carolyn Burke and Gillian C. Gill (Ithaca, N.Y.: Cornell University Press, 1993), 72–82.

exhortation.[106] Writing, as Stephanie Paulsell demonstrates, is a spiritual discipline.[107] Writing as it was practiced by medieval women may seem foreign to us today because their writing was neither proprietary nor commoditized. Instead writing functioned for them as an embodied spiritual practice that was but one piece of an entire way of life, centered on the love of God experienced through Christ and neighbor. In this way of writing, hermeneutics functioned as an expression of faith as women creatively interpreted the written Christian biblical and theological tradition for theological, spiritual, and ethical ends. In writing, they both practice and interpret the incarnation: they live into the Word-made-flesh as they write themselves into the Christian tradition.

Writing is rooted in the deep soil of divine love. It is divine love that enables our words, that keeps us held securely within the apophatic tension of impossible and necessary speech. For Christians, it is the grace manifest in the incarnation of the Word that invites and encourages our meager words. "Touched by the world's sensible bodies, at once intimate and mysterious, we seek the courage and the faith to write boldly, even as we attend with tenderness and tenacity to the questions at theology's apophatic threshold: Who are we to speak? Who are we to remain silent?"[108] Grace facilitates our words as the incarnation enables our writing, to the other, and the Other, out of love. For Kristeva, it is maternal love that exceeds, informs, and evokes our words; for Cixous and Irigaray, it is the embodied and proximate love of another that both compels and limits speech; for Hadewijch, Angela, and Porete, it is the love of God, Lady Love, the beloved Christ who brings them to the impossible limits of language, whose Word embodies their words and whose flesh speaks to their flesh. The incarnation sprouts up from below, in the bodies and words of many. We grow like plants toward the sunlight, becoming divine as we become fully human, in our flesh, and in our words.

---

[106] See Derek Krueger, *Writing and Holiness: The Practice of Authorship in the Early Christian East* (Philadelphia: University of Pennsylvania Press, 2004), 1–10.

[107] Stephanie Paulsell, "Writing as a Spiritual Discipline," in *The Scope of Our Art: The Vocation of the Theological Teacher*, ed. L. Gregory Jones and Stephanie Paulsell (Grand Rapids: Eerdmans, 2002), 17–31.

[108] Hughes, "Intimate Mysteries," 366.

Bibliography

Ahlgren, Gillian. "Teresa of Avila and Angela of Foligno: Ecstatic Sisters." *Magistra: A Journal of Women's Spirituality in History* 10, no. 1 (2004): 88–116.

Allison, Dorothy. *Two or Three Things I Know for Sure*. New York: Dutton, 1995.

Angela of Foligno. *Angela of Foligno: Complete Works*. Translated by Paul Lachance, O.F.M. New York: Paulist Press, 1993.

Aquinas, Thomas. *Summa Theologica*. Translated by Fathers of the English Dominican Province. 5 vols. New York: Benzinger Brothers, 1948.

Aristotle. *The Basic Works of Aristotle*. Edited by Richard McKeon. New York: Modern Library, 2001.

Armour, Ellen T. *Deconstruction, Feminist Theology, and the Problem of Difference: Subverting the Race/Gender Divide*. Chicago: University of Chicago Press, 1999.

Athanasius. *On the Incarnation: The Treatise De Incarnatione Verbi Dei*. Translated by A Religious of C.S.M.V. Crestwood, N.Y.: St. Vladimir's Seminary, 1998.

Babinsky, Ellen. "Christological Transformation in *The Mirror of Souls*, by Marguerite Porete." *Theology Today* 60 (2003): 34–48.

Bacon, Hannah. "A Very Particular Body: Assessing the Doctrine of Incarnation for Affirming the Sacramentality of Female Embodiment." In *Women and the Divine: Touching Transcendence*, edited by Gillian Howie and J'annine Jobling, 227–51. New York: Palgrave Macmillan, 2009.

Bakhtin, Mikhail. *The Dialogic Imagination*. Edited by Michael Holquist. Translated by Caryl Emerson and Michael Holquist. Austin: University of Texas Press, 1981.

Barthes, Roland. "The Death of the Author." In *Image-Music-Text*, translated by Stephen Heath, 142–48. New York: Hill & Wang, 1977.

Beattie, Tina. "Feminism, Vatican Style." *The Tablet*. August 7, 2004. http://www.thetablet.co.uk/article/2190. Accessed May 15, 2012.

Berg, Elizabeth L. "The Third Woman." *Diacritics* 12 (1982): 11–20.

Berry, Philippa. "The Burning Glass: Paradoxes of Feminist Revelation in *Speculum*." In *Engaging with Luce Irigaray*, edited by Carolyn Burke, Naomi Schor, and Margaret Whitford, 229–46. New York: Columbia University Press, 1994.

Boesel, Chris, and Catherine Keller. *Apophatic Bodies: Negative Theology, Incarnation, and Relationality*. New York: Fordham University Press, 2010.

Boeve, Lieven. "Christus Postmodernus: An Attempt at Apophatic Christology." In *The Myriad Christ: Plurality and the Quest for Unity in Contemporary Christology*, edited by T. Merrigan and J. Haers, 577–93. Leuven: Leuven University Press, 2000.

Boon, Jessica A. "Trinitarian Love Mysticism: Ruusbroec, Hadewijch, and the Gendered Experience of the Divine." *Church History* 72, no. 3 (2003): 484–503.

Bradley, Arthur. *Negative Theology and Modern French Philosophy*. New York: Routledge, 2004.

Brintnall, Kent L. *Ecce Homo: The Male-Body-in-Pain as Redemptive Figure*. Chicago: University of Chicago Press, 2012.

Brock, Rita Nakashima. *Journeys by Heart: A Christology of Erotic Power*. New York: Crossroad, 1988.

Budick, Sanford, and Wolfgang Iser, eds. *Languages of the Unsayable: The Play of Negativity in Literature and Literary Theory*. Stanford: Stanford University Press, 1987.

Burns, Charlene P. E. *Divine Becoming: Rethinking Jesus and the Incarnation*. Minneapolis: Fortress, 2002.

Butler, Judith. *Bodies That Matter: On the Discursive Limits of "Sex."* New York: Routledge, 1993.

———. *Gender Trouble: Feminism and the Subversion of Identity*. New York: Routledge, 1990.

Bynum, Caroline Walker. *Fragmentation and Redemption: Essays on Gender and the Human Body in Medieval Religion*. New York: Zone Books, 1991.

———. *Holy Feast and Holy Fast: The Religious Significance of Food to Medieval Women*. Berkeley: University of California Press, 1987.

———. "Introduction: The Complexity of Symbols." In *Gender and Religion: On the Complexity of Symbols*, edited by Caroline W. Bynum, Stevan Harrell, and Paula Richman, 1–20. Boston: Beacon, 1988.

———. *Jesus as Mother: Studies in the Spirituality of the High Middle Ages*. Berkeley: University of California Press, 1982.

Caputo, John D. *The Prayers and Tears of Jacques Derrida: Religion without Religion.* Bloomington: Indiana University Press, 1997.

Cardinal, Marie. *Les Mots Pour Le Dire.* Paris: Grasset, 1975.

———. *The Words to Say It: An Autobiographical Novel.* Translated by Pat Goodheart. Cambridge, Mass.: Van Vactor & Goodheart, 1983.

Carney, Sheila. "Exemplarism in Hadewijch: The Quest for Full-Grownness." *Downside Review* 103, no. 353 (1985): 276–95.

Carson, Anne. *Decreation: Poetry, Essays, Opera.* New York: Vintage, 2005.

Certeau, Michel de. *Heterologies: Discourse on the Other.* Translated by Brian Massumi. Minneapolis: University of Minnesota Press, 1985.

———. *The Mystic Fable.* Translated by Michael B. Smith. Chicago: University of Chicago Press, 1992.

Chance, Jane. *Gender and Text in the Later Middle Ages.* Gainesville: University Press of Florida, 1996.

Chanter, Tina. *Ethics of Eros: Irigaray's Rewriting of the Philosophers.* New York: Routledge, 1995.

Cheah, Pheng, and Elizabeth Grosz. "The Future of Sexual Difference: An Interview with Judith Butler and Drucilla Cornell." *Diacritics* 28, no. 1 (1998): 19–42.

———. "Of Being-Two: Introduction." *Diacritics* 28, no. 1 (1998): 8–9.

Chopp, Rebecca S. *The Power to Speak: Feminism, Language, God.* New York: Crossroad, 1989.

Christ, Carol P. "Embodied, Embedded Mysticism: Affirming the Self and Others in a Radically Interdependent World." *Journal of Feminist Studies in Religion* 24, no. 2 (2008): 159–67.

———. *She Who Changes: Re-imagining the Divine in the World.* New York: Palgrave Macmillan, 2004.

Chung Hyun Kyung. *Struggle to Be the Sun Again: Introducing Asian Women's Theology.* Maryknoll, N.Y.: Orbis Books, 1990.

Cixous, Hélène. *"Coming to Writing" and Other Essays.* Edited by Deborah Jenson. Translated by Sarah Cornell et al. Cambridge, Mass.: Harvard University Press, 1991.

———. "The Laugh of the Medusa." In *New French Feminisms,* edited by Elaine Marks and Isabelle de Courtivron. Translated by Keith Cohen and Paula Cohen, 245–64. New York: Schocken Books, 1980.

———. "Le rire de la Méduse." *L'Arc* 61 (1975): 39–54.

———. "Sorties." In Hélène Cixous and Catherine Clément, *The Newly Born Woman.* Translated by Betsy Wing. Minneapolis: University of Minnesota Press, 1986.

Cixous, Hélène, and Catherine Clément. *La Jeune Née.* Paris: Union Générale d'Éditions, 1975.

―――. *The Newly Born Woman*. Translated by Betsy Wing. Minneapolis: University of Minnesota Press, 1986.

Coakley, Sarah. "What Does Chalcedon Solve and What Does It Not? Some Reflections on the Status and Meaning of the Chalcedonian 'Definition.'" In *The Incarnation: An Interdisciplinary Symposium on the Incarnation of the Son of God*, edited by Stephen T. Davis, Daniel Kendall, S.J., and Gerald O'Collins, S.J., 143–63. Oxford: Oxford University Press, 2002.

Coakley, Sarah, and Charles M. Stang, eds. *Re-thinking Dionysius the Areopagite*. Oxford: Wiley Blackwell, 2009.

Colledge, Edmund. "Liberty of Spirit: 'The Mirror of Simple Souls.'" In *Theology of Renewal*, vol. 2, edited by L. K. Shook, 100–17. Dorval, Quebec: Palm, 1968.

Collins, Patricia Hill. *Black Feminist Thought*. 2nd ed. New York: Routledge, 2000.

Cone, James H. *God of the Oppressed*. Rev. ed. Maryknoll, N.Y.: Orbis, 1997.

Congregation for the Doctrine of the Faith. "Letter to the Bishops of the Catholic Church on the Collaboration of Men and Women in the Church and in the World." May 31, 2004. http://www.vatican.va/roman_curia/congregations/cfaith/documents/rc_con_cfaith_doc_20000626_message-fatima_en.html. Accessed May 15, 2012.

"Controversial Hymns Challenge US Methodists' View of God." Voice of America. July 2, 2002. http://www.voanews.com/content/a-13-a-2002-07-02-48-controversial-66290592/541141.html. Accessed July 15, 2012.

Copeland, M. Shawn. *Enfleshing Freedom: Body, Race, and Being*. Minneapolis: Fortress, 2010.

Coward, Harold, and Toby Foshay, eds. *Derrida and Negative Theology*. Albany: State University of New York Press, 1992.

Crenshaw, Kimberlé. "Demarginalizing the Intersection of Race and Sex: A Black Feminist Critique of Antidiscrimination Doctrine, Feminist Theory, and Antiracist Politics." In *Feminist Legal Theory: Readings in Law and Gender*, edited by T. K. Bartlett and R. Kennedy, 57–80. Boulder, Colo.: Westview: 1991.

Crisp, Oliver D. *Divinity and Humanity: The Incarnation Reconsidered*. Cambridge: Cambridge University Press, 2007.

Cullinan, Colleen Carpenter. "In Pain and Sorrow: Childbirth, Incarnation, and the Suffering of Women." *CrossCurrents* 58, no. 1 (2008): 95–107.

Culpepper, Emily. "Philosophia: Feminist Methodology for Constructing a Female Train of Thought." *Journal of Feminist Studies in Religion* 3, no. 2 (1987): 7–16.

Daggers, Jenny. "Luce Irigaray and 'Divine Women': A Resource for Postmodern Feminist Theology?" *Feminist Theology* 14 (1997): 35–50.

Daly, Mary. *Beyond God the Father: Toward a Philosophy of Women's Liberation.* Boston: Beacon, 1973.

————. "The Women's Movement: An Exodus Community." *Religious Education* 67 (1972): 327–33.

Daróczi, Anikó. *Hadewijch: Ende hieromme swighic sachte.* Amsterdam-Antwerp: Atlas, 2002.

Datta, Kitty Scoular. "Female Heterologies: Women's Mysticism, Gender-Mixing and the Apophatic." In *Self/Same/Other: Re-visioning the Subject in Literature and Theology,* edited by Heather Walton and Andrew W. Hass, 125–36. Sheffield, UK: Sheffield Academic, 2000.

Delphy, Christine. "The Invention of French Feminism: An Essential Move." *Yale French Studies* 87 (1995): 190–221.

Derrida, Jacques. *Of Grammatology.* Translated by Gayatri Chakravorty Spivak. Baltimore, Md.: Johns Hopkins University Press, 1974.

————. *Writing and Difference.* Translated by Alan Bass. Chicago: University of Chicago Press, 1978.

Didi-Huberman, Georges. *Invention of Hysteria: Charcot and the Photographic Iconography of the Salpêtrière.* Translated by Alisa Hartz. Cambridge, Mass.: MIT Press, 2003.

Dinshaw, Carolyn, and David Wallace, eds. *The Cambridge Companion to Medieval Women's Writings.* Cambridge: Cambridge University Press, 2003.

Douglas, Kelly Brown. *The Black Christ.* Maryknoll, N.Y.: Orbis Books, 1993.

Dreyer, Elizabeth. *Passionate Spirituality: Hildegard of Bingen and Hadewijch of Brabant.* Mahwah, N.J.: Paulist Press, 2005.

Dronke, Peter. *Women Writers of the Middle Ages: A Critical Study of Texts from Perpetua († 203) to Marguerite Porete († 1310).* Cambridge: Cambridge University Press, 1984.

Dubois, Danielle. "Spiritual Practice and Learned Traditions in Marguerite Porete's *Mirouer des simples ames.*" Ph.D. diss., Johns Hopkins University, 2012.

Duchen, Claire. *Feminism in France: From May '68 to Mitterand.* New York: Routledge, 1986.

Duclow, Donald. "The Hungers of Hadewijch and Eckhart." *Journal of Religion* 80 (2000): 421–41.

Eckhart, Meister. "Commentary on Exodus." In *Meister Eckhart: Teacher and Preacher,* edited by Bernard McGinn, 41–146. Mahwah, N.J.: Paulist Press, 1986.

————. *The Essential Sermons, Commentaries, Treatises, and Defense.* Translated by Edmund Colledge and Bernard McGinn. Mahwah, N.J.: Paulist Press, 1981.

Eiesland, Nancy L. *The Disabled God: Toward a Liberatory Theology of Disability*. Nashville: Abingdon, 1994.

Engel, Mary Potter, Carol P. Christ, et al. "Roundtable Discussion: 'Mysticism and Feminist Spirituality.'" *Journal of Feminist Studies in Religion* 24, no. 2 (2008): 143–87.

Farley, Wendy. *Eros for the Other: Retaining Truth in a Pluralistic World*. University Park: Pennsylvania State University Press, 1996.

———. *Gathering Those Driven Away: A Theology of Incarnation*. Louisville, Ky.: Westminster John Knox, 2011.

———. *Tragic Vision and Divine Compassion: A Contemporary Theodicy*. Louisville, Ky.: Westminster John Knox, 1990.

———. *The Wounding and Healing of Desire: Weaving Heaven and Earth*. Louisville, Ky.: Westminster John Knox, 2005.

Ferrante, Joan M. *To the Glory of Her Sex: Women's Roles in the Composition of Medieval Texts*. Bloomington: Indiana University Press, 1997.

Feuerbach, Ludwig. *The Essence of Christianity*. Translated by George Eliot. 1841. Reprint, Amherst, N.Y.: Prometheus Books, 1989.

Fiddes, Paul S. "The Quest for a Place Which Is 'Not-a-Place': The Hiddenness of God and the Presence of God." In *Silence and the Word: Negative Theology and Incarnation*, edited by Oliver Davies and Denys Turner, 35–60. Cambridge: Cambridge University Press, 2008.

Field, Sean L. *The Beguine, the Angel, and the Inquisitor: The Trials of Marguerite Porete and Guiard of Cressonessart*. Notre Dame, Ind.: Notre Dame University Press, 2012.

Finke, Laurie. *Feminist Theory, Women's Writing: Reading Women Writing*. Ithaca, N.Y.: Cornell University Press, 1992.

Foucault, Michel. "What Is an Author?" In *The Foucault Reader*, edited by Paul Rabinow, 101–20. Translated by Josué V. Harari. New York: Pantheon Books, 1984.

Fraeters, Veerle. Foreword to *Hadewijch: Writer, Beguine, Love Mystic*, by Paul Mommaers. Translated by Elisabeth Dutton. Leuven: Peeters, 2004.

Francis, Richard. *Ann the Word: The Story of Ann Lee, Female Messiah, Mother of the Shakers, the Woman Clothed with the Sun*. New York: Arcade, 2000.

Franke, William, ed. *On What Cannot Be Said: Apophatic Discourses in Philosophy, Religion, Literature, and the Arts*. Notre Dame, Ind.: University of Notre Dame Press, 2007.

Freud, Sigmund. *Dora: An Analysis of a Case of Hysteria*. New York: Collier Books, 1963.

———. *Totem and Taboo; Some Points of Agreement between the Mental Lives of Savages and Neurotics*. Translated by James Strachey. New York: Norton, 1950.

Fuss, Diana. *Essentially Speaking: Feminism, Nature & Difference.* New York: Routledge, 1989.

Gathogo, Julius. "Christology in African Women's Theology." *Africa Theological Journal* 31, no. 2 (2008): 75–92.

Gebara, Ivone. *Longing for Running Water: Ecofeminism and Liberation.* Minneapolis: Fortress, 1999.

Grabes, Herbert. *The Mutable Glass: Mirror Imagery in Titles and Texts of the Middle Ages and English Renaissance.* Cambridge: Cambridge University Press, 1982.

Grant, Jacquelyn. *White Women's Christ and Black Women's Jesus: Feminist Christology and Womanist Response.* Atlanta: Scholars, 1989.

Grijp, Louis P. "De zingende Hadewijch." In *Een zoet akkoord: Middeleeuwse lyriek in de Lage Landen,* edited by Frank Willaert, 72–93. Amsterdam: Prometheus, 1992.

Grosz, Elizabeth. "Irigaray and the Divine." In *Transfigurations: Theology and the French Feminists,* edited by C. W. Maggie Kim, Susan M. St. Ville, and Susan M. Simonaitis, 199–214. Minneapolis: Fortress, 1993.

———. *Sexual Subversions: Three French Feminists.* Sydney: Allen & Unwin, 1989.

———. *Volatile Bodies: Toward a Corporeal Feminism.* Bloomington: Indiana University Press, 1994.

Grundmann, Herbert. *Religious Movements in the Middle Ages: The Historical Links between Heresy, the Mendicant Orders, and the Women's Religious Movement in the Twelfth and Thirteenth Century, with the Historical Foundations of German Mysticism.* Translated by Steven Rowan. 1935. Reprint, Notre Dame, Ind.: University of Notre Dame Press, 1995.

Guarnieri, Romana. "Lo *Specchio delle anime semplici* e Margherita Poirette." *L'Osservatore Romano.* June 16, 1946.

Guest, Tanis M. *Some Aspects of Hadewijch's Poetic Form in the "Strofische Gedichten."* The Hague: Martinus Nijhoff, 1975.

Hadewijch. *Brieven.* 2 vols. Edited by Jozef van Mierlo, S.J. Antwerp: Standaard, 1947.

———. *Hadewijch: The Complete Works.* Translated by Mother Columba Hart, O.S.B. Mahwah, N.J.: Paulist Press, 1980.

———. *Mengeldichten.* Edited by Jozef van Mierlo, S.J. Antwerp: Standaard, 1952.

———. *Strophische Gedichten.* 2 vols. Edited by Jozef van Mierlo, S.J. Antwerp: Standaard, 1942.

———. *Visionen.* 2 vols. Edited by Jozef van Mierlo, S.J. Louvain: Vlaamsch Boekenhalle, 1924, 1925.

Hadot, Pierre. *Philosophy as a Way of Life: Spiritual Exercises from Socrates to Foucault*. Translated by Michael Chase. Oxford: Blackwell, 1995.

Hampson, Daphne. *Theology and Feminism*. Cambridge, Mass.: Blackwell, 1990.

Hartsock, Nancy. "The Feminist Standpoint: Developing the Ground for a Specifically Feminist Historical Materialism." In *Discovering Reality*, edited by Sandra Harding and Merrell Hintikka, 283–305. Dortrecht: Reidel, 1983.

Haught, John. *God after Darwin: A Theology of Evolution*. Boulder, Colo.: Westview, 2000.

Heine, Ronald. "Reading the Bible with Origen." In *The Bible in Greek Christian Antiquity*, edited by Paul M. Blowers, 131–48. Notre Dame, Ind.: University of Notre Dame Press, 1997.

Heyward, Carter. *The Redemption of God: A Theology of Mutual Relation*. Eugene, Ore.: Wipf & Stock, 2010.

Hick, John. *The Metaphor of God Incarnate: Christology in a Pluralistic Age*. 2nd ed. Louisville, Ky.: Westminster John Knox, 2006.

Hollywood, Amy M. "Inside Out: Beatrice of Nazareth and Her Hagiographer." In *Gendered Voices: Medieval Saints and Their Interpreters*, edited by Catherine M. Mooney, 78–98. Philadelphia: University of Pennsylvania Press, 1999.

———. "Preaching as Social Practice in Meister Eckhart." In *Mysticism and Social Transformation*, edited by Janet Ruffing, 76–90. Syracuse, N.Y.: Syracuse University Press, 2001.

———. "Queering the Beguines: Mechtild, Hadewijch, Porete." In *Queer Theology: Rethinking the Western Body*, edited by Gerard Loughlin, 163–75. Malden, Mass.: Blackwell, 2007.

———. *Sensible Ecstasy: Mysticism, Sexual Difference, and the Demands of History*. Chicago: University of Chicago Press, 2002.

———. "Sexual Desire, Divine Desire; Or, Queering the Beguines." In *Toward a Theology of Eros: Transfiguring Passion at the Limits of Discipline*, edited by Virginia Burrus and Catherine Keller, 119–33. New York: Fordam University Press, 2006.

———. *The Soul as Virgin Wife: Mechthild of Magdeburg, Marguerite Porete, and Meister Eckhart*. Notre Dame, Ind.: University of Notre Dame Press, 1995.

———. "Suffering Transformed: Marguerite Porete, Meister Eckhart, and the Problem of Women's Spirituality." In *Meister Eckhart and the Beguine Mystics: Hadewijch of Brabant, Mechthild of Magdeburg, and Marguerite Porete*, edited by Bernard McGinn, 87–113. New York: Continuum, 1994.

———. " 'Who Does She Think She Is?' Christian Women's Mysticism." *Theology Today* 60 (2003): 5–15.

Holmes, Emily A., and Wendy Farley, eds. *Women, Writing, Theology: Transforming a Tradition of Exclusion*. Waco, Tex.: Baylor University Press, 2011.

Hopkins, Gerard Manley. *Poems and Prose of Gerard Manley Hopkins*. Edited by W. H. Gardner. Baltimore, Md.: Penguin Books, 1953.

Hughes, Krista E. "Intimate Mysteries: The Apophatics of Sensible Love." In *Apophatic Bodies: Negative Theology, Incarnation, and Relationality*, edited by Chris Boesel and Catherine Keller, 349–66. New York: Fordham University Press, 2010.

Irigaray, Luce. *Ce sexe qui n'en est pas un*. Paris: Éditions de Minuit, 1977.

———. "Égales à qui?" *Critique* 43, no. 480 (1987): 420–37.

———. "Equal to Whom?" In *The Essential Difference*, edited by Naomi Schor and Elizabeth Weed. Translated by Robert L. Mazzola, 63–81. Bloomington: Indiana University Press, 1994.

———. "Ethical Gestures toward the Other." *Poligrafi* 57, no. 15 (2010): 3–23.

———. *An Ethics of Sexual Difference*. Translated by Carolyn Burke and Gillian C. Gill. Ithaca, N.Y.: Cornell University Press, 1993.

———. *I Love to You: Sketch of a Possible Felicity in History*. Translated by Alison Martin. New York: Routledge, 1996.

———. "Je—Luce Irigaray." Interview by Elizabeth Hirsh and Gary A. Olson. *Hypatia* 10, no. 2 (1995): 93–114.

———. *Key Writings*. London: Continuum, 2004.

———. *Parler n'est jamais neutre*. Paris: Minuit, 1985.

———. *Sexes and Genealogies*. Translated by Gillian C. Gill. New York: Columbia University Press, 1993.

———. *Sexes et parentés*. Paris: Minuit, 1987.

———. *Speculum de l'autre femme*. Paris: Éditions de Minuit, 1974.

———. *Speculum of the Other Woman*. Translated by Gillian C. Gill. Ithaca, N.Y.: Cornell University Press, 1985.

———. *This Sex Which Is Not One*. Translated by Catherine Porter. Ithaca, N.Y.: Cornell University Press, 1985.

———. *To Be Two*. Translated by Monique M. Rhodes and Marco F. Cocito-Monoc. New York: Routledge, 2001.

———. "Toward a Divine in the Feminine." In *Women and the Divine: Touching Transcendence*, edited by Gillian Howie and J'annine Jobling, 13–25. New York: Palgrave Macmillan, 2008.

Isasi-Díaz, Ada María. *La Lucha Continues: Mujerista Theology*. Maryknoll, N.Y.: Orbis Books, 2004.

Isherwood, Lisa. "The Embodiment of Feminist Liberation Theology: The Spiralling of Incarnation." *Feminist Theology* 12, no. 2 (2004): 140–56.

Jacobs, Harriet A. *Incidents in the Life of a Slave Girl*. 1861. Reprint, New York: Oxford University Press, 1988.

Jantzen, Grace. *Becoming Divine: Towards a Feminist Philosophy of Religion*. Bloomington: Indiana University Press, 1999.

————. *Power, Gender and Christian Mysticism*. Cambridge: Cambridge University Press, 1995.

Joh, Wonhee Anne. "Authoring a Multiplicity of Selves and No-Self." *Journal of Feminist Studies in Religion* 24, no. 2 (2008): 169–72.

————. *Heart of the Cross: A Postcolonial Christology*. Louisville, Ky.: Westminster John Knox, 2006.

John of the Cross. *The Dark Night of the Soul*. Translated by E. Allison Peers. New York: Doubleday, 1990.

Johnson, Elizabeth A. *Quest for the Living God: Mapping Frontiers in the Theology of God*. New York: Continuum, 2007.

————. "Redeeming the Name of Christ." In *Freeing Theology: The Essentials of Theology in Feminist Perspective*, edited by Catherine Mowry LaCugna, 115–37. San Francisco: Harper, 1993.

————. *She Who Is: The Mystery of God in Feminist Theological Discourse*. New York: Crossroad, 1997.

Jones, Ann Rosalind. "Writing the Body: Toward an Understanding of *l'Écriture Féminine*." In *The New Feminist Criticism: Essays on Women, Literature, and Theory*, edited by E. Showalter, 361–77. New York: Pantheon, 1985.

Jones, Serene. "Divining Women: Irigaray and Feminist Theologies." *Yale French Studies* 87 (1995): 42–67.

————. *Trauma and Grace: Theology in a Ruptured World*. Louisville, Ky.: Westminster John Knox, 2009.

Jordan, Mark D. "God's Body." In *Queer Theology: Rethinking the Western Body*, edited by Gerard Loughlin, 281–92. Oxford: Blackwell, 2007.

Joy, Morny. *Divine Love: Luce Irigaray, Women, Gender and Religion*. Manchester: Manchester University Press, 2006.

Joy, Morny, Kathleen O'Grady, and Judith L. Poxon, eds. *Religion in French Feminist Thought: Critical Perspectives*. New York: Routledge, 2003.

Kaminski, Phyllis H. "Mysticism Embodied Differently: Luce Irigaray and the Subject of Incarnate Love." *Religious Studies and Theology* 17, no. 2 (1998): 59–79.

————. "What the Daughter Knows: Re-thinking Women's Religious Experience with and against Luce Irigaray." In *Encountering Transcendence: Contributions to a Theology of Christian Religious Experience*, edited by Lieven Boeve, Hans Geybels, and Stijn Van den Bossche, 57–82. Leuven: Peeters, 2005.

Kerckvoorde, Colette M. van. *An Introduction to Middle Dutch*. New York: Mouton de Gruyter, 1993.

Kim, C. W. Maggie, Susan M. St. Ville, and Susan M. Simonaitis, eds. *Transfigurations: Theology and the French Feminists*. Minneapolis: Fortress, 1993.

Kocher, S. [Zan]. *Allegories of Love in Marguerite Porete's Mirror of Simple Souls*. Turnhout: Brepols, 2008.

Kramer, Heinrich, and James Sprenger. *The Malleus Maleficarum*. 1484. Translated by Montague Summers. New York: Dover, 1971.

Kristeva, Julia. *Histoires d'amour*. Paris: Denoël, 1983.

———. *Powers of Horror: An Essay on Abjection*. Translated by Leon S. Roudiez. New York: Columbia University Press, 1982.

———. *La Révolution du langage poetique*. Paris: Éditions du Seuil, 1974.

———. *Revolution in Poetic Language*. Translated by Margaret Waller. New York: Columbia University Press, 1984.

———. *Tales of Love*. Translated by Leon S. Roudiez. New York: Columbia University Press, 1987.

Krueger, Derek. *Writing and Holiness: The Practice of Authorship in the Early Christian East*. Philadelphia: University of Pennsylvania Press, 2004.

Lacan, Jacques. *Écrits: A Selection*. New York: Norton, 1977.

———. *Feminine Sexuality: Jacques Lacan and the école freudienne*. Edited and translated by Juliet Mitchell and Jacqueline Rose. London: Macmillan, 1982.

Lacan, Jacques, and Jacques-Alain Miller. *Séminaire XX: Encore. Le Séminaire De Jacques Lacan*. Paris: Seuil, 1975.

Lachance, Paul, O.F.M. *The Spiritual Journey of the Blessed Angela of Foligno according to the Memorial of Frater A*. Rome: Pontificium Athenaeum Antonianum, 1984.

Lanzetta, Beverly J. *Radical Wisdom: A Feminist Mystical Theology*. Minneapolis: Fortress, 2005.

Laqueur, Thomas. *Making Sex: Body and Gender from the Greeks to Freud*. Cambridge, Mass.: Harvard University Press, 1990.

Larrington, Carolyne. *Women and Writing in Medieval Europe: A Sourcebook*. New York: Routledge, 1995.

Lerner, Robert E. *The Heresy of the Free Spirit in the Later Middle Ages*. Los Angeles: University of California Press, 1972.

Little, J. P. "Simone Weil's Concept of Decreation." In *Simone Weil's Philosophy of Culture: Readings toward a Divine Humanity*, edited by Richard H. Bell, 25–51. Cambridge: Cambridge University Press, 1993.

Lochrie, Karma. "The Language of Transgression: Body, Flesh and Word in Mystical Discourse." In *Speaking Two Languages: Traditional Disciplines and Contemporary Theory in Medieval Studies*, edited by Allen J. Frantzen, 124–29. Albany: State University of New York Press, 1991.

———. *Margery Kempe and Translations of the Flesh*. Philadelphia: University of Pennsylvania Press, 1991.

———. "Mystical Acts, Queer Tendencies." In *Constructing Medieval Sexuality*, edited by Karma Lochrie, Peggy McCracken, and James A. Schultz, 180–200. Minneapolis: University of Minnesota Press, 1997.

Lorde, Audre. "Poetry Is Not a Luxury." In *Sister Outsider: Essays and Speeches*, 36–39. Trumansburg, N.Y.: Crossing, 1985.

————. *Sister Outsider: Essays and Speeches*. Trumansburg, N.Y.: Crossing, 1984.

————. "Uses of the Erotic: The Erotic as Power." In *Sister Outsider: Essays and Speeches*, 53–59. Trumansburg, N.Y.: Crossing, 1985.

Lucas, Elona K. "Psychological and Spiritual Growth in Hadewijch and Julian of Norwich." *Studia Mystica* 9, no. 3 (1986): 3–20.

Marks, Elaine, and Isabelle de Courtivron, eds. *New French Feminisms: An Anthology*. New York: Schocken Books, 1980.

Mazzoni, Cristina. "On the (Un)Representability of Woman's Pleasure: Angela of Foligno and Jacques Lacan." In *Gender and Text in the Later Middle Ages*, edited by Jane Chance, 239–62. Gainesville: University Press of Florida, 1996.

————. *Saint Hysteria: Neurosis, Mysticism, and Gender in European Culture*. Ithaca, N.Y.: Cornell University Press, 1996.

McDonnell, E. W. *The Beguines and Beghards in Medieval Culture, with Special Emphasis on the Belgian Scene*. New Brunswick, N.J.: Rutgers University Press, 1954.

McFague, Sallie. *The Body of God: An Ecological Theology*. Minneapolis: Fortress, 1993.

McGinn, Bernard. *The Flowering of Mysticism: Men and Women in the New Mysticism (1200–1350)*. Vol. 3 of *The Presence of God: A History of Western Christian Mysticism*. New York: Crossroad, 1998.

————. *The Foundations of Mysticism: Origins to the Fifth Century*. Vol. 1 of *The Presence of God: A History of Western Christian Mysticism*. New York: Crossroad, 1991.

————. "The Four Female Evangelists of the Thirteenth Century: The Invention of Authority." In *Deutsche Mystik im abendländischen Zusammenhang*, edited by Walter Haug and Wolfram Schneider-Lastin, 175–94. Tübingen: Niemeyer, 2000.

————, ed. *Meister Eckhart and the Beguine Mystics: Hadewijch of Brabant, Mechthild of Magdeburg, and Marguerite Porete*. New York: Continuum, 1994.

————. "Suffering, Emptiness, and Annihilation in Three Beguine Mystics." In *Homo Medietas: Aufsätze zu Religiosität, Literatur und Denkformen des Menschen vom Mittelalter bis in die Neuzeit*, edited by Claudia Brinker-von der Heyde and Niklaus Largier, 155–74. Bern: Peter Lang, 1998.

Mechthild of Magdeburg. *The Flowing Light of the Godhead*. Translated by Frank J. Tobin. New York: Paulist Press, 1998.

Miles, Margaret. *The Word Made Flesh: A History of Christian Thought*. Oxford: Blackwell, 2005.

Milhaven, John Giles. *Hadewijch and Her Sisters: Other Ways of Loving and Knowing*. Albany: State University of New York Press, 1993.

Miller, Julie B. "Eroticized Violence in Medieval Women's Mystical Literature: A Call for a Feminist Critique." *Journal of Feminist Studies in Religion* 15, no. 2 (1999): 25–48.

Moi, Toril. *Sexual/Textual Politics: Feminist Literary Theory*. London: Methuen, 1995.

Le Moine et la Sorcière. DVD. Directed by Suzanne Schiffman. Cambridge, Mass.: Lara Classics, Inc., 1987.

Mommaers, Paul. *Hadewijch: Writer, Beguine, Love Mystic*. Translated by Elisabeth M. Dutton. Leuven: Peeters, 2004.

————. *The Riddle of Christian Mystical Experience: The Role of the Humanity of Jesus*. Leuven: Peeters, 2003.

Mooney, Catherine M. "The Authorial Role of Brother A. in the Composition of Angela of Foligno's Revelations." In *Creative Women in Medieval and Modern Italy*, edited by E. Ann Matter and John Coakley, 34–63. Philadelphia: University of Pennsylvania Press, 1994.

————, ed. *Gendered Voices: Medieval Saints and Their Interpreters*. Philadelphia: University of Pennsylvania Press, 1999.

Mount Shoop, Marcia W. "Embodying Theology: Motherhood as Metaphor/ Method." In *Women, Writing, Theology: Transforming a Tradition of Exclusion*, edited by Emily A. Holmes and Wendy Farley, 233–52. Waco, Tex.: Baylor University Press, 2011.

Mulder, Anne-Claire. *Divine Flesh, Embodied Word: "Incarnation" as a Hermeneutical Key to a Feminist Theologian's Reading of Luce Irigaray's Work*. Amsterdam: Amsterdam University Press, 2006.

Murk-Jansen, Saskia. *The Measure of Mystic Thought: A Study of Hadewijch's Mengeldichten*. Gèoppinger Arbeiten Zur Germanistik 536. Gèoppingen: Kèummerle, 1991.

Newman, Barbara. *From Virile Woman to WomanChrist: Studies in Medieval Religion and Literature*. Philadelphia: University of Pennsylvania Press, 1995.

————. *God and the Goddesses: Vision, Poetry, and Belief in the Middle Ages*. Philadelphia: University of Pennsylvania Press, 2003.

————. "The Heretic Saint: Guglielma of Bohemia, Milan, and Brunate." *Church History* 74, no. 1 (2005): 1–38.

Niebuhr, R. R. *Schleiermacher on Christ and Religion*. New York: Scribner, 1964.

Norris, Richard A., Jr., trans. and ed. *The Christological Controversy*. Philadelphia: Fortress, 1980.

Oduyoye, Mercy Amba. "Jesus Christ." In *Hope Abundant: Third World and Indigenous Women's Theology*, edited by Kwok Pui-lan, 167–85. Maryknoll, N.Y.: Orbis Books, 2010.

Origen. *On First Principles.* Translated by G. W. Butterworth. New York: Harper & Row, 1966.

O'Sullivan, Robin. "Model, Mirror, and Memorial: Imitation of the Passion and the Annihilation of the Imagination in Angela da Foligno's *Liber* and Marguerite Porete's *Mirouer des simples âmes.*" Ph.D. diss., University of Chicago Divinity School, 2002.

Paulsell, Stephanie. "Dreaming the King, Writing God: Hope, Desire, and Fiction in Marguerite Porete's *Mirror of Simple Souls.*" In *Literature, Religion, and East/West Comparison*, edited by Eric Ziolkowski, 63–74. Newark: University of Delaware Press, 2005.

———. *Honoring the Body: Meditations on a Christian Practice.* San Francisco: Jossey-Bass, 2002.

———. "Writing as a Spiritual Discipline." In *The Scope of Our Art: The Vocation of the Theological Teacher*, edited by L. Gregory Jones and Stephanie Paulsell, 17–31. Grand Rapids: Eerdmans, 2002.

Petroff, Elizabeth. *Body and Soul: Essays on Medieval Women and Mysticism.* New York: Oxford University Press, 1994.

Pineda-Madrid, Nancy. "On Mysticism, Latinas/os, and the Journey: A Reflection in Conversation with Mary Engel." *Journal of Feminist Studies in Religion* 24, no. 2 (2008): 178–83.

Plato. *The Collected Dialogues of Plato.* Edited by Edith Hamilton and Huntington Cairns. Princeton, N.J.: Princeton University Press, 1961.

Porete, Marguerite. *Marguerite Porete: The Mirror of Simple Souls.* Translated by Ellen L. Babinsky. New York: Paulist Press, 1993.

———. *Le mirouer des simples âmes / Speculum simplicium animarum.* Edited by Romana Guarnieri and Paul Verdeyen. Corpus Christianorum Continuatio Mediaevalis 69. Turnhout: Brepols, 1986.

Porette, Margaret. *The Mirror of Simple Souls.* Translated by Edmund Colledge, O.S.A., J. C. Marler, and Judith Grant. Notre Dame, Ind.: University of Notre Dame Press, 1999.

Poxon, Judith L. "Corporeality and Divinity: Irigaray and the Problem of the Ideal." In *Religion in French Feminist Thought: Critical Perspectives*, edited by Morny Joy, Kathleen O'Grady, and Judith Poxon, 41–50. London: Routledge, 2003.

Priest, Ann-Marie. "Woman as God, God as Woman: Mysticism, Negative Theology, and Luce Irigaray." *Journal of Religion* 83, no. 1 (2003): 1–23.

Pseudo-Dionysius. *The Complete Works.* Translated by Colm Luibhéid and Paul Rorem. New York: Paulist Press, 1987.

Raab, Kelley A. *When Women Become Priests: The Catholic Women's Ordination Debate.* New York: Columbia University Press, 2000.

Rambo, Shelly. *Spirit and Trauma: A Theology of Remaining*. Louisville, Ky.: Westminster John Knox, 2010.

Rambuss, Richard. *Closet Devotions*. Durham, N.C.: Duke University Press, 1998.

Ray, Darby Kathleen. *Incarnation and Imagination: A Christian Ethic of Ingenuity*. Minneapolis: Fortress, 2008.

Reineke, Martha J. " 'This is My Body': Reflections on Abjection, Anorexia, and Medieval Women Mystics." *JAAR* 58, no. 2 (1990): 245–65.

Reynaert, Joris. "Hadewijch: Mystic Poetry and Courtly Love." In *Medieval Dutch Literature in Its European Context*, edited by Erik Kooper, 208–25. Cambridge: Cambridge University Press, 1994.

Rich, Adrienne. "As if Your Life Depended on It." In *What is Found There: Notebooks on Poetry and Politics*, 32–33. New York: Norton, 1993.

————. "Compulsory Heterosexuality and Lesbian Existence." In *Blood, Bread, and Poetry: Selected Prose, 1979–1985*, 23–75. New York: Norton, 1986.

————. *Of Woman Born: Motherhood as Experience and Institution*. New York: Norton, 1986.

Robinson, Joanne Maguire. *Nobility and Annihilation in Marguerite Porete's Mirror of Simple Souls*. Albany: State University of New York Press, 2001.

Ruddick, Sara. *Maternal Thinking: Toward a Politics of Peace*. Boston: Beacon, 1989.

Rudy, Gordon. *Mystical Language of Sensation in the Later Middle Ages*. New York: Routledge, 2002.

Ruether, Rosemary Radford. *Gaia and God: An Ecofeminist Theology of Earth Healing*. San Francisco: HarperCollins, 1992.

————. *Introducing Redemption in Christian Feminism*. Sheffield, UK: Sheffield Academic, 1998.

————. *Sexism and God-Talk: Toward a Feminist Theology*. Boston: Beacon, 1983.

Ruffing, Janet, ed. *Mysticism & Social Transformation*. Syracuse, N.Y.: Syracuse University Press, 2001.

Sargent, Michael G. "The Annihilation of Marguerite Porete." *Viator* 28 (1997): 253–79.

Saussure, Ferdinand de. *Course in General Linguistics*. Translated by Wade Baskin. 1959. Reprint, New York: Columbia University Press, 2011.

Schleiermacher, Friedrich. *The Christian Faith*. 1830. New York: T&T Clark, 1999.

————. *Christmas Eve: Dialogue on Incarnation*. Translated by Terrence N. Tice. Richmond, Va.: John Knox, 1967.

Schmiedel, Paul W. *The Johannine Writings*. Translated by Maurice A. Canney. London: Adam & Charles Black, 1908.

Schneider, Laurel. "Promiscuous Incarnation." In *The Embrace of Eros: Bodies, Desires, and Sexuality in Christianity*, edited by Margaret D. Kamitsuka, 238–44. Minneapolis: Fortress, 2010.

———. *Re-imagining the Divine: Confronting the Backlash against Feminist Theology*. Cleveland, Ohio: Pilgrim Press, 1998.

Schor, Naomi. "This Essentialism Which Is Not One: Coming to Grips with Irigaray." In *Engaging with Luce Irigaray: Feminist Philosophy and Modern European Thought*, edited by Carolyn Burke, Naomi Schor, and Margaret Whitford, 57–78. New York: Columbia University Press, 1994.

Schor, Naomi, and Elizabeth Weed, eds. *The Essential Difference*. Bloomington: Indiana University Press, 1994.

Schüssler Fiorenza, Elisabeth. *In Memory of Her: A Feminist Theological Reconstruction of Christian Origins*. New York: Crossroad, 1983.

———. *Jesus: Miriam's Child, Sophia's Prophet*. New York: Continuum, 1994.

Scott, Joan W. "The Evidence of Experience." *Critical Inquiry* 17 (1991): 773–97.

Sells, Michael Anthony. *Mystical Languages of Unsaying*. Chicago: University of Chicago Press, 1994.

Sentilles, Sarah. "The Pen Is Mightier: Sexist Responses to Women Writing about Religion." *Harvard Divinity Bulletin* 40, nos. 3–4 (2012): 42–51.

Showalter, Elaine. *Hystories: Hysterical Epidemics and Modern Media*. New York: Columbia University Press, 1997.

Simons, Walter. *Cities of Ladies: Beguine Communities in the Medieval Low Countries, 1200–1565*. Philadelphia: University of Pennsylvania Press, 2001.

Spearing, A. C. "Marguerite Porete: Courtliness and Transcendence in *The Mirror of Simple Souls*." In *Envisaging Heaven in the Middle Ages*, edited by Carolyn Muessig and Ad Putter, 120–36. New York: Routledge, 2009.

Spelman, Elizabeth V. *Inessential Woman: Problems of Exclusion in Feminist Thought*. Boston: Beacon, 1988.

Steinfels, Peter. "Cries of Heresy after Feminists Meet." *The New York Times*. May 14, 1994. http://www.nytimes.com/1994/05/14/us/cries-of-heresy-after -feminists-meet.html?src=pm. Accessed July 15, 2012.

Stewart, Dianne M. *Three Eyes for the Journey: African Dimensions of the Jamaican Religious Experience*. New York: Oxford University Press, 2005.

Summit, Jennifer. *Lost Property: The Woman Writer and English Literary History, 1380–1589*. Chicago: University of Chicago Press, 2000.

———. "Women and Authorship." In *The Cambridge Companion to Medieval Women's Writings*, edited by Carolyn Dinshaw and David Wallace, 92–105. Cambridge: Cambridge University Press, 2003.

Suydam, Mary A. "The Touch of Satisfaction: Visions and the Religious Experience According to Hadewijch of Antwerp." *Journal of Feminist Studies in Religion* 12, no. 2 (1996): 5–27.

Tanner, Kathryn. "In the Image of the Invisible." In *Apophatic Bodies: Negative Theology, Incarnation, and Relationality*, edited by Chris Boesel and Catherine Keller, 117–34. New York: Fordham University Press, 2010.

———. *Theories of Culture: A New Agenda for Theology*. Minneapolis: Fortress, 1997.

Tertullian. "On the Apparel of Women." Translated by S. Thelwall. In *Ante-Nicene Fathers: Translations of the Writings of the Fathers down to A.D. 325*, edited by Alexander Roberts and James Donaldson. Vol. 4, 14–25. Buffalo, N.Y.: Christian Literature Publishing, 1885.

Their, Ludger, O.F.M., and Abele Calufetti, O.F.M., eds. *Il Libro della Beata Angela da Foligno*. Grottaferrata (Rome): Editiones Collegii S. Bonaventurae ad Claras Aquas, 1985.

Torjesen, Karen. *Hermeneutical Procedure and Theological Method in Origen's Exegesis*. Berlin: De Gruyter, 1986.

Tracy, David. "Writing." In *Critical Terms for Religious Studies*, edited by Mark C. Taylor, 383–93. Chicago: University of Chicago Press, 1998.

Turner, Denys. *The Darkness of God: Negativity in Christian Mysticism*. Cambridge: Cambridge University Press, 1995.

———. "The Darkness of God and the Light of Christ: Negative Theology and Eucharistic Presence." *Modern Theology* 15, no. 2 (1999): 143–58.

———. "Dionysius and Some Late Medieval Mystical Theologians of Northern Europe." In *Re-thinking Dionysius the Areopagite*, edited by Sarah Coakley and Charles M. Stang, 121–35. Oxford: Wiley Blackwell, 2009.

Vargas, Alicia. "The Construction of Latina Christology: An Invitation to Dialogue." *Currents in Theology and Mission* 34, no. 4 (2007): 271–77.

Vattimo, Gianni. *After Christianity*. Translated by Luca D'Isanto. New York: Columbia University Press, 2002.

———. *Belief*. Translated by Luca D'Isanto and David Webb. Stanford, Calif.: Stanford University Press, 1999.

Verdeyen, Paul. "Le Procès d'inquisition contre Marguerite Porete et Guiard de Cressonessart (1309–1310)." *Revue d'histoire ecclésiastique* 81 (1986): 47–94.

Voss Roberts, Michelle. *Dualities: A Theology of Difference*. Louisville, Ky.: Westminster John Knox, 2010.

Walsh, Lisa. "Writing (into) the Symbolic: The Maternal Metaphor in Hélène Cixous." In *Language and Liberation: Feminism, Philosophy, and Language*, edited by Christina Hendricks and Kelly Oliver, 347–65. Albany: State University of New York Press, 1999.

Warner, Marina. *Alone of All Her Sex: The Myth and the Cult of the Virgin Mary*. New York: Knopf, 1976.

Watt, Diane. *Medieval Women's Writing: Works by and for Women in England, 1100–1500*. Cambridge: Polity, 2007.

Weil, Simone. *First and Last Notebooks*. Translated by Richard Rees. New York: Oxford University Press, 1970.

———. *The Simone Weil Reader*. Edited by George A. Panichas. New York: David McKay, 1977.

Wessley, Stephen. "The Thirteenth-Century Guglielmites: Salvation through Women." In *Medieval Women*, edited by Derek Baker, 289–303. Oxford: Blackwell, 1978.

Whitford, Margaret. *Luce Irigaray: Philosophy in the Feminine*. New York: Routledge, 1991.

Wiethaus, Ulrike. "Learning as Experiencing: Hadewijch's Model of Spiritual Growth." In *Faith Seeking Understanding: Learning and the Catholic Tradition*, edited by George C. Berthold, 89–106. Manchester, N.H.: Saint Anselm College Press, 1991.

———, ed. *Maps of Flesh and Light: The Religious Experience of Medieval Women Mystics*. Syracuse, N.Y.: Syracuse University Press, 1993.

Williams, Delores S. *Sisters in the Wilderness: The Challenge of Womanist God-Talk*. Maryknoll, N.Y.: Orbis Books, 1993.

Williams, Rowan. "Origen: Between Orthodoxy and Heresy." In *Origeniana Septima*, edited by W. A. Bienert and U. Kühneweg, 3–14. Leuven: Leuven University Press, 1999.

Wiseman, Wendy. "In the Beginning: Kristeva, Cixous, and the Abject Mother of Metaphysics." Paper presented at the annual meeting of the American Academy of Religion, Philadelphia, Pa., November 21, 2005.

Woolf, Virginia. *A Room of One's Own*. New York: Harcourt Brace Jovanovich, 1929.

———. *Three Guineas*. New York: Harcourt Brace, 1938.

Zum Brunn, Emilie. "Self, Not-Self, and the Ultimate in Marguerite Porete's 'Mirror of Annihilated Souls.'" In *God, the Self, and Nothingness: Reflections Eastern and Western*, edited by Robert E. Carter, 81–88. New York: Paragon House, 1990.

INDEX